'e

edited by Allen J. Scott · London papers in regional science · a pion publication

studies in regional science

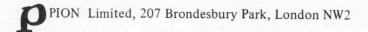

PION Limited, 207 Brondesbury Park, London NW2

SBN : 85086 008 3

Set on IBM 72 Composers by Pion Limited, London.
Printed in Great Britain by J.W.Arrowsmith Limited, Bristol.

CONTENTS

Spatial Data and Time Series Analysis   1
C.W.J.Granger

The Problem of Spatial Autocorrelation   25
A.D.Cliff and J.K.Ord

On the Optimal Partitioning of Spatially Distributed Point Sets   57
A.J.Scott

Reducing the Travel Time in a Transport Network   73
T.M.Ridley

The Integration of Accounting and Location Theory   89
Frameworks in Urban Modelling
A.G.Wilson

Alternate Urban Population Density Models: An Analytical   105
Comparison of Their Validity Range
E.Casetti

Some Factors Influencing the Income Distribution   117
of Households within a City Region
M.J.H.Mogridge

Regional Econometric Models: A Case Study of Nova Scotia   143
S.Czamanski

International and Interregional Economic Co-operation and   181
Planning by Linked Computers
T.O.M.Kronsjö

Two-stage Planning in the Irish Context   201
M.Ross

CONTRIBUTORS

E.Casetti
Department of Geography, Ohio State University, Columbus, Ohio.

A.D.Cliff
Department of Geography, University of Bristol, Bristol.

S.Czamanski
Department of City and Regional Planning, Cornell University, Ithaca, N.Y.

C.W.J.Granger
Department of Economics, University of Nottingham, Nottingham.

T.O.M.Kronsjö
Centre for Russian and East European Studies, University of Birmingham, Birmingham.

M.J.H.Mogridge
Centre for Environmental Studies, 5 Cambridge Terrace, Regent's Park, London, N.W.1.

J.K.Ord
Department of Geography, University of Bristol, Bristol.

T.M.Ridley
Department of Highways and Transportation, Greater London Council, Queensborough House, 12 Albert Embankment, London, S.E.1.

M.Ross
The Economic and Social Research Institute, 73 Lower Baggot Street, Dublin 2.

A.J.Scott
Department of Geography, University of Toronto, Toronto.

A.Wilson
Centre for Environmental Studies, 5 Cambridge Terrace, Regent's Park, London, N.W.1.

PREFACE

The collection of studies which follows represents the principal proceedings of the Annual Conference, held in London, August 1968, of the British Section of the Regional Science Association.

These studies are a representative section across the entire field of enquiry of Regional Science. They range in content from considerations, of regional and spatial theory, to mathematical techniques of analysis, empirical analyses, and the manifestation of all of these elements in planning. They will be of direct relevance to all economists, geographers, statisticians, planners, and indeed all social analysts whose primary interest is in the spatial and regional components of social and economic variation.

The studies should be seen within the wider context of a broad ongoing effort of research in Regional Science all over the world. It is hoped that the contributions contained in the present volume may at once help to quicken and consolidate that effort. In particular, it is hoped that much of this effort will be recorded in the periodic conferences of the British Section of the Association, and published in a series of volumes, of which this is the first.

AJS

Spatial Data and Time Series Analysis

C.W.J.GRANGER
University of Nottingham

Introduction

Consider some section of a plane, the points of which can be fixed by measurements on rectangular Cartesian co-ordinates and denoted by (p, q). At certain points, suppose that values of some random variable are recorded and denoted by $X(p_i, q_i)$ for the point (p_i, q_i). Thus, for example, we might measure wind speed at a number of meteorological stations. The values are not only of interest in themselves but possibly the most relevant information is contained in the spatial relationships between the readings. One might ask, for instance, whether or not values at adjacent points appear to be more correlated than values at points not near to each other. The problem with which we shall eventually be concerned in this paper is how such spatial data should be analysed. When looking at such a problem it is clearly sensible to ask how it has been solved using data which have a similar structured form, at least superficially. The analysis of time series data has a long history and has reached an advanced stage of development and so one can study if the lessons learnt in that field can be applied to spatial data. The first major section of the paper will summarise certain aspects of modern time series analysis and then in later sections some generalisations will be considered that might be applicable to spatial data. A number of examples of the use of the suggested techniques will also be presented. It should be noted that the analysis will not be concerned directly with the actual location of the points at which measurements are recorded.

TIME SERIES ANALYSIS

The Analysis of a Single Time Series

Consider a variable whose value can be recorded at specified moments of time. If the variable can be recorded at every moment of time, it can be denoted by $x(t)$ and is called a continuous time series or stochastic process. An example would be temperature measured at some specific location. If the variable can be recorded only at equally spaced moments of time, such as weekly car production, it can be denoted by x_t and is called a discrete time series. Note that any continuous series can be recorded as a discrete series but not vice versa. Thus, for instance, temperature could be recorded every hour but car production could not be measured at every moment of time as it represents an accumulation over a set period of time. We shall discuss only discrete series as the theory is easier and because most data are actually of this form. It is important to distinguish the theoretical series of values X_t, ($t = ..., -1, 0, 1, ...$), that might have been obtained, which will be called the generating process, from the actual observed data $\{x_t, t = 1, ..., n\}$. The distinction is similar to that between population and sample in classical statistics. By the analysis of a series will be meant the estimation or discovery of important properties of the generating process by investigation of the data. It is generally considered to be too ambitious to attempt to make statements about the distribution of the generating process or subsets of it and so attention is usually fixed only on the first and second moments of the process, i.e. the mean $\mu(t) = E[X_t]$, variance $\sigma^2(t) = E[\langle X_t - \mu(t) \rangle^2]$ and covariances $\mu(t, s) = E[\langle X_t - \mu(t) \rangle \langle X_s - \mu(s) \rangle]$. If there were available a number of realisations of the process, that is, several observed series, then it might be possible to attempt to estimate all of these quantities. Unfortunately, it is usually the case that only a single sample or observed series is available and so it is not possible to estimate even the first and second moments for all t and s or even the values at times for which observations are available. Consequently, restrictions on the variability over time of these moments have to be assumed to exist before any worthwhile estimation can take place. The basic assumption on which virtually all time series analysis is founded is that of stationarity. A process is said to be (second-order) stationary if its mean and variance are constant over time and $\mu(t, s) = \mu(t - s)$. That is, the covariance between any two terms depends solely on the difference in time and not the absolute time at which they are recorded. The assumption of stationarity essentially says that the law that generates the data is constant over time. Given the assumption of stationarity, estimates can now be obtained of the covariances of the form

$$\hat{\mu}(k) = \frac{1}{n-k} \sum_{t=k+1}^{n} (x_t - \bar{x})(x_{t-k} - \bar{x})$$

where

$$\bar{x} = \frac{1}{n} \sum_{t=1}^{n} x_t$$

although more sophisticated estimates are sometimes used.

The estimated covariances generally contain all of the relevant information about the series that will be used but various transformations of the sequence $\hat{\mu}(k)$, ($k = 0, 1, ...$) have been found to be more useful in that they are easier to interpret. Most of the earlier interpretations occur in connection with various plausible models that have been suggested for the underlying generating process. It will be found useful if we list some of these models:

Purely random or white noise series

A series is said to be a purely random series (or a white noise) if $\hat{\mu}(k) = 0$, $(k \neq 0)$, i.e. X_t and X_s are uncorrelated for all $t \neq s$. X_t will then be a set of uncorrelated random variables, each from the same distribution, as one might find for instance in a table of random numbers. One point about such a sequence that might be noted is that X_t cannot be predicted by any linear sum of past values of the series.

Linear cyclic model

$$X_t = \sum_{j=1}^{m} c_j \cos(\omega_j t + \theta_j) + \epsilon_t$$

where ϵ_t is a white noise series. The point about this model is that it consists of a sum of purely cyclical components with amplitudes c_j, frequencies ω_j (i.e. periods $2\pi/\omega_j$) and phases θ_j together with a white noise residual. This model has now been largely abandoned in economics, although not entirely, but is still important in meteorological, geological and technological series. The problem of how to estimate the parameters of the model was solved at the turn of the century by Schuster (1900) who pointed out that the function

$$I_n(\omega) = \frac{1}{n}\left[\left(\sum_{j=1}^{n} x_j \cos 2\pi\omega j\right)^2 + \left(\sum_{j=1}^{n} x_j \sin 2\pi\omega j\right)^2\right]$$

has sharp peaks at $\omega = \omega_j$, the unknown frequencies, and that the heights of the peaks were proportional to c_j^2, the squares of the unknown amplitudes. This function is known as the periodogram.

Autoregressive model

$$X_t = \sum_{j=1}^{m} a_j X_{t-j} + \epsilon_t$$

so that X_t is formed by a linear sum of earlier X's plus a white noise residual. Such a model will be found to contain no strictly cyclical components and so, if the periodogram is formed from data generated in this fashion, the resulting diagram takes on a form that is of little direct use, partly due to the unfortunate statistical properties of the periodogram. The coefficients a_j in the autoregressive model can be found by least squares, i.e. the $\hat{a}_j$'s are chosen so as to minimise

$$J = \sum_{t=m+1}^{n}\left(x_t - \sum_{j=1}^{m} a_j X_{t-j}\right)^2.$$

The solution involves the inversion of a matrix of covariances.

Other models can also be suggested, such as a mixture of the autoregressive and linear cyclic models. In economics, such a mixed model has frequently been proposed, in that it has been suggested that an economic variable can be usefully decomposed into the components:

trend + business cycles + seasonal + (autoregressive) residual. The object of such analysis is, then, to determine the properties of each component.

In the 1940's, some work by Wiener, Kolmogoroff and others suggested a new approach which both generalised earlier methods and also enabled considerable advances to be made in interpretations of the analysis. However, the new method, known as spectral analysis, involves more complicated mathematics and so is more difficult to explain. An attempt has been made elsewhere in some detail (Granger and Hatanaka, 1965). All that will be attempted here is to provide the basic formulae and then attempt to explain them in terms of analogies.

The two formulae which provide the basis of the whole method are the so-called spectral representation of the covariance sequence

$$\mu(\tau) = E[X_t \overline{X_{t-\tau}}] = \int_{-\pi}^{\pi} \exp(i\tau\omega) \, dF(\omega) \tag{1}$$

and the spectral representation of the series, called for convenience the Cramér representation

$$X_t = \int_{-\pi}^{\pi} \exp(it\omega) \, dz(\omega) \tag{2}$$

where $z(\omega)$ is a complex random function having the properties

$$E[dz(\omega) \, dz(\lambda)] = 0, \qquad \omega \neq \lambda$$
$$= dF(\omega), \qquad \omega = \lambda$$

and where $F(\omega)$ is a distribution function multiplied by a positive constant, so that $F(\omega_1) \geqslant F(\omega_2)$ for all $\omega_1 \geqslant \omega_2$ and $F(-\pi) = 0$.

Anyone unfamiliar with Fourier transforms or complex random functions is likely to find these formulae awsome. It is possible, however, to explain the basic ideas underlying the formulae fairly simply. Consider a time series made up of a number of purely cyclical components with amplitudes a_j, frequencies† ω_j and phases θ_j, i.e.

$$X_t = \sum_{j=1}^{m} a_j \cos(t\omega_j + \theta_j) \tag{3}$$

and suppose that for any particular realisation of the process (i.e. any observed sample), the a_j and θ_j's are selected at random from some given distributions. One might consider for instance, all the a_j's coming from normal distributions with zero means, so that $a_j \sim N(0, \sigma_j^2)$ and all the θ_j's from rectangular distributions on $[-\pi, \pi]$. Further, suppose that all the a_j's and θ_j's are independent of one another. For any particular realisation the a_j's and θ_j's will be fixed at the start and will remain constant, but in terms of the underlying generating process X_t they will be

---

† 'Frequency' ω corresponds to 'period' $p = 2\pi/\omega$.

random variables. Thus, X_t is the finite sum of independent components, each of which has associated with it a different frequency. By direct evaluation, one finds that

$$\text{var}(X_t) = \tfrac{1}{2} \sum \sigma_j^2$$

and

$$\mu(\tau) = \text{cov}(X_t, X_{t-\tau}) = \tfrac{1}{2} \sum \sigma_j^2 \cos \tau \omega_j$$

so that the importance of each component can be measured in terms of the contribution it makes ($\tfrac{1}{2}\sigma_j^2$) to the total variance of X_t. Similarly, one can represent the sequence $\mu(\tau)$, ($\tau = 0, 1, 2, ...$), by

$$\mu(\tau) = \int_{-\pi}^{\pi} \cos \tau \omega \, d F(\omega)$$

where $F(\omega)$ is a step function, with steps of size $\tfrac{1}{2}\sigma_j^2$ at ω_j and flat everywhere else. This latter equation is a real version of Equation (1).

Suppose now that we consider a generalisation of this model so that the *number* of components becomes extremely large and the contribution made to the variance of X_t by any one component becomes small. We could then talk about the contribution made to var(X_t) by all components with frequencies in some given band of frequencies. If we add up the contributions to var(X_t) made by all components with frequencies less than or equal to ω_0, this is then equal to the function $F(\omega_0)$ introduced above. It is seen that as all frequencies must lie in the region $(-\pi, \pi)$, that $F(-\pi) = 0$ and $F(\pi) = \text{var}(X_t)$.

A simpler version of Equation (1) is:

$$\mu(\tau) = \int_{-\pi}^{\pi} \cos \tau \omega \, f(\omega) \, d\omega. \tag{4}$$

Here $f(\omega)$ is the derivative of $F(\omega)$ and is called the power spectral density function or power spectrum. It arises in the limit considered above when no one component makes a finite contribution to var(X_t) but the sum of components with frequencies in any small band do make a finite contribution. The distinction is similar to that between the frequency function for a continuous random variable whereas if one has a discrete random variable no such frequency function exists.

To summarise, the model considered has the following two properties: (a) the series X_t is decomposed into a large (uncountable) number of independent components, each of which is associated with a different frequency; (b) the relative importance of any group of components is measured by their contribution to var(X_t). In particular, if no one component makes a finite contribution, then the contribution of all components with frequencies in the band (ω, $\omega + d\omega$) is $f(\omega)d\omega$, where $f(\omega)$ is the power spectrum.

The Basic Notions of Spectral Analysis

As the spectral concept is not a particularly easy one, this section is devoted to giving an analogy that has been found useful in the past.

We consider the total amount of sound (or noise) coming over a very wide radio band. If we had a very crude instrument which transformed all the noise into sounds audible to the human ear, the resulting cacophony would resemble the type of (stationary) time series that we are usually trying to analyze; that is, it is built up of many components, and we would like to know more about each component. Just as the ear can filter out sounds and concentrate on a particular one, so can a radio concentrate on a particular wave-band. Everyone has at some time swung the dial of a radio set across a wave-band, and the experience there gained can be used in an explanation of the spectrum. Suppose that we have a simple radio set that does not emit the actual words or sounds found at any frequency but only indicates the total power (or amount) of sound. By this we mean in effect that our simple radio set has the ability to look at one wave-length (frequency) at a time without being distracted by what is to be found at other frequencies. If we used our set when no stations were broadcasting, it would not register a zero amount of sound at every point but rather a small, constant amount. This is due to all the "atmospherics" and internally produced noise of the set and thus corresponds to receiving a purely random signal. If, however, some stations are broadcasting at that time, theoretically each will be sending signals at one frequency only. The radio will now show the small, constant (background) noise at all frequencies except at a finite number (corresponding to the number of stations) where it will record the individual power put out by that station. The radio will thus find the position of the frequencies at which the stations are broadcasting together with the strength of signal being received at these frequencies. In practice, the sound from a particular station is not to be found at a single point only but rather is spread around the point, although with decreasing power. Figures 1, 2, and 3 illustrate the three types of signals discussed above.

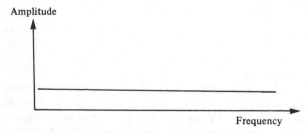

Figure 1. Random signal only.

We now define a *spectrum* as a diagram showing the size of the amplitude at each frequency to be found in a particular time series. It should not be surprising to learn that it may be proved that perfect knowledge of a spectrum will determine the *properties* of a time series, but not its actual values, due to the probabilistic elements involved. In any case, the spectrum will certainly show which are the important components of the series.

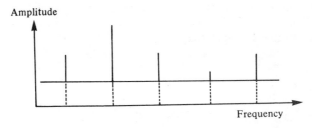

Figure 2. Theoretical signal when stations are broadcasting.

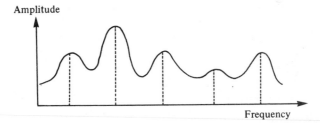

Figure 3. Actual signal when stations are broadcasting.

Figures 1–3 illustrate certain types of time series: Figure 1 is, of course, the spectrum of a purely random, independent series (white noise), Figure 2 is the theoretical spectrum of the linear cyclic model, whereas Figure 3 represents the perfect estimate (should such a thing exist) of the spectrum of a time series of finite length generated by the linear cyclic model. (Figure 3 corresponds to the shape that Schuster hoped his periodogram would take.)

It might be noted that even if the stations were broadcasting as in Figure 2, a real radio is unable to concentrate on a single wave-length, but rather gives the output over a small wave-band, centred on this wave-length, possibly with weights decreasing from the centre of the band outward. Thus, even if the stations were broadcasting as in Figure 2 the radio's output would resemble Figure 3. This situation is identical to that when we attempt to estimate the spectrum; having only a finite amount of data available, we are forced to estimate the spectrum over a finite number of frequency bands.

Suppose that our simplified radio is now attached to a radio telescope, which is directed towards some point in the Milky Way. It is possible

that the resulting plot of power against frequency would look like
Figure 1 or 3, but it is also plausible to expect a more complicated result
as shown in Figure 4 or 5. It is clear that such "spectra", as we may
now think of them, cannot arise from series which are derived from a
linear cyclic model. On the other hand, it is perfectly possible for a
series from a linear regressive model to produce such a smooth spectrum,
although a smooth spectrum does not necessarily indicate that a linear
regressive model is the correct one. Many more complicated systems
could also produce a similar shape.

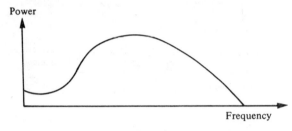

Figure 4.

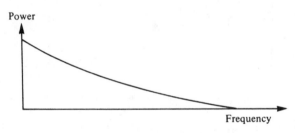

Figure 5.

By examining a spectrum the important *bands* of frequencies may be
seen although little can be said about the underlying generating process
(except, perhaps, that it is doubtful that it is linear cyclic).

It must be emphasized that the above analogy has been presented only
to help understand the ideas involved in the concept of a spectrum and,
like all analogies, it must not be taken too far.

It is seen then, that the spectrum will suggest the type of model that
might be fitted to the data; a very flat spectrum would suggest a white
noise (purely random), a smooth spectrum would suggest an autoregressive model but any sharp spikes would indicate the possible presence of
purely cyclical components.

One other use of the spectrum is to specify the effect of a linear filter
on the data. Suppose a series X_t is given with spectrum $f(\omega)$ and that a
second series Y_t is formed by

$$Y_t = \sum c_j X_{t-j}$$

then Y_t is said to be a filtered version of X_t and it can be shown that the spectrum of Y_t is given by $f_Y(\omega) = c(\omega)f(\omega)$ where

$$c(\omega) = \left| \sum c_j \exp(-ij\omega) \right|^2 \qquad (5)$$

It is seen that by choosing the c_j's properly, the spectrum of Y_t can be made to have approximately any desired shape. In particular, one can reduce in importance or remove completely any purely cyclical component. Thus, suppose X_t is measured monthly and has a seasonal component. Then if

$$Y_t = \tfrac{1}{12} \sum_{j=1}^{12} X_{t-j}$$

it can be shown that Y_t will have no seasonal component. Of course, the effect of such a filter will have other consequences and these can be determined by Equation (5).

This idea is also useful in dealing with trends. In practice, there is no generally accepted and satisfactory definition of what is meant by a trend. It is normally taken to be a very smooth component, either continually increasing or continually decreasing and is usually taken to be well represented by some simple function of time, such as a linear, exponential or polynomial function. One point about such functions is that they never repeat themselves, so that they can be said to have an infinite period and hence a zero frequency. It is thus seen that trend terms, in theory at least, only affect the spectrum at zero frequency. Thus, if a filter is devised which cuts out low frequencies to a large extent, this filter will effectively remove trend. One way of doing this, for instance, is to form a moving average of the series X_t, that is,

$$Z_t = \frac{1}{2m+1} \sum_{j=-m}^{m} X_{t-j}$$

and then forming $X_t - Z_t$. It is also possible to remove trends by regression techniques, that is by estimating the trend curve from the data and then subtracting it. However, the side effects of this procedure are less easily investigated.

The problem of how, given some data, a spectrum is estimated is too complicated to go into here. A number of computer programs exist for this purpose.

The Analysis of Two or More Series

Consider now two stationary series X_t and Y_t. The methods introduced above can be easily generalised to analyse the relationship between such a pair of series. The autoregressive model, for instance, generalises into the pair of equations

$$X_t = \sum a_j X_{t-j} + \sum b_j Y_{t-j} + \epsilon_t$$
$$Y_t = \sum c_j X_{t-j} + \sum d_j Y_{t-j} + \eta_t .$$

However, it is often easier to interpret relationships through a generalisation of the spectral methods, known as cross-spectral analysis. For the sake of exposition, suppose that each series is decomposed into $m+1$ components, each of which is associated with a frequency (or narrow frequency range), i.e.

$$X_t = \sum_{j=0}^{m} X_{jt}$$

$$Y_t = \sum_{j=0}^{m} Y_{jt}.$$

We know from above that any pair of X components is uncorrelated, i.e.

$$E[X_{jt}X_{kt}] = 0, \quad (j \neq k),$$

(taking $E[X_t] = 0$) and similarly for any pair of Y components. If the pair of series X_t, Y_t are so-called jointly stationary, that is their relationship does not change over time, then it follows that any non-corresponding pairs of components, one from X_t and one from Y_t, are uncorrelated, i.e.

$$E[X_{jt}Y_{kt}] = 0, \quad (j \neq k).$$

It then follows that any relationship between the series can be measured solely in terms of the relationship between corresponding components, i.e. X_{jt} and Y_{jt}, $(j = 0, ..., m)$, in the present simplified model.

This relationship can be constructed from just two parts, the square of the correlation between X_{jt} and Y_{jt}, for each j, known as the *coherence* and the phase-difference between them, remembering that they are associated with identical frequencies. If coherence is plotted against frequency a *coherence-diagram* is obtained. This diagram measures for each frequency the strength of the relationship between corresponding components. A value near zero indicating no relationship, a value near one suggesting an almost perfect relationship. The phase-diagram being the plot of the phase-difference against frequency can be interpreted in terms of the time lag of one component to the corresponding component in the other series. Thus, for instance, if $Y_t = X_{t-k}+Z_t$, where Z_t is a series uncorrelated (having zero coherence) with X_t, then the phase-diagram will be the straight line $k\omega$, and so the extent of the time lag k can be measured directly from the slope of the line. It should be noted that if the series are measured monthly, for instance, then k can be some fraction of a month and could still be estimated. This kind of interpretation is really only relevant when one series is essentially lagging the other. If feedback is occurring between the series, the problems become much more complex.

To state these results formally:

$$\mu^{xy}(\tau) = E[X_t Y_{t-\tau}] = \int_{-\pi}^{\pi} \exp(i\tau\omega)\, c_r(\omega)\, d\omega$$

where $c_r(\omega)$ is the cross-spectrum.

Coherence is defined by

$$C(\omega) = \frac{|c_r(\omega)|^2}{fx(\omega)fy(\omega)}$$

and phase defined by

$$\phi(\omega) = \tan^{-1}\frac{\text{Imaginary part of } c_r(\omega)}{\text{Real part of } c_r(\omega)}.$$

Again, these techniques can be generalised to the case of several jointly stationary series. One can define and interpret concepts such as the partial cross-spectrum, so that the relationship between two series can be discussed *after* all the relevant data about them contained in the other series has been subtracted.

Further details about all of the above techniques, together with some further developments, practical problems and applications to economics, can be found in the references given at the end of this paper.

THE ANALYSIS OF SPATIAL DATA

A number of writers have suggested that many of the concepts introduced above for time series can be extended immediately to spatial data, (see for instance Bartlett, 1955, p.188, Whittle, 1963, 1954, and Priestley, 1964). Mathematically, the argument proceeds as follows: Let the variables p, q each take the values $..., -2, -1, 0, 1, 2, ...$ and let X_{pq} be the value taken by a random variable at the grid-point (p, q). Thus, for instance, a rectangular grid could be placed on a map and X_{pq} could be the height above sea-level measured at each point where two grid-lines cross. Suppose that the mean value of X_{pq} is constant for all p, q and is then subtracted, so that we can consider $E[X_{pq}] = 0$ for all p, q. If this mean varied from one point to another it might be possible to consider such variation as a trend-term. This is discussed further below. The spatial process X_{pq} is said to be spatially stationary if

$$\mu(\tau, k) = E[X_{pq}X_{p-\tau, q-k}]$$

i.e. the covariance between two X values depends only on the differences in coordinates and not on the actual p, q values.

It is easy to see how one would estimate these covariances or the corresponding spatial correlations. Given data x_{pq}, $(p = 1, ..., m;$ $q = 1, ..., n)$, an estimate of $\mu(\tau, k)$ would be

$$\hat{\mu}(\tau, k) = \frac{1}{mn} \sum_{\substack{p = \tau, ..., m \\ q = k, ..., n}}^{n} (x_{pq} - \bar{x})(x_{p-\tau, q-k} - \bar{x})$$

and an estimate of the correlation coefficient would be

$$\hat{\rho}(\tau, k) = \frac{\hat{\mu}(\tau, k)}{\hat{\mu}(0, 0)}.$$

Rather than divide the sum by mn it will sometimes be better to divide by $(m-\tau)(n-k)$. Here

$$\bar{x} = \frac{1}{mn} \sum_{s,\,t} x_{st}.$$

These correlation coefficients may be quite large in number, and it is tempting to try to summarise or transform them. Following the time series analogy, some of the writers mentioned above have suggested estimating spectra. The formal mathematical model gives

$$\mu(\tau, k) = \int_{-\pi}^{\pi} \int_{-\pi}^{\pi} \exp i\tau\omega \exp ik\lambda \, dF(\omega, \lambda)$$

where $F(\omega, \lambda)$ is a bivariate distribution. If F contains no steps (or singularities in its derivate) then the bivariate power spectrum can be defined by

$$f(\omega, \lambda) = \frac{\partial^2 F(\omega, \lambda)}{\partial\omega\partial\lambda}.$$

In particular, if $f(\omega, \lambda) = $ constant this means that $\mu(\tau, k) = 0$, (all $\tau, k \neq 0$), and so the X_{pq} are a purely random, non-interconnected set of random numbers placed on a grid, i.e. a spatial white noise process.

Using two spatial processes X_{pq}, Y_{pq} it is possible to define a bivariate cross-spectrum and the other functions derived from it. Alternatively an attempt might be made to build a model to explain the inter-relationships between neighbouring X_{pq}'s.

For a time series, the simplest model of inter-related terms is the first order autoregressive scheme

$$X_t = aX_{t-1} + \text{white noise.}$$

For spatial processes a similar and reasonably simple model would be

Model A: $X_{pq} = aX_{p-1,\,q} + bX_{p+1,\,q} + cX_{p,\,q-1} + dX_{p,\,q+1} + \epsilon_{pq}$

where ϵ_{pq} is a spatial white noise process. We immediately encounter the first major problem concerned with spatial processes, apart from their relative complexity. For the time series and model there exists a natural causal mechanism. The past can cause the future but the future cannot cause the past. No such causal mechanism applies naturally to spatial processes. This leads to a number of difficulties. Whereas it is easy to simulate time series models on a computer it is by no means easy to form an example of a spatial process generated even by the above simple model. It is possible, however, to generate models having (virtually) the same spatial correlations. It is possible to find a spatial autoregressive model for X_{pq} involving only (possibly infinite) linear sums of X_{jk} with $j < p$, any k and X_{pk}, $k < q$, which has the same spatial correlations and hence the same bivariate spectrum. The model would be of the form

Model B: $X_{pq} = \sum_{\substack{j < p \\ k}} a_{jk} X_{jk} + \sum_{k < q} a_{pk} X_{pk} + \epsilon_{pq},$

The forms of the two models may be illustrated as in Figures 6 and 7. The heavy dots in these two Figures denote the location of variables which enter into the model, the empty circle representing the location of X_{pq}. The fact that we are not able to distinguish between this pair of models using covariance or spectral techniques means that causal interpretation of such models becomes extremely difficult. (This equivalence of models has been discussed by Wiener, 1949, p.78, and Whittle, 1954.)

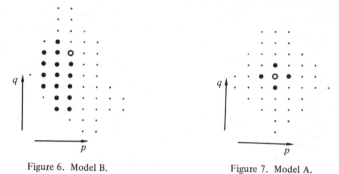

Figure 6. Model B.   Figure 7. Model A.

If an attempt is made to estimate the coefficients of model A by minimising

$$U = \sum_{pq} (x_{pq} - ax_{p-1, q} - bx_{p+1, q} - cx_{p, q-1} - dx_{p, q+1})^2$$

with respect to the parameters a, b, c and d absurd results are obtained. Whittle (1954) has shown that in fact kU should be minimised with respect to the parameters, where U is as before and contains the data, and k is a very complicated mathematical function of a, b, c and d and does not contain data. The resulting equations are not simple to solve. It is clear that many of the methods, which prove to be useful in dealing with time series, are vastly more complicated when generalised in an attempt to deal with data from spatial processes.

A similar remark applies when considering discontinuous spectra, a very full mathematical study of which has been made by Priestley (1964). For a time series, a discontinuity in the spectrum corresponds to a purely periodic component in the series, such as a time invariate seasonal component. For spatial processes there are many possible discontinuities in the bivariate spectrum, the majority of which have no simple interpretations. Two types which may be interpreted are straight line and point discontinuities. The line discontinuity corresponds to a spatial wave, like a sheet of corrugated iron. The point discontinuity corresponds to a spatial cycle, having many evenly placed peaks and an appearance like the bottom of an egg-box. Although such shapes may be of some relevance to geological or biological data, it is doubtful whether they are of any importance for spatially distributed economic data.

When real data are considered the already complicated problems of estimation and interpretation become even more difficult. Real economic data of the sort examined in Regional Science are not usually recorded on any neat grid. Instead they are generally either values recorded at some arbitrary set of points (p_j, q_j) on the (pq) plane or they are the set of accumulations over specified economic or political regions. Thus, for instance, an example of the first type of data is wind speed recorded at various meteorological stations; an example of the second type is unemployment in each state, county or parish. The first type of data may be considered to be a sample from a continuous random variable $X(p, q)$ which exists at every point on the plane. The second type of data may be thought of as arising from a random variable which takes a value *not* at every point in the plane but for any small region in the plane, i.e. $X(p, q)dpdq$. The value for a whole county is then the integral of this variable over all the small regions which make up the county, i.e.

$$\iint_{county} X(p, q)dp\,dq.$$

A similar distinction may be made with time series data. Price, for instance, can in theory at least be recorded at any moment of time and the series actually observed, such as a closing stock market price, is a sample from the continuous flow of data. Production on the other hand is the accumulation of units produced over some specified time interval. Only on rare occasions does this distinction have any importance in time series analysis but this is likely to be less true for spatial data. Data arising in economic regional analysis are generally of the accumulated type. It is usual, of course, to transform this type of data into a facsimile of the continuous type by placing the numbers at the centroids of the regions or counties. The model however is worth bearing in mind when attempting to answer the question: what are measures of continuity or spatial correlation actually trying to measure?

The fact that actual data rarely occur on a grid makes model building, for instance, almost impossible. However, it is still possible to estimate spatial correlations and in a form that is probably more useful. When interpreting a set of spatial correlations, the relationships between points along the lines of a right-angled coordinate system are not really what is required. It is simpler to discuss correlations between points which are some set distance apart, possibly without referring to direction, i.e.
$\mu(r) = E[X_{pq}X_{uv}]$ where
$$r^2 = (p-u)^2+(q-v)^2.$$

However a more useful form is to consider a spatially stationary process such that
$$\mu(r, \theta) = E[X_{pq}X_{uv}]$$

where
$$r^2 = (p-u)^2 + (q-v)^2$$
and
$$\theta = \tan^{-1}\left(\frac{q-v}{p-u}\right).$$

Appendix I discusses estimation problems for such correlations given real data and an example is provided. Given such spatial correlations an estimated bivariate spectrum could also be obtained, given two spatial processes, and it would be possible to obtain an estimated bivariate cross-spectrum. Interpretation of these functions is, in general, not easy. In particular, it is doubtful if the bivariate cross-spectrum could be used to find spatially displaced relationships, being equivalent to the major use of the cross-spectrum to find leads or lags between a pair of time series.

Most of the functions that statisticians have introduced into the field of spatial processes, such as the generalised spectra, seem to have been introduced simply because the mathematics exists, and represent extensions of methods made familiar by time series analysis. Little or no thought seems to have been given to the usefulness, naturalness or interpretation of the functions. The concept of frequency, for instance, is a very natural one for a time sequence, but is very much less natural when related to spatial processes, although the mathematical tools allow its introduction. We have already seen the difficulties involved in interpreting even the simplest spatial model and the virtual impossibility of estimating such models from real data. It should be clear from what has been said so far that it is very easy to criticise the current methods of dealing with spatial data.

However, a much more telling criticism exists. All the possible methods developed so far rely heavily on an assumption of stationarity, that is, an assumption that the relationship between values of the processes is the same for *every* pair of points whose *relative* positions are the same. Thus, for example, if direction did not matter, the degree to which these variables were related would depend only on the distance between the points. The relationship between values measured at Oxford and London will be the same as between values measured at two Lincolnshire villages 55 or so miles apart. The correlation between unemployment figures in New York and Philadelphia will be the same as between two small mid-Western towns roughly a hundred miles apart. This assumption of stationarity on the plane is completely unrealistic for economic variables. Attempts might be made to use measures of 'distance', other than a purely spatial measure. The values entering into an estimate of a correlation might be weighted in some way to allow for differences in the size of towns or regions. To succeed properly such methods presume considerable knowledge about the variable under study and increase the complexity of how to interpret the results. The theoretical or population correlation between values of an economic variable measured at various points will in general vary considerably from one location to another, particularly in the neighbourhood of large conurbations, such as London or Los Angeles. If the assumption of stationarity is discarded there is little reason to sum over pairs of similarly placed points across the plane to form estimates of spatial correlation. At best one can hope for some average relationship, at worst a meaningless number will result.

What is to be done? An answer can be found by considering more carefully what one is attempting to do when forming statistics such as spatial correlations. By considering the interpretation hoped for from these statistics some kind of answer arises, as will be shown below.

THE ANALYSIS OF SPATIAL DATA OVER TIME

Suppose that data are available from a stationary spatial process and that a set of estimates of spatial correlations are formed by some method such as that outlined in Appendix I. The question is, what can be done with these estimates? Given sufficient statistical expertise one might be able to test whether any single coefficient were significantly non-zero or if some set of coefficients were non-zero. A theoretically zero value is easily interpreted as indicating no (linear) relationship between the variables used in forming the correlation. But what if the test rejects a hypothesis that the true value is zero? This would suggest that there is then some kind of relationship operating and this is in itself of interest. However, the next stage is to ask whether the form of the relationship found cannot be expressed in a more useful manner. For the analogous situation with time series, the serial correlations by themselves are extremely difficult to interpret. Interpretation only becomes satisfactory when these serial correlations are related to specific kinds of models or are transformed into spectra. However, as explained in the previous section, this is by no means easy to do with spatial correlations.

The big temptation with any significantly non-zero correlation coefficient is to attempt to imply causality from it. However a spatial correlation coefficient, like most other correlation coefficients, cannot, in fact, prove anything about causality. An exception to this rule is the serial correlation coefficients derived from time series. Due to time-ordering resulting in the self-evident fact that the future cannot cause the past, causal interpretations can on occasions be given to serial correlations. It has been argued elsewhere, (Granger and Hatanaka, 1965), that a testable form of causality can only be derived from time-ordered sequences of observations. This is not an appropriate place to go into the suggested theory of testing for causality.

We now turn to a class of data for which the majority of the problems discussed above can probably be solved. Suppose that there is given a set of observations $X(p, q; t)$ of a spatial process observed at spatial locations with coordinates (p, q) and at a sequence of times $t = 1, ..., n$.

Thus, there are a number of time series of values for the variable at each available location. Suppose, further, for the time being, that the process is not spatially stationary but that for each location it is time-stationary. We can now apply all of the theory of multivariate time series as discussed in the first section. Auto-serial correlations and spectra can be formed for any one series, cross-serial correlations and cross-spectra can be formed for any pair of series and partial correlations and partial spectra can be formed for any pair of series given any set of other series. The outcome will be very many correlations or spectral functions and care will have to be taken in summarising and presenting the results. The interpretation of any coherence diagram, for instance, will have to be both in terms of frequency and also of the relative spatial positions of the two time series used. In Appendix II an example of this type of analysis is given using unemployment data. A similar method has been successfully used in an investigation of the term structure of interest rates, (Granger and Rees, 1968).

With spatial-time data, currently available techniques can be used; in fact all the methods devised for analysing stationary and non-stationary series become available. It must be admitted that the proposed method of investigation, (that of analysing the series in pairs or within small sets), does not make complete use of the spatial aspect of the data, at least not until interpretation of the results is begun. However, it is now possible to build models which are stationary over time but not necessarily stationary over space and it is possible to begin thinking in terms of causal structures. It is also quite easy to generalise the method to deal with pairs of spatial processes measured at constant time intervals, such as employment and production measured monthly, for some group of economic or political units within a country. The amount of data available has to be sufficient for a time-series analysis to be carried out, (say 40 terms or more), but a large number of spatially separated series is not required. The amount of data handling necessary would be extensive and a large computer and modern methods of computation would need to be employed (c.f. Jenkins and Watt, 1968). However, the effort is likely to prove worthwhile.

References

Bartlett, M.S., 1955, *An Introduction to Stochastic Processes* (Cambridge University Press, Cambridge).

Bartlett, M.S., 1964, "The Spectral Analysis of Two-dimensional Point Processes", *Biometrika*, **51**, 299–311.

Granger, C.W.J., and Hatanaka, M., 1965, *Spectral Analysis of Economic Time Series*, (Princeton University Press, Princeton).

Granger, C.W.J., and Rees, H., 1968, "Spectral Analysis of the Term Structure of Interest Rates", *Review of Economic Studies*, **35**, 67–76.

Jenkins, G.M., and Watts, D.G., 1968, *Spectral Analysis and its Applications* (Holden Day, New York).

Priestley, M.B., 1964, "The Analysis of Two-dimensional Stationary Processes with Discontinuous Spectra", *Biometrika*, **51**, 195–217.

Schuster, A., 1900, "The Periodogram of Magnetic Declination", *Transactions of the Cambridge Philosophical Society*, **18**, 107.

Whittle, P., 1954, "On Stationary Processes in the Plane", *Biometrika*, **41**, 434–449.

Whittle, P., 1963, *Prediction and Regulation* (English University Press, London).

Wiener, N., 1949, *The Extrapolation, Interpolation and Smoothing of Stationary Time-Series* (John Wiley, New York).

APPENDIX I

AN ESTIMATE OF SPATIAL CORRELATION

Consider a stationary continuous spatial process $X(p, q)$ defined at all points (p, q) on the plane. Let the spatial covariance between $X(p, q)$, $X(u, v)$ where the points (p, q) and (u, v) are distance r apart and at angle θ be

$$\mu(r, \theta) = \text{cov}[X(p, q) X(u, v)]$$

where

$$r^2 = (p-u)^2 + (q-v)^2$$

and

$$\tan\theta = \frac{v-q}{u-p}.$$

As the process is stationary, $\text{var}[X(p, q)] = \tau_x^2$ is a constant for any (p, q) and the spatial correlation coefficient will be

$$\rho(r, \theta) = \frac{\mu(r, \theta)}{\tau_x^2}$$

If now data are available of the form $x(p_j, q_j)$ recorded at the given points (p_j, q_j), $(j = 1, ..., n)$, how can $\mu(r, \theta)$ be estimated and hence $\rho(r, \theta)$? As in general the points (p_j, q_j) will obey no particular pattern, it will be quite impossible to estimate $\rho(r, \theta)$ for *every* r and θ. In fact, for most combinations of r and θ there will be no pairs (p_j, q_j), (p_k, q_k) which are separated by a distance r and at an angle θ. For values of r and θ where there is such a combination of observation points there will only very rarely be more than a single pair of such points. It is clear therefore that the most that can be hoped for is an estimate of the integral (or average) of $\mu(r, \theta)$ over some subset of r, θ values.

Divide the range of possible values for r $(0, \infty)$ into m sections R_j, $(j = 1, ..., m)$, where

$$R_1 \equiv 0 < r \leqslant r_1$$
$$R_2 \equiv r_1 < r \leqslant r_2$$
$$R_3 \equiv r_2 < r \leqslant r_3$$
$$\vdots$$
$$R_m \equiv r_m < r < \infty$$

Usually $r_1, r_2, ...$ will be equally spaced but not necessarily. Similarly, divide the range of possible value of θ $(0, 2\pi)$ into m' sections T_j, $(j = 1, ..., m')$ where

$$T_1 \equiv 0 \leqslant \theta \leqslant \theta_1$$
$$T_2 \equiv \theta_1 < \theta \leqslant \theta_2$$
$$\vdots$$
$$T_{m'} \equiv \theta_{m'} < \theta \leqslant 2\pi$$

A couplet (R_j, T_k) will represent a spatial segment and an attempt might be made to estimate 'average' convariances over such segments, i.e.

$$\mu(R_j, T_k) = \int_{\substack{r \in R_j \\ \theta \in T_k}} \mu(r, \theta)\, dr\, d\theta$$

Let

$$\bar{x} = \frac{1}{n}\sum_{j=0}^{n} x(p_j, q_j)$$

and

$$x'(p_j, q_j) = x(p_j, q_j) - \bar{x}$$

then an estimate for $\bar{\mu}(R_j, T_k)$ will be

$$\overline{m}(R_j, T_k) = \frac{1}{N_{jk}}\sum x'(p_a, q_a) x'(p_b, q_b)$$

summed over all a, b such that

$$r^2 = (p_a - p_b)^2 + (q_a - q_b)^2 \qquad \text{and } r \in R_j$$

$$\tan\theta = \frac{q_b - q_a}{p_b - p_a} \qquad \text{and } \theta \in T_k.$$

N_{jk} is the number of terms entering into the sum. Thus, the estimate is the product of all x values after subtraction of the overall mean, as summed over all pairs whose values are measured at points whose distance apart is between r_j and r_{j+1} and at an angle θ lying in the region T_k. In a sense, each point (p_a, q_a) is taken in turn and then other points; the specified distance and direction apart, are sought. If N_{jk} is not large enough for a reasonable estimate to be formed, the effective sample size can be increased by using a smoothed estimate of the form

$$\overline{\overline{m}}(R_j, T_k) = \frac{\sum_{L,m} a_{Lm} N_{Lm} \overline{m}(R_L, T_m)}{\sum_{L,m} a_{Lm} N_{Lm}}$$

where a_{Lm} are appropriate weights. A simple set to use is:

m

				$j-2$	$j-1$	j	$j+1$	$j+2$	
$k+2$	...	∘	∘	∘	∘	∘	∘	∘	...
$k+1$	...	∘	∘	$\frac{1}{16}$	$\frac{1}{8}$	$\frac{1}{16}$	∘	∘	...
k	...	∘	∘	$\frac{1}{8}$	$\frac{1}{4}$	$\frac{1}{8}$	∘	∘	...
$k-1$	...	∘	∘	$\frac{1}{16}$	$\frac{1}{8}$	$\frac{1}{16}$	∘	∘	...
$k-2$	...	∘	∘	∘	∘	∘	∘	∘	...

$$L$$

If the data suggest that it is necessary, a polynomial trend should first be removed by least squares. The trend term is given by

$$t(p, q) = \sum_{L, m} b_{Lm} p^L q^m$$

where the coefficients b_{Lm} are found by minimising

$$I = \sum_a [X(p_a, q_a) - t(p_a, q_a)]^2.$$

An *Algol* computer program has been used to form estimates of spectral correlation for any number of sectors and rings, and with smoothing and trend removal if necessary. The program has been written to find R_{min}, the smallest distance between any two data-recording points and R_{max}, the largest distance. The rings then divide $R_{max} - R_{min}$ into any required number of equi-sized segments.

As an example of the use of this program three sets of spatial data were investigated. These data consist of: the percentage capital income, (X), the percentage of all workers who are agricultural workers, (Y), and the percentage of all land that is arable land, (Z), recorded in 1962 for the 90 administrative units of France†. A quadratic spatial trend term of the form

$$T(p, q) = a + bq + cp + dp^2 + epq + fq^2$$

was fitted for each variable by least squares regression and subtracted from the data. The instantaneous correlation coefficients, ignoring spatial arrangements (i.e. assuming zero distance between the locations of

† Data are taken from: *Annuaire Statistique de la France*, Institut National de la Statistique et des Etudes Economiques, 1963.

all data points) are:

$$\text{corr}(X, Y) = -0\cdot693$$
$$\text{corr}(X, Z) = -0\cdot146$$
$$\text{corr}(Y, Z) = 0\cdot017$$

The last of these is surprisingly small, and probably the removal of the quadratic trend terms removed any relationship between the two variables Y and Z.

The spatial correlations found were all very small. Four sectors and five rings were used, the rings being of equal size, splitting the minimum distance of 1 and the maximum distance of 211 between recording points into five equal sections. For the variable X, the estimated spatial correlations were:

	Sector 1 (East to North)	Sector 2 (North to West)	Average over all sectors
Inner ring	0·02	0·08	0·05
2nd ring	−0·11	−0·03	−0·07
3rd ring	−0·00	0·05	0·02
4th ring	0·10	−0·11	−0·02
5th ring	no estimate	0·04	0·04
Average over all rings	−0·03	0·01	

(Due to symmetry the results for sector 3 are the same as sector 1, those for sector 4 are the same as for sector 2.)

The other two variables gave similar results. It must be concluded that, after removal of quadratic spatial trend terms, the variables seem to be spatial white noise or purely random processes.

The set of spatial cross-correlations between X and Y was found to be:

	Sector 1 (E to N)	Sector 2 (N to W)	Sector 3 (W to S)	Sector 4 (S to E)	Average over all sectors
Inner ring	0·03	−0·07	−0·02	−0·04	−0·03
2nd ring	0·06	0·11	0·05	0·01	0·06
3rd ring	−0·01	−0·11	−0·02	−0·01	−0·04
4th ring	−0·07	0·17	−0·04	0·05	0·05
Outer ring	no estimate	−0·24	no estimate	−0·02	−0·13
Average over all rings	0·02	0·01	0·01	0·00	

These figures are all so small that no spatial relationship seems to exist between these two variables, after trend removal. A fuller report on these and other calculations is under preparation.

APPENDIX II

AN EXAMPLE OF SPATIAL TIME-SERIES ANALYSIS: UNEMPLOYMENT DATA

The data used for the example are monthly unemployment figures, seasonally adjusted, for the period August 1958 to March 1965 taken over seven major regions of the U.K., i.e. London and the South-east, East and South, South-west, Wales, North-west, North and Scotland. The figures are taken from the monthly Digest of Statistics, where more precise definitions of the boundaries of the regions can be found. It was not possible to use some of the other regions, such as Midlands or Yorkshire, due to boundary changes. The series used are rather short for a proper time-series study but are sufficient for an illustrative example. Spectra were estimated for each series and cross-spectra for each pair. The spectra were all similar in shape, falling from a high value at low frequency to a low value at high frequency. The cross-spectra are of most interest in the spatial context as the resulting coherence diagrams enable us to examine the degree to which pairs of series are related. The coherence diagrams are also generally similar in shape, being rather constant as frequency increases but with a clear drop in level for very high frequencies. For such shaped coherence diagrams a convenient summary measure of the amount to which two series are related is the average of the estimated coherences, the average being taken over the frequencies. The Table below shows the average coherences between the unemployment series for each pair of regions.

	London and South-east	East and South	South-west	Wales	North-west	North	Scotland
London & S.E.	–	0·8185	0·7743	0·6538	0·7120	0·6859	0·6441
East & South	0·8185	–	0·8186	0·6289	0·5967	0·6729	0·5530
South-west	0·7743	0·8186	–	0·6309	0·5880	0·5806	0·5337
Wales	0·6538	0·6289	0·6309	–	0·5492	0·4321	0·4827
North-west	0·7120	0·5967	0·5880	0·5492	–	0·5137	0·5655
North	0·6859	0·6729	0·5806	0·4321	0·5137	–	0·5827
Scotland	0·6441	0·5530	0·5337	0·4827	0·5655	0·5827	–

The Table is of course symmetric about the main diagonal.

It is seen from the Table that although the coherence diagrams have the same *shapes* they do vary in average *height*. The degree of relatedness might be expected to diminish as distance between the regions increases. This is generally true, for the figures in any row or column decrease with distance from the main diagonal. However, it is seen that the figures also generally decrease in average size as one goes down the rows.

Thus it appears that the series are more highly related for neighbouring areas in the South than for the North. London and the South-west have an average coherence of only $0 \cdot 51$. This strongly suggests that there is *no spatial stationarity* for this set of spatial (and time) variables. If the figures are taken at their face values (i.e. ignoring possible sampling errors and the idea of significant differences) the Northern series seem to be more related to the London series than to each other, possibly reflecting the dominant position played by London and the South in determining the economic prosperity of the country. No significant leads or lags were found although there was a slight indication that both the South-west and Wales were leading both the North and Scotland. Further analysis with longer series should give better information about possible leads and such a study is being planned.

Although this study is only intended as an illustrative example, it does indicate the kind of results and interpretations that should arise from the use of time-series methods with spatial data. Given data for more areas it should be possible to derive more sophisticated spatial models to account for the results obtained.

The Problem of Spatial Autocorrelation [†]

A.D.CLIFF and J.K.ORD
University of Bristol

Introduction

Consider a two dimensional study area which has been partitioned into n' non-overlapping regions that exhaust the study area, such as, for example, counties within a country. Let the value of a variate, X, in the typical county, i, be x_i. We call all n counties for which an x_i exists non-vacant counties. All $n' - n$ counties for which an x_i does not exist are termed vacant counties. In this paper, a statistic is presented which tests for spatial autocorrelation between the x_i in the n counties. While the particular geographic formulation of counties within a country is used, the statistic may be applied to any two or more dimensional space which is either partitioned into an exhaustive set of non-overlapping regions by a regular or irregular lattice into which the x_i are mapped; or for which the x_i are point rather than area based data. Note further that the statistic does not require the x_i to be the observed values for the counties or points. Any convenient values may be used such as normal scores, ranks, or binary data.

The remainder of the paper comprises five sections. First, autocorrelation is defined for spatially arranged data. The fundamental difference between autocorrelation in spatial data, as opposed to unidimensional data such as time series, is discussed. The attempts of Moran (1950), and Geary (1954), to develop a statistic which measures spatial autocorrelation are outlined, and the limitations of the measures they propose are examined. Ways of avoiding the weaknesses inherent in the Moran and Geary statistics are discussed. Second, a statistic is presented which eliminates these weaknesses. Third, the distribution theory of the statistic is developed and the statistic is shown to be asymptotically normal as n increases. Fourth, some empirical applications for the statistic are considered. Data for the Irish Republic first presented in Geary (1954), and reproduced in Table 2, are tested for spatial autocorrelation. Population changes in the City of Bristol and surrounding areas are also investigated using data drawn from the Preliminary Report of the 1961

† The authors wish to thank Mrs. Barbara Gratrix, Mrs. Anne Kempson, Mr. R.Oliver, and Mrs. Mary Reynolds for assistance in the preparation of this paper. All computations were performed at the Bristol University Computer Unit.

Population Census. The results obtained from both analyses are compared with the values given by the Moran and Geary statistics. The statistic is then used as a test for spatial autocorrelation in the residuals from a regression on areally arranged data. Fifth, the conclusions of the paper are discussed, and the directions of research into the problem of spatial autocorrelation which are being followed by the present writers are outlined.

PREVIOUS MEASURES OF SPATIAL AUTOCORRELATION

The Spatial Autocorrelation Problem

We define spatial autocorrelation for a county system in the following way. It is assumed that the x_i in each of the n counties are separate observations on X, and that each x_i is drawn from the same population. If every pair of x_i is uncorrelated, then the data are said to lack spatial autocorrelation. Conversely, if the x_i are not pairwise uncorrelated, then the data are said to be spatially autocorrelated.

The problem of determining whether geographic data are spatially autocorrelated is fundamentally different from measuring autocorrelation in stationary time series. This is due to the fact that the variate of a time series is influenced only by past values, while for a spatial process, dependence extends in all directions. Thus Whittle (1954, p.434) has commented:

"At any instant in a time series we have the natural distinction of past and future, and the value of the observation at that instant depends only upon past values. That is, the dependence extends only in one direction: backwards.... [In] the more general two dimensional case of [say] a field, a dab of fertilizer applied at any point in the field will ultimately affect soil fertility in *all* directions."

Several attempts have been made in the literature to develop a statistic which tests whether or not county data are spatially autocorrelated. Most of this work has focused upon autocorrelation in two and k-colour maps where only nominal and ordinal data can be used[1]. However, measures of spatial autocorrelation which can handle nominal, ordinal and interval data have been considered in detail only by Moran (1950), Geary (1954) and Whittle (1954).

The Moran and Geary approaches

The tests for spatial autocorrelation in county data proposed by Moran (1950) and Geary (1954) are now outlined. Whittle (1954) extends spectral methods to study regular two dimensional point patterns.

---

[1]Statistics for the analysis of two and k-colour maps have been reviewed by Dacey (1965) and have been discussed in detail by Cliff (1969).

This is an essentially different approach to that adopted by Moran and Geary, and is not considered further here.

The statistics given by Moran and Geary test for autocorrelation between the x_i in contiguous non-vacant counties of a county system. The x_i may be measured on a nominal, ordinal or interval scale. Two non-vacant counties are taken to be contiguous if they have a boundary of positive, non-zero length in common. Let $[\delta_{ij}]$ be a connexion matrix in which $\delta_{ij} = 1$ if the ith and jth non-vacant counties are contiguous, and $\delta_{ij} = 0$ otherwise. If two non-vacant counties are contiguous, they are said to be linked by a join. Let the number of non-vacant counties contiguous to the ith non-vacant county be L_i. Then we define

$$A = \tfrac{1}{2} \sum_{i=1}^{n} L_i, \tag{1}$$

$$D = \tfrac{1}{2} \sum_{i=1}^{n} L_i (L_i - 1). \tag{2}$$

Moran's coefficient for interval-scaled x_i only [2]

Moran (1950) has proposed the following estimator of a correlation coefficient between the x_i in contiguous non-vacant counties:

$$r = \left(\frac{n}{A}\right) \frac{\displaystyle\sum_{i=1}^{n} \sum_{j=i+1}^{n} z_i z_j \delta_{ij}}{\displaystyle\sum_{i=1}^{n} z_i^2} \tag{3}$$

$$= \left(\frac{n}{A}\right) I, \tag{4}$$

where $z_i = x_i - \bar{x}$ and the x_i are assumed to be identically normally distributed. Since Moran is concerned only with a test for the presence of spatial autocorrelation, it is sufficient to consider a test using I alone. Based upon a result of Koopmans (1942), Moran shows that, under the assumption of no spatial autocorrelation,

$$E(I^p) = \frac{E[(\text{numerator of } I)^p]}{E[(\text{denominator of } I)^p]}, \tag{5}$$

for any positive integer, p. From Equation (5), the first two crude moments of I are, (Moran, 1950):

$$E(I) = -A/n(n-1), \tag{6}$$

and

$$E(I^2) = \frac{\{A(1+2\rho^2)+2D(\rho+2\rho^2)+3[A(A-1)-2D]\rho^2\}(n-1)}{n^2(n+1)}, \tag{7}$$

---

[2] The following description of Moran's coefficient is a generalisation of Moran's results discussed in Dacey (1965) and Cliff (1969).

where $\rho = -(n-1)^{-1}$. The variance of I is computed from

$$\text{Var}(I) = E(I^2) - [E(I)]^2. \tag{8}$$

To test for autocorrelation between the x_i in contiguous non-vacant counties in a county map, the quantity

$$\frac{I - E(I)}{\sqrt{\text{Var}(I)}} \tag{9}$$

is evaluated as a standard normal deviate. Moran (1950) shows that the distribution of I is asymptotically normal as n increases.

Generalisation of Moran's results

Moran's results can be generalised to handle interval data for which no assumption about the distribution of the x_i has been made. The same generalisation also permits nominal and ordinal data to be handled by his coefficient. The required generalisation defines r as in Equation (3) and uses the principle of randomisation to derive the moments of r. The first and second crude moments of r using randomisation are a special case of Equations (32) and (38) in which $w_{ij} = 1$ if counties i and j are contiguous and $w_{ij} = 0$ otherwise.

Geary's coefficient for interval scaled x_i only

An alternative measure of autocorrelation between the x_i in contiguous non-vacant counties has been suggested by Geary (1954, p.116). Geary's statistic, c, is defined as (using our notation):

$$c = \frac{(n-1)\sum_{\substack{i=1 \\ i \neq j}}^{n}\sum_{j=1}^{n}(x_i - x_j)^2 \delta_{ij}}{4A\sum_{i=1}^{n} z_i^2}. \tag{10}$$

Note that Geary's statistic is based upon the squared differences between the x_i as opposed to the cross-products of the deviations of the x_i from $\bar{x}$ in Moran's statistic.

Like Moran, Geary assumes that the x_i are identically normally distributed. Based upon this assumption, Geary (1954, p.121) shows that, for a county system with no spatial autocorrelation, the expectation of c is

$$E(c) = 1, \tag{11}$$

and the variance of c is

$$\text{Var}(c) = \frac{(2A+D)(n-1) - 2A^2}{(n+1)A^2}. \tag{12}$$

To test for autocorrelation between the x_i in contiguous non-vacant counties, the quantity,

$$\frac{E(c) - c}{\sqrt{Var(c)}},$$ (13)

is evaluated as a standard normal deviate. Geary (1954, pp.122–24) shows that the distribution of c is asymptotically normal as n increases.

Generalisation of Geary's results

As with Moran's statistic, Geary's results can also be generalised using randomisation. Geary's c will then test for autocorrelation in nominal and ordinal scaled x_i, and also in interval scaled x_i for which no distributional assumptions are made. Define c as in Equation (10). For a county system with no spatial autocorrelation, the expectation of c using randomisation is (Geary, 1954, p.118)

$$E(c) = 1,$$ (14)

and the variance of c is

$$Var(c) = \frac{1}{n(n-2)(n-3)2A^2} [2A^2\{-(n-1)^2 b_2 + (n^2 - 3)\}$$

$$+ 2A(n-1)\{-(n-1)b_2 + n^2 - 3n + 3\}$$ (15)

$$+ (D+A)(n-1)\{(n^2 - n + 2)b_2 - (n^2 + 3n - 6)\}],$$

where b_2 is the sample kurtosis [see Equation (37)].

The test for spatial autocorrelation remains that given in Equation (13), and it is known (Geary, 1954, p.118) that the distribution of c under randomisation is asymptotically normal as n increases.

Limitations

The normal and randomised measures of spatial autocorrelation developed by Moran and Geary have some important weaknesses. First, as Dacey (1965) has noted, the statistics are biased measures of spatial autocorrelation, since they are invariant over certain topological transformations of the underlying county structure. Dacey illustrates this point as follows: Consider a county map, P_0, with a connexion matrix $[\delta_{ij}]$, an assigned set of values, x_0, and an index value, I_0, (Moran's statistic), or c_0 (Geary's statistic). Without changing $[\delta_{ij}]$ or x_0, it is possible to transform P_0 topologically and produce a new county map, P_1, with $I_1 = I_0$, $c_1 = c_0$, and for which the degree of spatial autocorrelation is unchanged. For example, P_1 may be constructed from P_0 by the rule that county boundaries are shortened if the counties separated by the boundary have values of opposite sign, and are increased in length if the counties have values of the same sign. Alternatively, the area of counties may be changed so that the area of, say, counties with positive values is increased, and the area of counties with negative values is decreased.

However, I and c are invariant over such topological transformations because the only element of the underlying county structure which they incorporate is the connexion matrix. No account is taken of size and shape characteristics of the counties. I and c are, therefore, biased measures of correlation.

A second important weakness of the Moran and Geary statistics is that in their present form they can only be used to test for first order correlation between the x_i. That is, they only test for correlation between the x_i in contiguous counties. Thus spatial autocorrelative schemes between each county and its second and higher order contiguous neighbours[3] would be undetected by these statistics.

Method of overcoming limitations

The topological invariance of I and c, and the fact that these statistics test only for first order correlation between the x_i, can be eliminated by weighting. For example, consider first the problem of topological invariance. Dacey (1965, p.29) has suggested, with regard to Moran's statistic, that I could be weighted by the area of each non-vacant county in a study lattice and by the lengths of common boundaries between contiguous non-vacant counties. Dacey gives a correlation coefficient

$$r' = \left(\frac{n}{A}\right) \frac{\frac{1}{2} \sum_{\substack{i=1 \\ i \neq j}}^{n} \sum_{j=1}^{n} \delta_{ij} \alpha_i \beta_{i(j)} z_i z_j}{\sum_{i=1}^{n} \alpha_i z_i^2}, \qquad (16)$$

$$= \left(\frac{n}{A}\right) I', \qquad (17)$$

where   and

$$\alpha_i = \frac{a_i}{\sum_{i=1}^{n} a_i} \qquad\qquad \beta_{i(j)} = \frac{b_{ij}}{\sum_{i=1}^{n} b_{ij}}.$$

[3] It will be recalled that two counties are contiguous if they have a common boundary of positive, non-zero length. Thus in the diagram below, counties i and j, j and k, and k and l are contiguous. Two counties, for example i and k, are second order contiguous neighbours if they have no common boundary of positive, non-zero length, but there exists a county, j, such that i and j are contiguous and j and k are contiguous. Using similar definitions for third and higher order contiguous neighbours, it is evident, for example, that i and l are third order contiguous neighbours. These definitions are not unique, and alternative schemes might consider two counties to be contiguous if they have a common boundary or vertex.

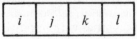

Here, a_i equals the area of the ith non-vacant county, b_{ij} denotes the length of the common boundary between the ith and jth non-vacant counties. Like Moran, Dacey assumes that the x_i are identically normally distributed. Because Equation (5) does not hold for Equation (16), it has not proved possible to derive any moments for I'.

As regards the fact that I and c provide tests for first order spatial autocorrelative schemes only, we note that once the principle of using a general set of weights is adopted, this limitation can also be overcome. A set of weights can be constructed which, unlike $[\delta_{ij}]$ in the Moran and Geary approaches, do not depend solely on joins between counties, and which may be varied to suit circumstances[4]. In particular, first, second, and higher order 'contacts' may be studied in turn to yield a correlogram-type analysis. This approach is particularly meaningful in regular lattices.

We now present a statistic which employs a general set of weights to overcome the problem of invariance. The set of weights also ensures that the statistic can be used to test for any order of spatial autocorrelation between the x_i in a county system.

THE PROPOSED STATISTIC

Basic Properties

A correlation type coefficient should possess certain basic properties if it is to serve as an analytic tool. These are (a) a constant, or very nearly constant, expected value under the null hypothesis of no correlation; (b) that the statistic should have a bounded fixed range. For example, Pearson's r lies in the interval $-1 \leqslant r \leqslant 1$; (c) that it should be possible to develop the distribution theory of the statistic, at least as far as evaluating the first two moments.

Choice of weights

The Geary and Moran statistics use binary weights, δ_{ij}, to operationalise the concept of contiguity. The present approach, by allowing an investigator to *choose* a set of weights which he deems appropriate from *prior* considerations, allows greater flexibility, particularly with regard to natural barriers, county size, and so on. Further, if different hypotheses are proposed about the degree of contact between neighbouring areas, alternative sets of weights might be used to investigate these hypotheses. Caution must be exercised here to avoid the pitfalls of spurious correlation and bogus cause–effect relationships.

---

[4] An equivalent approach is to generalise the concept of a join. For example, we can put $\delta_{ij} = 1$ if two counties are second order contiguous neighbours and $\delta_{ij} = 0$ otherwise. The forms of the statistics and their moments are unaltered, although the numerical values of A and D will clearly be different.

The form of the statistic

Consider a population described by the variate X, from which a sample of size n is drawn. The sample values $x_1, x_2, ..., x_n$ have mean $\bar{x}$. The deviations of the observations from the sample mean are denoted by

$$z_i = x_i - \bar{x}.$$

Let the effect of county i on county j be denoted by the weight w_{ij}. Then the proposed statistic has the form

$$r = \frac{n \sum_{(2)} w_{ij} z_i z_j}{W \sum_{(1)} z_i^2}, \tag{18}$$

where $\sum_{(1)}$ is equivalent to $\sum_{i=1}^{n}$; $\sum_{(2)}$ is equivalent to $\sum_{j=1}^{n} \sum_{\substack{i=1 \\ i \neq j}}^{n}$; and $W = \sum_{(2)} w_{ij}$.

The statistic is put in this form to leave the denominator invariant under random permutations. Otherwise, the moments of r cannot be evaluated. As shown in Equation (32), the statistic also satisfies property (a) described above. Unfortunately, property (b) is not met. However, it is shown in Appendix I that the limits of r may be evaluated for any particular sets of $\{z_i\}$ and $\{w_{ij}\}$ and further that

$$\max|r| \leqslant 1 \text{ whenever}$$
$$W^2 \text{Var}(z_i) \geqslant n^2 \text{Var}(\sum_{j \in J} w_{ij} z_j) \tag{19}$$

where $J \equiv J(i)$ is the set of counties contiguous to county i.

The structure of the weights

The amount of interaction between any two counties may depend, for example, on the distance between them (say between their geographic or demographic centres), the length of common boundary between the counties and so on. The factors which are most important will depend on the study. Thus in an urban area, the contact between two zones may depend on the frequency of public transport services.

Suppose it is decided that the relevant variables which measure the amount of interaction between any pair of counties are distance between county centres and length of common boundary between counties. A system of weights based on these variables is now outlined.

Let the distance between the centres of counties i and j be d_{ij}, where distance may be defined by the Euclidean or other appropriate metric. Further, suppose that the proportion of the perimeter[5] of i which is in

---

[5]We exclude from the perimeter of county i those parts which coincide with the boundary of the study area.

contact with county j is $q_i(j)$. We note that

$$\sum_{j \in J} q_i(j) = 1,$$

where J is defined as in Equation (19). The weighting system is then defined as some function, g, of d_{ij} and $q_i(j)$, that is,

$$w_{ij} = g[d_{ij}, q_i(j)]. \tag{20}$$

For the empirical work on the Irish Republic below, we have taken

$$w_{ij} = d_{ij}^{-1} q_i(j), \tag{21}$$

which is a special case of

$$w_{ij} = d_{ij}^{-\alpha} [q_i(j)]^\beta, \tag{22}$$

where α and β are parameters. Positive values of α and β give greater weight to pairs of counties which have shorter distances between their centres and which have long common boundaries. It should be noted that Equation (22) gives positive weights only to counties which are contiguous.

Other forms could be used for Equation (20). For example, an exponential function might replace the Pareto form which we have used for distance. The choice of functional form for w_{ij} must lie with the investigator, but it is felt that Equation (22) is a reasonable choice in the present study. More generally, for distance, the exponential decay function or the Pareto form with $\alpha > 2$ seem to put excessive emphasis on "near" counties.

Finally, we observe that only rarely will $w_{ij} = w_{ji}$. The obvious exception to this occurs when the study area is split into regular units such as squares or hexagons.

The weights which have been constructed are then substituted into Equation (18). There may be some value in first standardising these weights. For example, they could be scaled so that

$$\sum_{j \in J} w_{ij} = w_i. = 1, \qquad i = 1, ..., n, \tag{23}$$

implying that $W = n$. Under this standardisation the quantity

$$\sum_{j \in J} w_{ij} z_j \tag{24}$$

represents a value for z_i 'suggested' by the counties contiguous to i. See Appendix I for further discussion of quantity (24).

THE DISTRIBUTION THEORY FOR r

Before deriving the moments of r, it is necessary to specify the underlying population model for the $\{x_i\}$ and to decide the basis from which statistical inferences are to be made.

The population model

The model of the population process which generates the set of values $\{x_i\}$ of variate X may be formulated in two ways:

(a) There exists a single population, described by the variate X, from which n drawings are made to give the county sample values $\{x_i\}$. Then, under the null hypothesis, we assume that the set of values $\{x_i\}$ is distributed in the plane in such a way that they are not spatially autocorrelated.

(b) Each x_i is an observation on X_i for county i. The X_i are identically distributed, or, if we are interested in the first k moments of r, have their first $2k$ moments identical. Under the null hypothesis all the X_i are pairwise uncorrelated.

In this and earlier sections either model is valid. However, model (a) is used throughout this part of the paper as it seems conceptually simpler.

The basis of inference

We recall that Moran, in order to derive the moments of his correlation coefficient, assumed that the $\{x_i\}$ were identically normally distributed. This ensures that the term in the denominator of Equation (3)

$$\sum_{(1)} z_i^2 \qquad (25)$$

is distributed as a χ^2 variable, and permits the expectations of powers of the numerator and the denominator of the correlation coefficient, Equation (3), to be evaluated separately. Conversely, Geary (1954) considers the $n!$ possible permutations of the set of $\{z_i\}$ over the county system, for which the term (25) in the denominator of his coefficient, Equation (10), is invariant.

Either method is acceptable as a way of enabling the investigator to evaluate the moments of the coefficient, but the basis of any inference is different. Using the normality assumption we consider all possible values which the set of $\{X_i\}$ might take, while the method of random permutations compares the observed location of each x_i in the county system with the set of all possible locations for the same set of $\{x_i\}$.

If the alternative hypothesis under the normality assumption is that the $\{X_i\}$ are jointly distributed according to the usual form of the multivariate normal distribution, then for all $\{X_i\}$ to be pairwise uncorrelated is equivalent to their being independent. For other distributions this may not be so.

Evaluation of the moments of r

For convenience, we repeat Equation (18),

$$r = \frac{n \sum_{(2)} w_{ij} z_i z_j}{W \sum_{(1)} z_i^2} . \qquad (26)$$

By randomising over the set of all possible spatial configurations of the sample values we know that

$$E(r^p) = \left(\frac{n}{W \sum_{(1)} z_i^2}\right)^p E(T^p), \tag{27}$$

for any p, where

$$T = \sum_{(2)} w_{ij} z_i z_j, \tag{28}$$

since (25) is invariant over permutations of the z_i.

We define the $2j$th sample moment as

$$m_{2j} = n^{-1} \sum_{(1)} z_i^{2j}. \tag{29}$$

Expectation of r

Since $\sum_{(1)} z_i = 0$, then

$$\sum_{(1)} z_j^2 = - \sum_{(2)} z_i z_j. \tag{30}$$

It follows, using Equation (29), that

$$E(z_i z_j) = -m_2 (n-1)^{-1}, \tag{31}$$

and therefore

$$E(T) = - \sum_{(2)} w_{ij} m_2 (n-1)^{-1},$$

implying that

$$E(r) = -(n-1)^{-1}. \tag{32}$$

The second crude moment of r

From Equation (28), the second crude moment of T is

$$E(T^2) = E\left[\tfrac{1}{2} \sum_{(2)} (w_{ij} + w_{ji})^2 z_i^2 z_j^2 \right.$$
$$+ \sum_{(3)} (w_{ij} + w_{ji})(w_{ik} + w_{ki}) z_i^2 z_j z_k$$
$$\left. + \sum_{(4)} w_{kl} z_i z_j z_k z_l \right], \tag{33}$$

where, in addition to the summation notation used earlier we set

$$\sum_{(3)} \equiv \sum\sum\sum_{i \neq j \neq k}, \text{ where } i, j, k \text{ range over } [1,n]$$

and

$$\sum_{(4)} \equiv \sum\sum\sum\sum_{i \neq j \neq k \neq l}, \text{ where } i, j, k, l \text{ range over } [1,n],$$

and so on.

Taking the expectations of the terms in the $\{z_i\}$ we find that, for $i \neq j \neq k \neq l$,

$$E(z_i^2 z_j^2) = (nm_2^2 - m_4)/(n-1)$$

$$E(z_i^2 z_j z_k) = (2m_4 - nm_2^2)/(n-1)^{(2)} \qquad (34)$$

$$E(z_i z_j z_k z_l) = (3nm_2^2 - 6m_4)/(n-1)^{(3)}$$

where $n^{(s)} = n(n-1), ..., (n-s+1)$.

Further, the sums of the weights in Equation (33) may be reduced in the following ways:

$$\sum_{(3)}(w_{ij}+w_{ji})(w_{ik}+w_{ki}) = \sum_{(1)}(w_{i.}+w_{.i})^2 - \sum_{(2)}(w_{ij}+w_{ji})^2$$

$$= S_2 - 2S_1; \qquad (35)$$

$$\sum_{(4)}w_{ij}w_{kl} = W^2 + \tfrac{1}{2}\sum_{(2)}(w_{ij}+w_{ji})^2 - \sum_{(1)}(w_{i.}+w_{.i})^2$$

$$= W^2 + S_1 - S_2; \qquad (36)$$

where

$$w_{i.} = \sum_{j=1}^{n} w_{ij}, \qquad w_{.j} = \sum_{i=1}^{n} w_{ij} \quad \text{and} \quad W = \sum_{(2)}w_{ij}.$$

Using the results of Equations (35) and (36) together with those of Equation (34) it may be shown that

$$E(T^2) = \frac{m_2^2[n\{(n^2-3n+3)S_1 - nS_2 + 3W^2\} - b_2\{(n^2-n)S_1 - 2nS_2 + 6W^2\}]}{n^{(4)}n} \qquad (37)$$

where the sample kurtosis is $b_2 = m_4/m_2^2$.

Excluding constants, the denominator of r^2 is $\left(\sum_{(1)}z_i^2\right)^2$, which is invariant under random permutations, being equal to $(nm_2)^2$. Finally we find that

$$E(r^2) = \frac{[n\{(n^2-3n+3)S_1 - nS_2 + 3W^2\} - b_2\{(n^2-n)S_1 - 2nS_2 + 6W^2\}]}{(n-1)^{(3)}W^2} \cdot (38)$$

If $E(r^2)$ is evaluated using the assumption that the $\{x_i\}$ are normally distributed, then we find

$$E(r^2) = \frac{(n^2 S_1 - nS_2 + 3W^2)}{(n^2-1)W^2}. \qquad (39)$$

Knowing the mean and variance we may express r as a standardised deviate with mean zero and variance one. As a first step, this deviate may be tested using the normal curve, since it is shown below that r has asymptotically a normal distribution. However, the approach to normality of the distribution of r as n increases is likely to be slow[6]. To

---

[6]For example Pearson's r is asymptotically normally distributed, but it requires a large value of n, say 500, before the distribution is acceptably close to the normal curve. These comments also apply to the Moran and Geary coefficients.

evaluate the validity of a normality assumption when n is small, we need to know more about the probability distribution of r. As a first step towards this, the third crude moment of r has been evaluated by methods similar to those of the earlier part of this section. The third crude moment, using randomisation is

$$E(r^3) = (Wm_2)^{-3} \sum [(\text{coefficient in cell } i,j) \times (\text{function of weights at the}$$
$$\text{left of row } i) \times (\text{moment function at the head of column } j)],$$
$$(40)$$

where the rows, columns and cells referred to are those of Table 1 and the summation is carried out over the six rows and four columns of that Table. For convenience, we write $u_{ij} = w_{ij} + w_{ji}$ and $u_i = w_{i.} + w_{.i}$, in Table 1 and in the remainder of this section.

If it is assumed that the x_i are normally distributed, the theory of symmetric functions yields the results

$$n^3 E(m_6) = 15(n-1)^3 K_2^3$$
$$n^3 E(m_4 m_2) = 3(n-1)^2(n+3)K_2^3$$
$$n^3 E(m_3^2) = 6(n-1)(n-2)K_2^3 \qquad (41)$$
$$n^3 E(m_2^3) = (n^2-1)(n+3)K_2^3$$

where K_2 is the second cumulant, or variance. Substituting Equation (41) into the numerator and denominator of $E(r^3)$ we find that, under normality,

$$E(r^3) = \frac{[-3(n-1)(n-5)S_3 + 2n^3 S_5 - 3n^2 S_7 + 3S_8]}{2(n-1)(n+1)(n+3)W^3}. \qquad (42)$$

The asymptotic distribution for r

We assume that, for all i and j, (a) u_{ij}/W, u_i/W are all $O(n^{-1})$ or less; (b) the first six sample moments of the standardised deviate are $O(1)$ or less. Both these assumptions will generally hold in practice. The coefficients asterisked in Table 1 correspond to the terms in Equation (40) which are $O(n^{-2})$; all other terms in Equation (40) are $O(n^{-3})$ or less, provided (a) and (b) hold. We note that the terms in m_3^2 are of a lower order in n if the underlying population is symmetric.

From Equation (38) it is readily established that the variance of r is $O(n^{-1})$ when assumptions (a) and (b) hold. Therefore the Pearson coefficient, $\beta_1 = \mu_3^2/\mu_2^3$, is $O(n^{-1})$. Likewise, using assumption (a) and extending (b) to cover the first eight moments, it is evident that

$$\beta_2 - 3 = (\mu_4/\mu_2^2) - 3 \text{ is } O(n^{-1}).$$

By extending (b) to cover the first $2k$ sample moments, we may show

TABLE 1. Coefficients of terms in the numerator of μ'_3 for r, evaluated using randomisation.

Functions of weights	Code	$m_6/(n-1)^{(5)}$	$nm_2m_4/(n-1)^{(5)}$	$nm_3^2/(n-1)^{(5)}$	$n^2m_2^3/(n-1)^{(5)}$
$\frac{1}{2}\sum_{(2)}u_{ij}^2$	S_3	$-n^4+2n^3-23n^2+166n-120$	$6n^3-150n+180$	$n^4-8n^3+31n^2-64n$ *	$-12n^2+72n-90$
$\sum_{(2)}u_iu_{ij}^2$	S_4	$6n^3-6n$	$-3n^3-18n^2+75n-90$	$-3n^3+12n^2-45n+60$	$9n^2-36n+45$
$\sum_{(3)}u_{ij}u_{jk}u_{ki}$	S_5	$2n^3-6n^2+4n$	$-3n^3+21n^2-60n+60$	$-60n^2+30n-40$	$n^3-9n^2+29n-30$ *
$\sum_{(1)}u_i^3$	S_6	$-6n^2-18n$	$3n^2+27n-30$	$2n^2+6n$	$-9n+15$
$\frac{1}{2}W\sum_{(1)}u_{ij}^2 + \sum_{(2)}u_iu_ju_{ij}$	S_7	$-18n+18n$	$15n^2-27n+30$	$6n^2-6n$	$-3n^2+9n-15$ *
$3Wn\sum_{(1)}u_i^2-5W^3$	S_8	24	-18	-8	3

* indicates terms of $0(n^{-2})$.

that

$$\lim_{n \to \infty} \beta_k = (2k)!/2^k(k!), \quad k \text{ even}$$
$$= 0, \quad k \text{ odd}$$

establishing that the distribution of r tends to normality as n increases.

EMPIRICAL WORK

Geary's Irish Data

To illustrate the use of the Moran, Geary, and the proposed correlation coefficients, county data for the Irish Republic given in Geary (1954) were tested for first order spatial autocorrelation. The data are reproduced here in Table 2. Note that county Dublin was excluded from the computations because of the highly urbanised nature of that county compared with the other counties in the Irish Republic. The location of the counties of the Irish Republic is shown in Figure 1. The serial letters on the map correspond with the serial letters against the county names in Table 2. The number in each county is the value of L_i for that county.

Recall that the moments of the Moran, Geary, and the proposed correlation coefficients can be evaluated using either randomisation or by assuming that the x_i are normally distributed. Since it was desired to test the coefficients under both these assumptions, the sample measures of skewness and kurtosis, b_1 and b_2, were calculated for all data sets and tested for significant departures from normality. Variables (1), (2), (3), (4), (6), and (7) were found to be non-normal at the 0·01 level. $\log_e$ transformations were carried out on all these variables except (2) and (3). b_1 and b_2 were then evaluated for the transformed variables. The transformations were sufficient to 'eliminate' the non-normality in all cases. The results are presented in Table 3. In the case of variables (2) and (3), more sophisticated transformations, such as $\tanh^{-1}$ on variable (3), would have been necessary to eliminate non-normality. Since such transformations require estimates of the range to be made from the data, which would lead to dependence among the sample county values, variables (2) and (3) were not transformed.

The Moran, Geary, and the proposed correlation coefficients were then evaluated for all raw and transformed data sets. The variances were computed for both the randomised and normal assumptions. In the case of the proposed correlation coefficient, solutions using unstandardised and standardised weights were calculated[7]. As discussed above the

---

[7]An algorithm which evaluates the Moran, Geary, and the proposed correlation coefficients has been written in Algol 60 for use on the Elliott 503. A listing of the programme is available from the authors on request.

TABLE 2. Data on Irish counties

Serial letter	County (incl. county borough)	Percentage number agricultural holdings in valuation groups (1950)			Per 1000 acres crops and pasture (1952)				Town and village population as percentage of total (1951)	Per 1000 population (1951)		Retail sales £ per person (1951)	Single males as % of all males aged 30-34 (1951)
		£2-£10	£10-£50	Above £50	Milch cows	Other cattle	Pigs	Sheep		Private cars registered (1952)	Radio licences (1952)		
		(1)	(2)	(3)	(4)	(5)	(6)	(7)	(8)	(9)	(10)	(11)	(12)
A	Carlow	31·8	46·9	21·3	67	252	56	531	40·2	43	169	66	60·3
B	Cavan	40·1	56·0	3·9	99	231	97	56	17·3	26	56	49	73·4
C	Clare	38·8	54·4	6·8	110	285	32	116	24·4	22	67	28	68·3
D	Cork	33·2	50·4	16·4	146	256	137	148	52·6	38	130	66	60·1
E	Donegal	69·8	25·9	4·2	102	248	22	463	18·9	21	80	45	62·4
F	Dublin	41·2	33·4	25·4	108	268	110	236	94·8	49	185	117	40·8
G	Galway	45·7	50·9	3·4	69	239	44	801	28·1	22	87	40	69·1
H	Kerry	51·4	45·1	3·5	194	283	84	354	26·7	20	76	41	68·2
I	Kildare	34·0	41·5	24·5	52	290	28	184	29·2	40	123	54	53·5
J	Kilkenny	25·0	50·6	24·4	91	283	63	157	31·1	41	82	45	64·8
K	Laoighis	32·7	51·7	15·6	69	269	54	87	26·7	38	121	46	67·2
L	Leitrim	60·2	38·4	1·4	102	231	37	84	13·7	20	70	29	73·4
M	Limerick	33·3	47·5	19·2	181	277	68	36	48·2	32	158	53	55·2
N	Longford	40·4	51·8	7·8	74	290	49	75	21·3	32	111	44	68·6
O	Louth	36·0	48·2	15·8	69	285	55	204	63·0	37	200	78	51·0
P	Mayo	68·0	30·8	1·2	97	289	50	393	18·5	17	84	37	67·4
Q	Meath	32·0	48·8	19·2	55	351	23	252	17·5	49	116	53	62·1
R	Monaghan	31·8	61·9	6·3	85	235	101	39	24·6	32	80	70	69·7
S	Offaly	31·2	55·7	13·1	55	262	50	112	35·6	33	110	55	65·2
T	Roscommon	44·6	51·7	3·7	66	275	24	299	13·2	22	115	28	74·9
U	Sligo	48·9	48·1	3·0	92	266	30	205	29·7	24	102	42	67·0
V	Tipperary	28·3	52·1	19·6	107	312	52	140	36·5	41	127	56	62·8
W	Waterford	34·3	39·1	23·6	122	292	96	199	56·4	41	164	74	54·6
X	Westmeath	28·4	54·4	17·2	43	323	25	188	35·8	37	157	57	56·9
Y	Wexford	27·0	52·1	20·8	64	219	68	288	34·6	34	122	66	56·4
Z	Wicklow	34·7	46·3	19·0	79	212	44	528	49·8	36	102	65	50·4

Reproduced with permission of The Institute of Statisticians

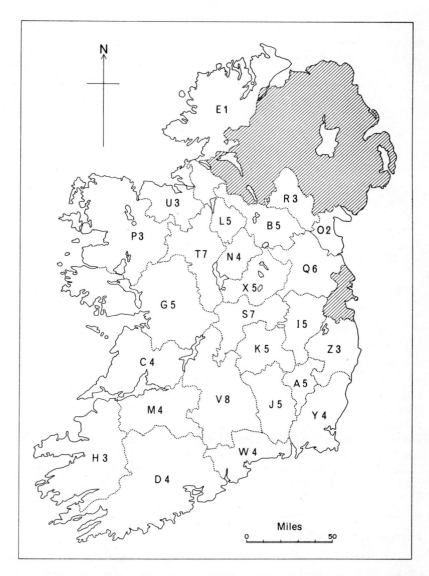

Figure 1. The Irish Counties showing serial letters and numbers of contiguous counties

unstandardised weights were of the form

$$w_{ij} = d_{ij}^{-1} q_i(j),\qquad\qquad(43)$$

while the standardised weights were obtained from the unstandardised
weights by application of Equation (23).   The unstandardised and standardised weighting matrices are given in Appendix II as Tables A1 and
A2 respectively.

TABLE 3. Sample Beta coefficients for Geary's Irish counties data

Variable	b_1	b_2	Transformation	b_1	b_2
(1)	1·675*	3·790	$\log_e$	0·688	2·883
(2)	1·295*	4·331			
(3)	0·000	1·508*			
(4)	1·682	4·294	$\log_e$	0·179	2·779
(5)	0·086	2·985			
(6)	1·138*	3·754	$\log_e$	0·008	2·212
(7)	1·842*	4·527	$\log_e$	0·042	2·421
(8)	0·473	2·619			
(9)	0·011	1·865			
(10)	0·343	2·730			
(11)	0·003	2·188			
(12)	0·068	2·034			

*Significant at the 0·01 level.
The variable numbers correspond to the numbers assigned in Table 2.

The results of the analysis appear in Tables 4, 5 and 6.[8]   The county
serial letters and the variable numbers used in Tables 4 and 5 correspond
with the serial letters and variable numbers of Table 2.   Note that for the
proposed correlation coefficient, the results in Tables 4–6 were computed from weights which had been calculated to eight decimal places.
The weights in Tables A1 and A2 have been rounded to four decimal
places for economy of space.   In the evaluation of the moments of the
Moran, Geary, and the proposed correlation coefficients, the following
hold: $n = 25$, $A = 55$, $D = 217$; with unstandardised weights,
$W = 0·84686672$, $S_1 = 0·01869986$, $S_2 = 0·12267319$; with standardised weights, $W = 25$, $S_1 = 15·849300$, $S_2 = 103·62041$.

Interpretation of Results

In the following discussion, attention is focused upon the performance
of the different correlation coefficients, rather than upon any explanation of why most of the variables display a high degree of spatial autocorrelation.   This aspect has been covered by Geary (1954, pp.133–37).

---

[8]The results for the Geary statistic on variables (1), (2), (3), (5), and (9) differ from those
presented in Geary (1954, p.134).   The correct results are the ones given here.

In Table 4, the results for variables (2), (5), (7), and (8) demonstrate most clearly the differences between the three coefficients. The results for variables (5) and (8) are of particular interest.

TABLE 4. Values of the standard deviates for Geary's Irish data

Variable	Moran		Geary		Proposed Statistic (unstandardised weights)		Proposed Statistic (standardised weights)	
	N	R	N	R	N	R	N	R
(1) Raw Data	3·7851	3·8779	4·3142	3·8990	3·3313	3·4150	3·8828	4·0277
Transformed Data	4·0965	4·1074	4·0841	4·0343	3·5786	3·5885	4·1268	4·1383
(2) Raw Data	1·0899	1·1317	2·7511	2·3771	1·3373	1·3902	1·4966	1·5742
(3) Raw Data	5·2011	4·9058	4·0178	4·6767	4·6620	4·5247	4·8300	4·7402
(4) Raw Data	5·1969	5·3919	4·3531	3·7709	4·1359	4·2957	4·6740	4·9126
Transformed Data	5·2420	5·2445	3·9211	3·9085	4·1958	4·1988	4·6502	4·6536
(5) Raw Data	0·5565	0·5595	-0·1707	-0·1668	2·1405	2·1511	1·9036	1·9346
(6) Raw Data	2·4807	2·5396	2·2928	2·0810	2·8333	2·9018	3·1573	3·2719
Transformed Data	2·3015	2·2723	2·0520	2·1893	2·5174	2·4842	2·8475	2·8096
(7) Raw Data	1·0188	1·0631	0·8689	0·7390	1·7326	1·8098	1·4572	1·5407
Transformed Data	1·2930	1·2827	1·5156	1·5767	2·3655	2·3458	2·0329	2·0158
(8) Raw Data	2·2759	2·2684	2·5475	2·5904	1·2169	1·2090	1·6091	1·6210
(9) Raw Data	4·4927	4·4008	3·2247	3·6012	3·8909	3·8072	4·1379	4·0945
(10) Raw Data	0·3156	0·3153	1·2294	1·2352	0·5957	0·5944	0·7818	0·7892
(11) Raw Data	3·4985	3·4512	3·1303	3·3520	2·9310	2·8898	3·0020	2·9931
(12) Raw Data	2·7349	2·6889	2·3382	2·5523	2·7563	2·7079	2·6807	2·6635

N indicates assumption of identically normally distributed x_j.
R indicates use of randomisation.

Variable 5: Spatial autocorrelation between the sample county values is suggested fairly strongly by the proposed correlation coefficient, whereas the Moran and Geary statistics support the null hypothesis. If the county values for the variable in the form, $z_i = x_i - \bar{x}$, are checked against the county locations shown in Figure 1, it will be found that the counties with a positive deviation lie in two unbroken belts running from west to east across the Irish Republic. The northern belt runs from county P to county O, and the southern belt connects counties H and J. The counties with a negative deviation comprise two zones. The first zone is the counties from E to R which form the border with Northern Ireland. The second zone runs west to east across the Republic between counties G and Z, thus separating the two belts of positive deviations.

The fact that the positive and negative deviations form such perfect spatial 'blocks' is highly suggestive of an autocorrelative structure.

TABLE 5. Results under randomisation of the Moran, Geary, and proposed correlation
coefficients for the Irish county system

	Moran		Geary		Proposed Statistic (unstandardised weights)		Proposed Statistic (standardised weights)	
	I	$\sigma(I)$	c	$\sigma(c)$	r	$\sigma(r)$	r	$\sigma(r)$
Expectation under H_0	-0·0917		1		-0·0417		-0·0417	
Variable								
(1) Raw Data	0·8964	0·2548	0·3477	0·1673	0·4560	0·1457	0·5384	0·1440
Transformed Data	0·9776	0·2604	0·3825	0·1531	0·4931	0·1490	0·5680	0·1473
(2) Raw Data	0·1928	0·2514	0·5840	0·1750	0·1581	0·1437	0·1819	0·1420
(3) Raw Data	1·2660	0·2686	0·3925	0·1299	0·6548	0·1539	0·6799	0·1522
(4) Raw Data	1·2649	0·2516	0·3418	0·1745	0·5762	0·1438	0·6566	0·1421
Transformed Data	1·2766	0·2609	0·4071	0·1517	0·5854	0·1493	0·6454	0·1476
(5) Raw Data	0·0536	0·2597	1·0258	0·1547	0·2781	0·1487	0·2427	0·1470
(6) Raw Data	0·5559	0·2550	0·6533	0·1666	0·3816	0·1459	0·4300	0·1442
Transformed Data	0·5091	0·2644	0·6897	0·1417	0·3346	0·1514	0·3790	0·1497
(7) Raw Data	0·1743	0·2502	0·8686	0·1778	0·2171	0·1430	0·1760	0·1413
Transformed Data	0·2458	0·2632	0·7708	0·1453	0·3118	0·1507	0·2587	0·1490
(8) Raw Data	0·5024	0·2619	0·6148	0·1487	0·1397	0·1500	0·1987	0·1483
(9) Raw Data	1·0811	0·2665	0·5124	0·1354	0·5396	0·1527	0·5765	0·1510
(10) Raw Data	-0·0093	0·2613	0·8141	0·1505	0·0473	0·1496	0·0751	0·1479
(11) Raw Data	0·8215	0·2646	0·5267	0·1412	0·3962	0·1515	0·4068	0·1498
(12) Raw Data	0·6222	0·2655	0·6465	0·1385	0·3701	0·1521	0·3588	0·1504

TABLE 6. Results under normality of the Moran,
Geary, and proposed correlation coefficients for the
Irish county system

Correlation Coefficient	Expectation under H_0	Standard Deviation
Moran's I	−0·0917	0·2610
Geary's c	1	0·1512
Proposed Statistic, r (unstandardised weights)	−0·0417	0·1494
Proposed Statistic, r (standardised weights)	−0·0417	0·1477

The actual values of I, c and r under normality are as
given in Table 5.

The failure of the Moran and Geary statistics, as opposed to the proposed coefficient, to detect this autocorrelation, may be attributed in large part to the different weighting schemes employed by the coefficients. For this variable, the proposed statistic, in contrast to the binary weights of the Moran and Geary coefficients, tends to give greater weight to those pairs of counties with similar z_i values. Such counties comprise the 'blocks' mentioned above.

Variable 8: The proposed correlation coefficient has much lower values of the standardised deviate than the Moran and Geary coefficients. This is because the contiguous counties with small differences between their sample values on this variable are grouped in the south and south west of the Republic. Since these counties are large, the d_{ij}^{-1} component of each county weight in the proposed coefficient is small. Therefore, these counties make only a minor contribution to the numerator of r. Conversely, binary weights do not detract so heavily from large counties, and so ensure larger values for I and c.

Variable 7: The marked differences between the results for the raw and transformed data are due to the disrupting influence of three large sample values in counties A, G, and Z in the raw data. Since counties contiguous to these three counties generally have large negative z_i values, the effect is to reduce the size of the standard deviates. The $\log_e$ transformation ensures a much smaller contribution to the coefficients for these counties by reducing the influence of these large values. The larger standardised deviates for the proposed correlation coefficient, as opposed to the Moran and Geary statistics, on both the raw and transformed data are again due to the different weighting schemes used.

Variable 2: The Geary statistic yields results of a different order of magnitude to the Moran and proposed correlation coefficients. There is no obvious reason for this, but we note that the data are highly negatively skewed.

. Consider now Tables 5 and 6. It can be seen that the range of values of the standard deviations under randomisation is much less for the Moran and proposed correlation coefficients than for the Geary statistic. The ranges of the randomised standard deviations, centred about their respective normal standard deviations, are: Moran, $(-0\cdot0035, +0\cdot0049)$; proposed coefficient, unstandardised weights, $(-0\cdot0045, +0\cdot0064)$; proposed coefficient, standardised weights, $(-0\cdot0045, +0\cdot0064)$; Geary, $(-0\cdot0266, +0\cdot0213)$.[9] These results suggest that the variance of the cross-product type of coefficient used in the Moran and proposed statistics is less affected by the distribution of the sample data than is the differences squared form used by Geary. This is because the coefficient of

[9]For the Moran statistic, the range has been multiplied by a factor of n/A to make it compatible with the Geary and proposed coefficients.

the b_2 term in the variance of the Geary statistic is $0(n^{-1})$, whereas for the other statistics, the coefficient of the b_2 term is $0(n^{-2})$. Recall from Table 3 that the three coefficients have been evaluated for raw data with sample b_2 values varying from $b_2 = 1 \cdot 508$ on variable (3) to $b_2 = 4 \cdot 527$ on variable (7).

In addition, there is some evidence from variables (4) and (7) in Table 5 that Geary's c is more affected by transformations of the data than are the other coefficients. This tendency is reinforced by the sensitivity, noted above, of the variance of Geary's c to transformations.

Population changes in the Bristol area

Data presented in Table 7 give the percentage changes in population for the City of Bristol and surrounding districts between 1951 and 1961. The data are drawn from the Preliminary Census Report (1961). The distances given in Table 7 are between the (approximate) demographic centres of the administrative districts. Three major hypotheses are investigated.

(1) Whether there has been any change in the distribution of population in the area. Here, all links shown in Figure 2 are taken into account.

(2) Whether there has been a drift of population from the city to surrounding districts. Here only the links between Bristol and each surrounding district shown in Figure 2 are considered.

(3) Whether the population changes in districts surrounding Bristol are first order spatially autocorrelated. Here links with Bristol are ignored, and only the links between contiguous pairs of surrounding districts shown in Figure 2 are considered.

These hypotheses were considered using the Moran, Geary and proposed coefficients, and the results appear in Table 8. The weighting function used for the proposed statistic was

$$w_{ij} = d_{ij}^{-\alpha}, \tag{44}$$

for $\alpha = 1$ and $\alpha = 2$.

Hypothesis 1. No strong pattern emerges and we look to the breakdown of links between hypotheses 2 and 3 to provide evidence of specific changes.

Hypothesis 2. The Moran and Geary statistics show no evidence of any population drift. The proposed statistic does, however, suggest a drift from Bristol to surrounding districts. The data show large increases in areas D, E, G, and J. These are all districts of relatively small area, close to Bristol, and they all lie to the east of the city. The greater weight given by the proposed coefficient to pairs of districts with near centres draws out this feature.

TABLE 7. Percentage population changes and inter-centre distances

Administrative Area	% change in population between 1951 and 1961	Distances between demographic centres of contiguous areas (in miles)
A. Bristol C.B.	- 1·5	
B. Bathavon R.D.	+ 9·3	A, 12·5; C, 8·1; D, 6·9; H, 13·4; J, 8·7.
C. Clutton R.D.	- 0·7	A, 8·7; B, 8·1; F, 8·7.
D. Keynsham R.D.	+83·0	A, 5·2; B, 6·9; J, 2·8.
E. Kingswood U.D.	+34·3	A, 4·4; G, 1·6; J, 1·1.
F. Long Ashton R.D.	+27·5	A, 5·3; C, 8·7.
G. Mangotsfield U.D.	+35·5	A, 4·8; E, 1·6; H, 6·1; J, 2·4.
H. Sodbury R.D.	+18·4	A, 10·8; B, 13·4; G, 6·1; I, 7·5; J, 7·0.
I. Thornbury R.D.	+18·7	A, 11·2; H, 7·5.
J. Warmley R.D.	+87·3	A, 5·3; B, 8·7; D, 2·8; E, 1·1; G, 2·4; H, 7·0.

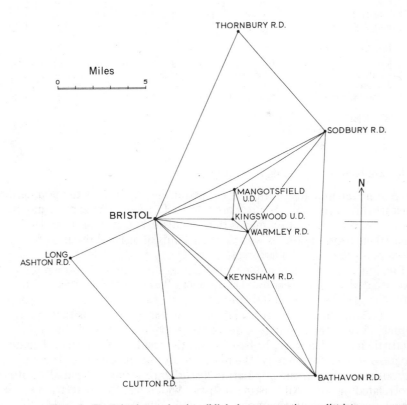

Figure 2. The Bristol area, showing all links between contiguous districts.

Hypothesis 3. The Moran statistic, unlike the Geary coefficient, provides slight evidence of similar changes in contiguous surrounding districts. The proposed statistic, with $\alpha = 1$, demonstrates more clearly the same effect. The contiguous fast growing districts to the east side of the city are chiefly responsible for this result.

TABLE 8.

Statistic	Value of Statistic		Standard Deviation		Standard Deviate	
	observed	expected under H_0	N	R	N	R
1. All links						
Moran, I	−0·0204	−0·2333	0·2667	0·2656	0·94	0·95
Geary, c	0·8313	1·0	0·2436	0·2784	0·69	0·61
proposed, $r, \alpha = 1$	0·1251	−0·1111	0·2178	0·2169	1·08	1·09
proposed, $r, \alpha = 2$	0·2444	−0·1111	0·4142	0·4131	0·86	0·86
2. Bristol–other only						
Moran, I	−0·1221	−0·1	0·1206	0·1245	−0·18	−0·18
Geary, c	1·0494	1·0	0·6030	0·6352	−0·08	−0·08
proposed, $r, \alpha = 1$	−0·3401	−0·1111	0·1820	0·1847	−1·26	−1·24
proposed, $r, \alpha = 2$	−0·5230	−0·1111	0·2425	0·2438	−1·70	−1·69
3. Non-Bristol links only						
Moran, I	0·1158	−0·1667	0·2787	0·2760	1·01	1·02
Geary, c	1·0559	1·0	0·2982	0·3066	−0·19	−0·18
proposed, $r, \alpha = 1$	0·3779	−0·125	0·2967	0·2903	1·69	1·73
proposed, $r, \alpha = 2$	0·3645	−0·125	0·4667	0·4559	1·05	1·07

N = Normality
R = Randomisation

The Analysis of Residuals from Regression

A fundamental assumption of regression analysis is that the population disturbance terms are not autocorrelated. For data having a geographic ordering, this assumption means that the disturbance terms must lack spatial autocorrelation, as well as other kinds of aspatial serial correlation. This point has been made forcefully by Geary (1954, 1963), in the case of regional econometric models. Although there are well known tests for aspatial serial correlation, [Durbin and Watson (1950, 1951), Theil and Nagar (1961)], no suitable test for *spatial* autocorrelation in the population disturbance terms is available. The reason for this is that in any practical case, the population disturbances will be unknown and a test statistic must, therefore, be based upon the residuals from the calculated regression. Unfortunately, the residuals are correlated under the null hypothesis whether the population disturbance terms are spatially auto-correlated or not. All existing statistics which test for correlation in the areal arrangement of geographic data, including those described in this paper, assume that data are uncorrelated spatially under the null hypothesis. However, provided that the regression contains only one or two independent variables, and the number of observations is not small, the correlation between the regression residuals under H_0 may be small and we could assume for convenience that they are in fact spatially uncorrelated under H_0. The residuals may then be tested for spatial autocorrelation using any of the statistics described in this paper. It must be emphasised that the results of such an analysis are only a guide as to whether the population disturbance terms are spatially autocorrelated or not, and no guarantees about significance levels can be made.

To illustrate the sort of study envisaged, regression analysis on variable (4) in Table 2 against certain obvious independent variables was carried out. The residuals were tested for spatial autocorrelation with all the correlation coefficients described in this paper. The standardised and unstandardised weights of Tables A1 and A2 were used with the proposed coefficient. The first independent variable tried was average rainfall in millimetres, 1916–50, which gave an R^2 of $0 \cdot 4051$. The rainfall data and the residuals for each county are summarised in Table 9. The results

TABLE 9. Rainfall data and regression residuals for the Irish county system

County	Rainfall,* mm	Residual	County	Rainfall,* mm	Residual
A	945·4	− 8·328	O	887·05	2·183
B	970·7	19·981	P	1290·75	−28·704
C	1145·4	5·498	Q	826·15	− 2·933
D	1204·0	32·950	R	935·4	11·130
E	1338·0	−30·597	S	892·45	−12·605
G	1144·0	−35·298	T	1063·75	−26·592
H	1413·6	50·376	U	1104·4	− 6·522
I	765·1	2·972	V	978·7	26·814
J	951·9	14·724	W	1124·0	20·619
K	908·7	− 0·975	X	954·5	−33·656
L	1237·7	−15·966	Y	1052·3	−26·922
M	1087·6	84·929	Z	1212·45	−35·283
N	989·75	− 7·798			

*Republic of Ireland: Meteorological Service. *"Average of rainfall for stations in Ireland, 1916-1950"*.

of the tests for autocorrelation are given in Table 10. It is evident from Table 10 that the residuals are highly autocorrelated spatially. Several other independent variables were tried in a multiple regression. In addition, transformations were carried out where necessary to ensure linear relations between the variables. In particular, a regression using rainfall, soil type, and access to urban markets gave an R^2 of $0 \cdot 5810$. The county-by-county spatial pattern of positive and negative residuals differed in only two counties from the residual pattern using rainfall alone, and the tests for autocorrelation on the residuals gave standardised deviates of the same order of magnitude as those in Table 10. The conclusion was therefore reached that the spatial autocorrelation in the residuals was probably due to inertia affecting the distribution of milch cows in Ireland, rather than to non-linear relationships between the variables or to a missing variable in the regression.

TABLE 10. Tests for autocorrelation on residuals

Coefficient	Standard Deviate	
	Assuming normal x_i	Under Randomisation
Moran	$4 \cdot 0273$	$4 \cdot 1629$
Geary	$3 \cdot 5232$	$3 \cdot 0876$
Proposed (Unstandardised Weights)	$3 \cdot 2361$	$3 \cdot 3500$
Proposed (Standardised Weights)	$3 \cdot 9354$	$4 \cdot 0754$

CONCLUSIONS AND DIRECTIONS FOR FUTURE RESEARCH

The main conclusions of the paper are now summarised and the directions of further research in this field which the authors believe necessary are listed.

1.   Use of weights. Ease of computation apart, there is no virtue in using binary weights. With a flexible system of weights, the researcher can highlight those features of a study area which he believes to be important. Alternatively, the effects of a natural or man made barrier (range of mountains, railway line and so on) can be investigated. Such factors as appear in the weights (for example, distances between centres) can be given different emphasis, to see how important they are in inter-area relationships. From a practical viewpoint, there seems little to be gained, in most cases, by standardising the weights, although there may be theoretical attractions (see Appendix I).

2.   The assumption that the data are drawn from a normal population does not seem to be crucial in evaluating the variance for the cross product coefficients. The simpler equation for the variance using the normal assumption may therefore be used without introducing an error of more than, say, 5% in the standard deviation when $|b_2 - 3| \leqslant 1 \cdot 5$. For the Geary statistic the error may be much larger.

3. All the statistics have a normal distribution asymptotically. However, no evidence exists to show how many regions should be in the study area before the asymptotic results may be applied as reasonable approximations to the distributions of the statistics. Further work, including an extensive numerical study, is needed.

4. The dependence among the sample estimators for the population regression residuals means that the statistics discussed in this paper cannot genuinely be used to search for autocorrelation in the residuals. An extension of the work begun by Moran (1950a) is required.

5. When analysing an existing regional system, the data available are often presented in such a way that the number of regions cannot be significantly increased by breaking down individual results. Even when this is possible, the meaning of the final results may be uncertain. Thus, the only way to obtain further information is to expand the analysis to look at changes over time, possibly by use of spectral analysis. The theoretical and computational difficulties in the way of such extensions are, at the least, formidable.

References

Census 1961: England and Wales, Preliminary Report, Her Majesty's Stationary Office, London.

Cliff, A.D., 1969, "Some Measures of Spatial Association in Areal Data", University of Bristol, Ph.D. Thesis (unpublished).

Durbin, J., and Watson, G.S., 1950, 1951, "Testing for Serial Correlation in Least Squares Regression", *Biometrika*, 37, 409-428; 38, 159-178.

Geary, R.C., 1954, "The Contiguity Ratio and Statistical Mapping", *The Incorporated Statistician*, 5, 115-145.

Geary, R.C., 1963, "Some Remarks about Relations between Stochastic Variables: A Discussion Document", *Review of the International Statistical Institute*, 31, 163-181.

Koopmans, T.C., 1942, "Serial Correlation and Quadratic Forms in Normal Variables", *Annals of Mathematical Statistics*, 13, 14-33.

Moran, P.A.P., 1950, "Notes on Continuous Stochastic Phenomena", *Biometrika*, 37, 17-23.

Moran, P.A.P., 1950a, "A Test for the Serial Independence of Residuals", *Biometrika*, 37, 178-181.

Republic of Ireland: Meteorological Service. *Average of Rainfall for Stations in Ireland, 1916-1950*, (Department of Transport and Power, Dublin).

Theil, H., and Nagar, A.L., 1961, "Testing the Independence of Regression Disturbances", *Journal of the American Statistical Association*, 56, 793-806.

Whittle, P., 1954, "On Stationary Processes in the Plane", *Biometrika*, 41, 434-449.

APPENDIX I

Using the notation of Equation (28), we consider

$$T = \sum_{(2)} w_{ij} z_i z_j \tag{A1}$$

Define the index $k = n(i-1)+j$, $\quad k = 1, ..., n^2$,
and put

$$\omega_k = w_{ij},$$

$$y_k \equiv y_{(i-1)n+j} = z_j,$$

$$v_k \equiv v_{j-n+1-ni} = z_i.$$

Then Equation (A1) becomes $\sum_k \omega_k y_k v_k$. Using the Cauchy–Schwarz

inequality, T has absolute value

$$|T| \leqslant \left\{ \sum_k \omega_k y_k^2 \sum_k \omega_k v_k^2 \right\}^{\frac{1}{2}} = T^*. \tag{A2}$$

This implies that r has absolute value

$$|r| \leqslant \frac{T^*}{\sum_{(1)} z_i^2}, \tag{A3}$$

taking $W = n$, without loss of generality, to simplify the working. Alternatively, we may express this as the proposition that r lies in the range $[-1, +1]$ whenever

$$\left(\sum_{(1)} w_{i.} z_i^2 \right) \left(\sum_{(1)} w_{.i} z_i^2 \right) \leqslant \left(\sum_{(1)} z_i^2 \right)^2, \tag{A4}$$

recalling that $W = n$ as before.

Thus, the range of r is exactly the interval $[-1, +1]$ if and only if $w_{i.} = w_{.i} = 1$ for all i. The weights matrix is then said to be of the doubly stochastic form familiar in the theory of Markov chains.

Again, we may write r in the form

$$r = \frac{\text{Cov}\left(\sum_j w_{ij} z_j, z_i \right)}{\left[\text{Var}\left(\sum_j w_{ij} z_j \right) \text{Var}(z_i) \right]^{\frac{1}{2}}} \times \left[\frac{\text{Var}\left(\sum_j w_{ij} z_j \right)}{\text{Var}(z_i)} \right]^{\frac{1}{2}} \tag{A5}$$

where $W = n$ as before. Then $\max |r| \leqslant 1$ whenever

$$\mathrm{Var}\left(\sum_j w_{ij}z_j\right) \leqslant \mathrm{Var}(z_i). \tag{A6}$$

Suppose, for example, that each observation consists of two components, one common to each county, the other part being uncorrelated with all other counties. That is,

$$z_i = a_i + b, \quad i = 1, ..., n$$

where

$$\mathrm{Var}(a_i) = \sigma^2, \mathrm{Cov}(a_i, a_j) = 0, \quad i \neq j$$

$$\mathrm{Var}(b) = \alpha^2, \mathrm{Cov}(a_i, b) = 0.$$

Then

$$\mathrm{Var}(z_i) = \sigma^2 + \alpha^2,$$

$$\mathrm{Var}\left(\sum_j w_{ij}z_j\right) = n^{-1}\sigma^2 \sum_{(2)} w_{ij}^2 + \alpha^2,$$

where these expectations are evaluated over the set of all possible sample configurations for the given set of z_i.

Then $\max |r| \leqslant 1$ when, from Equation (A6),

$$\sum_{(2)} w_{ij}^2 \leqslant n \tag{A7}$$

Equation (A7) certainly holds when $\max_{i,j} w_{ij} \leqslant 1$, which is true when the standardised weights with $w_{i.} = 1$ are used. Finally, we note that Equation (A6) implies that

$$\max |r| = \left[\frac{\mathrm{Var}\left(\sum_j w_{ij}z_j\right)}{\mathrm{Var}(z_i)}\right]^{\frac{1}{2}}$$

giving explicit bounds for r given any set of $\{z_i\}$ and weights $\{w_{ij}\}$.
Example: For variable (5) in Table 2 using standardised weights, we have $\mathrm{Var}\left(\sum_j w_{ij}z_j\right) = 358 \cdot 91$, and $\mathrm{Var}(z_i) = 1036 \cdot 72$, so that $\max r = 0 \cdot 589$.
Alternatively we can define r^* so that

$$\max |r^*| = 1.$$

Then the observed value $r = 0 \cdot 2427$ yields the value $r^* = 0 \cdot 412$.
This gives a more clear indication of the degree of correlation if assessed on the usual $[-1, +1]$ interval, but we cannot, of course, develop any distribution theory for r^* as the numerator and denominator are no longer independent.

APPENDIX II

This appendix contains the unstandardised and standardised weighting matrices used when analyzing Geary's Irish counties data.

TABLE A1. Unstandardised weighting matrix

County	Contiguous Counties and Weights					
A	I 0·0039	J 0·0142	K 0·0031	Y 0·0112	Z 0·0119	
B	L 0·0099	N 0·0061	Q 0·0089	R 0·0113	X 0·0006	
C	G 0·0134	H 0·0018	M 0·0103	V 0·0028		
D	H 0·0125	M 0·0084	V 0·0008	W 0·0030		
E	L 0·0186					
G	C 0·0087	P 0·0068	S 0·0010	T 0·0079	V 0·0013	
H	C 0·0021	D 0·0175	M 0·0046			
I	A 0·0034	K 0·0081	Q 0·0063	S 0·0068	Z 0·0110	
J	A 0·0111	K 0·0088	V 0·0086	W 0·0051	Y 0·0044	
K	A 0·0025	I 0·0074	J 0·0090	S 0·0185	V 0·0033	
L	B 0·0106	E 0·0008	N 0·0055	T 0·0079	U 0·0098	
M	C 0·0080	D 0·0077	H 0·0030	V 0·0095		
N	B 0·0079	L 0·0067	T 0·0105	X 0·0232		
O	Q 0·0324	R 0·0134				
P	G 0·0094	T 0·0049	U 0·0100			
Q	B 0·0083	I 0·0052	O 0·0087	R 0·0008	S 0·0008	X 0·0086
R	B 0·0319	O 0·0109	Q 0·0023			
S	G 0·0012	I 0·0044	K 0·0134	Q 0·0006	T 0·0010	V 0·0062	X 0·0088
T	G 0·0088	L 0·0049	N 0·0054	P 0·0039	S 0·0009	U 0·0054	X 0·0015
U	L 0·0100	P 0·0133	T 0·0089			
V	C 0·0016	O 0·0006	G 0·0012	J 0·0047	K 0·0018	M 0·0071	S 0·0046
							W 0·0055
W	D 0·0051	J 0·0071	V 0·0140	Y 0·0023		
X	B 0·0006	N 0·0179	Q 0·0092	S 0·0120	T 0·0022	
Y	A 0·0165	J 0·0083	W 0·0032	Z 0·0108		
Z	A 0·0139	I 0·0146	Y 0·0086			

TABLE A2. Standardised weighting matrix

County	Contiguous Counties and Weights
A	I 0·0874 J 0·3207 K 0·0699 Y 0·2540 Z 0·2680
B	L 0·2690 N 0·1658 Q 0·2426 R 0·3073 X 0·0153
C	G 0·4808 H 0·0617 M 0·3590 V 0·0985
D	H 0·5056 M 0·3411 V 0·0327 W 0·1206
E	L 1·0000
G	C 0·3392 P 0·2639 S 0·0394 T 0·3076 V 0·0499
H	C 0·0866 D 0·7218 M 0·1916
I	A 0·0959 K 0·2274 Q 0·1766 S 0·1907 Z 0·3095
J	A 0·2919 K 0·2312 V 0·2259 W 0·1345 Y 0·1166
K	A 0·0610 I 0·1808 J 0·2217 S 0·4558 V 0·0807
L	B 0·3057 E 0·0229 N 0·1604 T 0·2277 U 0·2833
M	C 0·2827 D 0·2732 H 0·1075 V 0·3365
N	B 0·1628 L 0·1387 T 0·2169 X 0·4816
O	Q 0·7080 R 0·2920
P	G 0·3881 T 0·2000 U 0·4119
Q	B 0·2560 I 0·1624 O 0·2685 R 0·0233 S 0·0249 X 0·2649
R	B 0·7075 O 0·2416 Q 0·0508
S	G 0·0348 I 0·1245 K 0·3742 Q 0·0177 T 0·0289 V 0·1748 X 0·2451
T	G 0·2871 L 0·1586 N 0·1748 P 0·1269 S 0·0306 U 0·1749 X 0·0471
U	L 0·3114 P 0·4126 T 0·2760
V	C 0·0602 D 0·0203 G 0·0432 J 0·1743 K 0·0649 M 0·2611 S 0·1713 W 0·2045
W	D 0·1797 J 0·2488 V 0·4901 Y 0·0814
X	B 0·0134 N 0·4288 Q 0·2196 S 0·2861 T 0·0521
Y	A 0·4254 J 0·2146 W 0·0810 Z 0·2791
Z	A 0·3740 I 0·3935 Y 0·2325

On the Optimal Partitioning of Spatially Distributed Point Sets †

A.J.SCOTT
University of Pennsylvania and University College London

The problem considered in this paper has the following general form: Given a set of points distributed in Euclidean N-space establish a partitioning of the points into a predetermined number of groups so as to optimize an objective function.

Several variations of this problem are well known. In particular, the problem has been discussed frequently in connection with the geographical problem of the optimal location of service centres such as warehouses, hospitals, or schools (Baumol and Wolfe, 1958; Cooper, 1963). Assume that m such facilities are to be located and that the population to be served consists of a set of n discrete points distributed in the plane. The problem is then to discover an m-fold partitioning of the set of customer points so that the sum of the distances between every point and its nearest central facility (whose location is also an element of the solution), is a minimum. It is understood that each central facility is unconstrained in its capacity. A number of approximative and heuristic approaches to the resolution of this special problem have been advanced, (Balinski, 1961; Cooper, 1964, 1967; Kuehn and Hamburger, 1963; Maranzana, 1964).

A second important special manifestation of this general problem is in the matter of taxonomic description (Sokal and Sneath, 1963). This problem consists in deriving an m-fold partitioning of a set of points distributed in Euclidean N-space such that some function of the set of intra-group or inter-group distances is optimized. A common objective function for such problems is to minimize the sum of squares of all intra-group distances, or to maximize the sum of squares of all inter-group distances. Again, several approximative resolutions of this problem have been proposed (e.g. Berry, 1961; Ward, 1963). A variant of this problem and a solution heuristic are described by Hess *et al.*, (1965).

In the account which follows an exact solution method for all problems of this sort is demonstrated. This is the method of backtrack

† This research was supported by the Federal Water Pollution Control Administration (Grant No. WP-00938), the National Science Foundation, Resources for the Future, and the Regional Science Research Institute. All computations were performed at the Computer Centre, University College London.

programming which is applied here to the solution of an exemplary case
formulated as a zero-one programming problem (Balas, 1965, 1967;
Golomb and Baumert, 1965). This method is sufficiently powerful to
be able to optimize any linear or monotonic non-linear objective function. Typically, however, the method also becomes computationally
over-extended as the size of the problem to be solved increases. Hence
an alternative, more efficient, solution algorithm is proposed. This
algorithm is shown by experiment to be exceptionally robust and to
converge with high probability on the true optimal solution for any
given problem.

Mathematical Specification of the Problem

For simplicity of exposition, certain restrictions are imposed upon the
problems discussed in the entire following account. These restrictions
are: (a) all problems are concerned with point sets distributed in the
plane, (b) the number of partitions required in any solution is always
two, (c) all points in any problem are of equal weight, and lastly, (d) exemplary problems are confined to a specific variation of the central facility location problem. Any of these restrictions may always be relaxed
without difficulty.

A generalized objective function for an optimal two-fold partitioning
of a two-dimensional point set may be written:
Minimize:

$$\phi = \sum_{i=1}^{n} f(\lambda_i^{(1)}, X_i, Y_i) + \sum_{i=1}^{n} f(\lambda_i^{(2)}, X_i, Y_i) \qquad (1)$$

where X_i and Y_i are the Cartesian coordinates of the ith point. The function, f, is any function which is monotonic non-decreasing with respect to
$\lambda_i^{(1)}$ and $\lambda_i^{(2)}$. This limitation on the function is necessitated by the structure of the backtrack programming algorithm which is considered subse-
quently. The terms $\lambda_i^{(1)}$ and $\lambda_i^{(2)}$ are solution variables such that:

$$\lambda_i^{(1)} + \lambda_i^{(2)} = 1, \qquad (2)$$

$$\lambda_i^{(1)}, \lambda_i^{(2)} = \begin{cases} 1 \\ 0 \end{cases}. \qquad (3)$$

Whenever $\lambda_i^{(1)} = 1$ then the ith point is assigned to the first group and
otherwise whenever $\lambda_i^{(1)} = 0$. Similarly, whenever $\lambda_i^{(2)} = 1$ then the ith
point is assigned to the second group and otherwise whenever $\lambda_i^{(2)} = 0$.
The constraint (2) ensures that each point is assigned to one and only
one group.

Now consider the special case of Equation (1) where it is required to
partition the total point set into two groups in such a way that (a) each
group has associated with it a centroid, such as median point or mean
point (see Neft, 1966), and (b) the sum over every group of the distances
from all points to their respective centroids is a minimum. Symbolically

such a problem may be written:

Minimize:

$$\phi = \sum_{i=1}^{n} \lambda_i^{(1)}[(C_x^{(1)} - X_i)^2 + (C_y^{(1)} - Y_i)^2]^{\frac{1}{2}}$$

$$+ \sum_{i=1}^{n} \lambda_i^{(2)}[(C_x^{(2)} - X_i)^2 + (C_y^{(2)} - Y_i)^2]^{\frac{1}{2}}$$

subject to Equations (2) and (3), and where $C_x^{(1)}$, $C_y^{(1)}$, $C_x^{(2)}$, $C_y^{(2)}$ are the coordinates of the two centroids. The values of these coordinates must be obtained as part of the solution to the problem. In what follows, the two centroids are defined as mean points or centres of gravity. Thus their coordinates are:

$$C_x^{(1)} \equiv \frac{\sum_{i=1}^{n} X_i \lambda_i^{(1)}}{\sum_{i=1}^{n} \lambda_i^{(1)}}, \qquad C_y^{(1)} \equiv \frac{\sum_{i=1}^{n} Y_i \lambda_i^{(1)}}{\sum_{i=1}^{n} \lambda_i^{(1)}}.$$

$$C_x^{(2)} \equiv \frac{\sum_{i=1}^{n} X_i \lambda_i^{(2)}}{\sum_{i=1}^{n} \lambda_i^{(2)}}, \qquad C_y^{(2)} \equiv \frac{\sum_{i=1}^{n} Y_i \lambda_i^{(2)}}{\sum_{i=1}^{n} \lambda_i^{(2)}}.$$

This specification of the centroids is perhaps less appealing than to define them as median centres (so that the sum of within-group distances from every point to its associated centroid would be a minimum). However, as existing methods for obtaining the values of the coordinates of a median centre are somewhat cumbersome (Kuhn and Kuenne, 1962) the simpler case is employed here.

Thus, the objective function of the specific problem, which is used to exemplify the methods described below, is to derive a two-fold partitioning of a given point set so as to minimize the sum of the distances from each point to the centre of gravity of the group to which that point belongs. Because this problem is used merely for purposes of exemplification, it is simply asserted here, without proof, that this objective function is indeed monotonic non-decreasing with respect to all solution variables.

A BACKTRACK PROGRAMMING FORMULATION OF THE PROBLEM

General properties of the backtrack algorithm

The optimal partitioning problem is a pure combinatorial problem. That is, the problem can always be solved in principle by direct examination of every combinatorial possibility for the given problem and extracting that solution which is optimal within the frame of reference of the

specified constraints. In practice, of course, such a procedure is imprac-
ticable for all but the smallest problems. However, this problem in pure
combinatorics can frequently be made tractable by the application of
backtrack programming procedures.

The backtrack programming algorithm consists essentially of an
ordered search over a combinatorial tree representing the solution space
of the entire problem. This search is composed of two elements: a
branching process, and a backtrack process, where the operation of any
one process is determined at each stage during the solution algorithm by
the application of a bounding mechanism. This mechanism prevents the
algorithm from searching for the optimal solution in sectors of the solution space which are known, *a priori*, not to contain the optimal solution.

Construction of a combinatorial tree for a general partitioning problem

Suppose, for simplicity, that it is desired to group four points labelled
a, b, c, d, into a two-fold partitioning and to evaluate directly every combinatorial possibility for this problem (see Figure 1). The method of
evaluation is to work through a combinatorial tree from a set of infeasible solutions towards a final set of feasible solutions, which are the solutions of interest here. A feasible solution is, in the present case, any
two-fold grouping which incorporates all n points in the problem. One
of these groups may be empty. Any two-fold grouping which incorporates less than all n points is termed infeasible.

The tree representing the complete set of solution possibilities for
this problem is built up as follows: the origin node of the tree consists
simply of the first point (point a). This is an infeasible grouping with an
implied second, but empty, group. Let this solution represent generation 1 of the tree. Now, point b is added into the system and a second
generation of combinations established. This second generation consists
of two solutions emanating out of the origin of the tree. These two solutions represent the two ways that the points a and b can be combined in
two groups: that is, either in a single group, ab, or as a/b, where the bar
represents a partition. In general, in the kth generation of the tree, the
kth point is introduced into the problem. This is effected in such a way
that every solution in generation k gives rise to two different descendants
in generation $k+1$. The tree is built up in this manner until the nth
generation of solutions is encountered. A set of terminal states is now
established. These terminal states represent every possible feasible solution, at least one of which will be optimal.

For a general two-fold partitioning problem of this sort, there will be a
total number of $\sum_{i=0}^{n-1} 2^i$ solutions within the combinatorial tree, and a total
of 2^{n-1} purely terminal states.

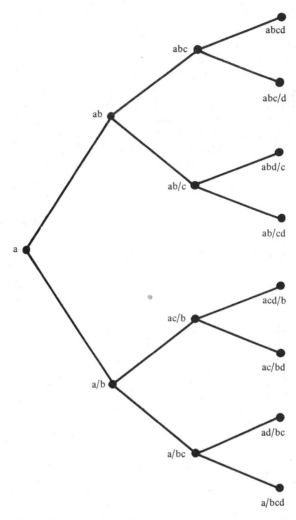

Figure 1. Combinatorial tree for evaluation of points a, b, c, d.

A backtrack programming algorithm

A systematic search over the combinatorial tree described above is put into effect. The search is initiated at the origin of the tree and is directed outwards and in a clockwise direction through the tree. Only one solution is examined at each stage, and after this examination the algorithm moves on to a descendant solution or backtracks to an antecedent solution. The orderly progression of the search is facilitated by the fact that any solution in generation $k + 1$ differs from its antecedent solution in generation k by possessing a single extra point. This means that it is possible to move in a systematic fashion forwards and backwards through the tree by adding or dropping, as the case may be, a point at a time.

As each solution within the tree is examined in turn, it is compared against an upper bound U on the value of the optimal objective function. The outcome of this comparison determines whether or not the optimal solution can occur as a direct descendant in the tree of the current solution. If not, the solution process backtracks towards the origin of the tree. Otherwise the solution process continues branching outwards.

Initially, U may be set equal to any arbitrarily high value. However, the efficiency of the backtrack algorithm is, to a large degree, dependent upon establishing very early during the solution process as strong an upper bound on the optimal solution as possible. Thus probably a better initial determination of U would be to set it equal to the objective function, ϕ, for a solution which is guessed to be close to optimal. It will be recalled that the objective function is determined by establishing a two-fold partitioning of the n points in the problem, and then summing the distances between each point and the centre of gravity of the group to which that point belongs.

As the search continues, successive values of ϕ are computed. Whenever a solution yielding the condition $\phi > U$ is encountered, then neither this solution (if it is feasible) nor any of its descendants (if it is infeasible) can be optimal. For, since the objective function of the problem is monotonic non-decreasing with respect to all solution variables, it follows that all such descendants must also yield solution values which exceed the value of U. However, the optimal value of ϕ is known to be less than U. Thus whenever the condition $\phi \geqslant U$ occurs, then the algorithm backtracks into the tree to the nearest combination from which a new and previously unexamined branch can be drawn.

Whenever the condition $\phi < U$ occurs two possibilities are open. Firstly, if the solution corresponding to this value of ϕ is infeasible, the algorithm simply continues branching outwards. Secondly, if the solution is feasible, then a new best upper bound on the value of the optimal solution has been discovered and the value of U is changed to this value of ϕ.

The algorithm continues its operation until the entire tree has been scrutinized in this way. On the termination of the algorithm, the current value of U represents the value of the final optimal solution.

Exact numerical solution of some optimal partitioning problems

A series of ten optimal partitioning problems was evaluated by the method of backtrack programming. Each of these problems consists of finding a two-fold partitioning of twenty randomly distributed points. The optimal solutions to two of these problems are depicted in Figures 2 and 3 where each group of points is indicated by a particular symbol.

For any problem of the sort investigated here the total number of different solutions within the corresponding combinatorial tree is a little

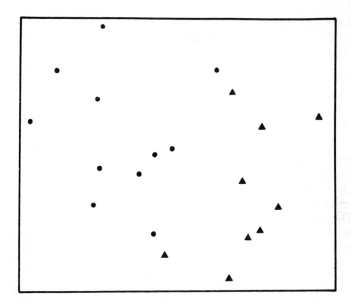

Figure 2.

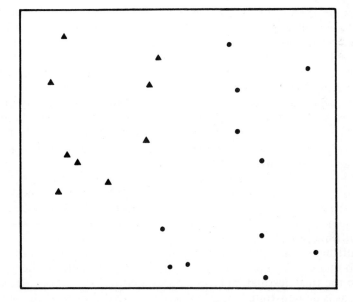

Figure 3.

over one million.   Even so, none of the problems examined required
more than two minutes of solution time on an IBM 360 computer.
Nevertheless, problems of this size are very close to being practically in-
soluble.   For example, one problem involving a two-fold partitioning of
twenty-five points required fifty minutes of computer time to achieve a
final solution.

AN ALGORITHM FOR APPROXIMATING SOLUTIONS TO THE OPTIMAL PARTITIONING PROBLEM

In view of the lengthy computations incurred by backtrack programming formulations of the optimal partitioning problem, rapid computational algorithms which give at least close approximations to optimality
would obviously be of great value.   One such algorithm is described below.   This algorithm was originally devised for the solution of certain
network problems (Scott, 1969).   However, the algorithm is certainly of
fairly general applicability to a wide class of zero-one programming problems.   In particular, it is shown to be an especially powerful method for
solving the optimal partitioning problem.

General principles of the approximative algorithm

Consider, again, the problem of finding an optimal two-fold partitioning of the four points a, b, c, d, and of directly evaluating every combinatorial possibility for this problem.   One way of arriving in an orderly
manner at every possible feasible combination is by means of the tree
structure depicted in Figure 1.   A second means is depicted in Figure 4.
Here, the combinatorial evaluation process involves moving progressively
through every combination containing 1, 2, ..., n elements in that order.
However, whereas in the combinatorial tree there is one and only one
path from the origin node to the optimal solution, in this second combinatorial process there are many.   This means that any attempt to trace a
continuous path through the network represented by Figure 4, from the
origin node to the optimal solution, can always be corrected to some
degree if it should appear to be deviating from its goal.   The approximative algorithm takes advantage of this feature and, in part, attempts to
trace out such a path by a process of local optimization.   At the same
time, the power of the algorithm is enhanced by the subsidiary operation
of a shuffling process which also seeks out local optima.   By means of
this shuffling process the algorithm jumps from path to path in the network so that the final path traced out by the algorithm from the origin
node to the final destination is, in fact, discontinuous.   These operations
ensure, as is demonstrated later by induction, that the algorithm will tend
to converge in the direction of the global optimum for the full problem.

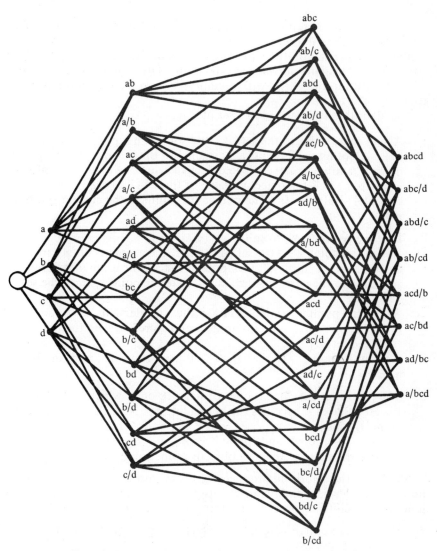

Figure 4. Combinatorial network for evaluation of points a, b, c, d.

Development of the approximative algorithm

Consider the sets $\{A\}$, $\{B\}$ and $\{G\}$ with elemental components, each representing a particular point, as follows:

$$\alpha_1, \alpha_2, ..., \alpha_i, ..., \alpha_{n_A} \in \{A\}$$

$$\beta_1, \beta_2, ..., \beta_i, ..., \beta_{n_B} \in \{B\}$$

$$\gamma_1, \gamma_2, ..., \gamma_i, ..., \gamma_{n_G} \in \{G\}$$

The sets $\{A\}$ and $\{B\}$ represent the two groups which are sought as a solution. During the solution period of the algorithm these two sets will contain only partial solutions to the partitioning problem. The set $\{G\}$ contains any elements not assigned to $\{A\}$ and $\{B\}$. On the termination of the algorithm the set $\{G\}$ will be empty. Given these definitions it follows that $n_A + n_B + n_G = n$.

The algorithm is described in a set of stages:

1. Assign some point to the set $\{A\}$, and some other point to the set $\{B\}$. All other $n-2$ points are assigned to the set $\{G\}$. Now $n_A = 1$, $n_B = 1$, and $n_G = n-2$. The objective value of the set $\{A\}$, $(\phi\{A\})$, is now zero as is the objective value of the set $\{B\}$, $(\phi\{B\})$, and $\phi = \phi\{A\} + \phi\{B\} = 0$. The number of points in the current solution is $J = n_A + n_B$.

2a. Delete any point, γ_i, from the set $\{G\}$.

2b. Assign the point γ_i to the set $\{A\}$ so that the elements of $\{A\}$ are $\alpha_1, \alpha_2, ..., \alpha_j, ..., \alpha_{n_A}, \gamma_i$. Compute and store the value of ϕ corresponding to the current solution. Delete the point γ_i from the set $\{A\}$.

2c. Assign the point γ_i to the set $\{B\}$ so that the elements of $\{B\}$ are $\beta_1, \beta_2, ..., \beta_j, ..., \beta_{n_B}, \gamma_i$. Compute ϕ and store. Delete the point γ_i from the set $\{B\}$.

2d. Return the point γ_i to the set $\{G\}$. Repeat steps 2a to 2d for all $\gamma_i \in \{G\}$.

3. The particular assignment of γ_i in stage 2b or 2c which yields the lowest value of ϕ becomes the new solution. Now this γ_i is deleted from $\{G\}$ and *either* $\alpha_{n_A+1} \leftarrow \gamma_i$ or $\beta_{n_B+1} \leftarrow \gamma_i$. The elements of $\{G\}$ are now re-ordered, and the indices n_A, n_B, n_G, and J up-dated. Denote the value of the new objective function by ϕ_J.

Stage 3 of the algorithm produces a forward motion of the solution process through the combinatorial network of the problem. At this juncture the shuffling procedure is brought into action:

4a. Delete any point, α_i, from the set $\{A\}$, and hold α_i in separate temporary storage.

4b. Delete any point, γ_j, from the set $\{G\}$.

4c. Assign the point γ_j to the set $\{A\}$ so that the elements of $\{A\}$ are $\alpha_1, \alpha_2, ..., \alpha_{i-1}, \alpha_{i+1}, ..., \alpha_{n_A}, \gamma_j$. Compute the value of ϕ and store. Delete the point γ_j from the set $\{A\}$.

4d. Return the point γ_j to $\{G\}$. Repeat steps 4b to 4d for all $\gamma_j \in \{G\}$.

4e. Return the point α_i to the set $\{A\}$. Repeat steps 4a to 4e for all $\alpha_i \in \{A\}$.

5a. Delete any point, β_i, from the set $\{B\}$, and hold β_i in separate temporary storage.

5b. Delete any point, γ_j, from the set $\{G\}$.

5c. Assign the point γ_j to the set $\{B\}$ so that the elements of $\{B\}$ are $\beta_1, \beta_2, ..., \beta_{i-1}, \beta_{i+1}, ..., \beta_{n_B}, \gamma_j$. Compute the value of ϕ and store. Delete the point γ_j from the set $\{B\}$.

5d. Return the point γ_j to $\{G\}$. Repeat steps 5b to 5d for all $\gamma_j \in \{G\}$.

5e. Return the point β_i to the set $\{B\}$. Repeat steps 5a to 5e for all $\beta_i \in \{B\}$.

6a. Delete any point, β_i, from the set $\{B\}$.

6b. Assign the point β_i to the set $\{A\}$ so that the elements of $\{A\}$ are $\alpha_1, \alpha_2, ..., \alpha_j, ..., \alpha_{n_A}, \beta_i$. Compute the value of ϕ and store. Delete the point β_i from the set $\{A\}$.

6c. Return the point β_i to the set $\{B\}$. Repeat steps 6a to 6c for all $\beta_i \in \{B\}$.

7a. Delete any point, α_i, from the set $\{A\}$.

7b. Assign the point α_i to the set $\{B\}$ so that the elements of $\{B\}$ are $\beta_1, \beta_2, ..., \beta_j, ..., \beta_{n_B}, \alpha_i$. Compute the value of ϕ and store. Delete the point α_i from the set $\{B\}$.

7c. Return the point α_i to the set $\{A\}$. Repeat steps 7a to 7c for all $\alpha_i \in \{A\}$.

8. If the lowest value of ϕ computed in one of the steps 4c, 5c, 6b, 7b is less than ϕ_J then a new best solution has been found. ϕ_J is now changed to this value of ϕ. In addition, depending upon which particular assignment (if any) gives rise to the new best solution, one of the four alternatives applies, respectively:

$\quad$ (a) $\alpha_i \leftarrow \gamma_j, \quad \gamma_j \leftarrow \alpha_i$

$\quad$ (b) $\beta_i \leftarrow \gamma_j, \quad \gamma_j \leftarrow \beta_i$

$\quad$ (c) $\alpha_{n_A+1} \leftarrow \beta_i, \quad \beta_i$ is deleted from $\{B\}$

$\quad$ (d) $\beta_{n_B+1} \leftarrow \alpha_i, \quad \alpha_i$ is deleted from $\{A\}$.

If necessary, the elements of any set are now re-ordered, and the indices n_A and n_B are up-dated. Note that whatever the outcome of stage 8 the quantities n_G and J remain unchanged.

9. If a new best solution has been discovered in step 8, return to step 4a. Otherwise continue on.

10. If the set $\{G\}$ is non-empty (i.e. if $n_A + n_B < n$) return to step 2a. Otherwise the operation of the algorithm is terminated.

On the termination of the algorithm the sets $\{A\}$ and $\{B\}$ will contain the full final solution.

Evaluation of the approximative algorithm

Although the approximative algorithm requires lengthy arithmetical operations to achieve a conclusion, it is nevertheless appreciably more efficient than the backtrack programming method. Once an initial starting position for the algorithm has been specified, its operation is entirely automatic. To some degree the specification of this starting position is an arbitrary matter. This problem is discussed in more detail below. A typical full solution sequence for the algorithm is shown in Figure 5. Points belonging to the set $\{G\}$ are shown by open circles; the sets $\{A\}$ and $\{B\}$ are shown as they are in Figures 2 and 3. Solution sets within Figure 5 which are displaced to the right represent solutions which have undergone a shuffling process. An unpromising starting position has been deliberately selected for the sample problem shown in Figure 5.

The optimal partitioning problems, which were solved exactly by the method of backtrack programming, are now used as a standard of comparison against which to judge the performance of the approximative algorithm. Recall that there were ten of these problems each involving a two-fold partitioning of a set of twenty randomly located points.

Initially, to avoid whatever difficulties that might be incurred in making a selection of a specific pair of points as a starting position for the algorithm, each twenty-point problem was solved repeatedly using every possible pair of points as a starting position. Thus, a total of $\binom{20}{2} = 190$

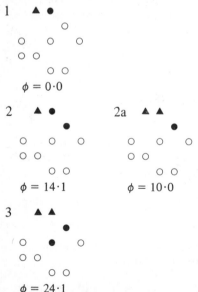

Figure 5. The approximative algorithm—a typical solution sequence (*continued over*).

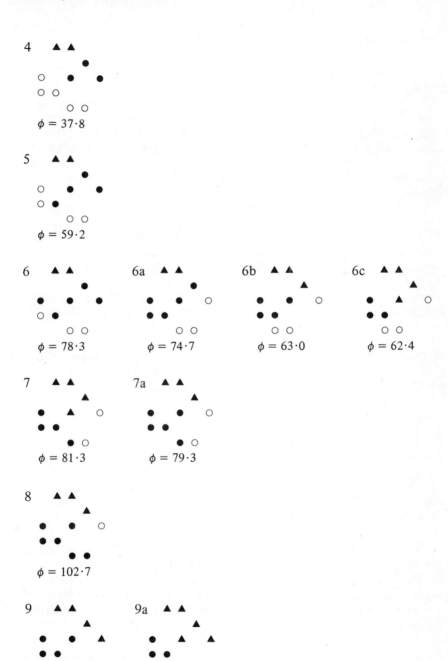

Figure 5. The approximative algorithm—a typical solution sequence.

solutions was computed by the approximative algorithm for each problem. The total set of 1900 solutions for all ten problems required seventy-five minutes of solution time on an IBM 360 computer. This is the equivalent of slightly less than 2·4 seconds per solution. The numerical results of these analyses were entirely beyond expectation. Of the 1900 different solutions computed, 1768 or 93·1% were completely optimal. There were, in fact, only two point sets which yielded sub-optimal solutions. In the one case, optimality was attained for 140 solutions out of a possible 190; the remaining 50 solutions converged onto a single objective function which deviated from optimality by only 0·1%. In the other case, full optimality was attained on 108 occasions, and the remaining 82 solutions again converged onto a single value; this value was 0·9% higher than optimal.

A secondary criterion of judgement of the performance of the algorithm is now applied: this consists in evaluating the algorithm against what is probably the best existing alternative approximative procedure for solving the optimal partitioning problem. This is Cooper's "elimination–alternate–correction" heuristic, (Cooper, 1967). The performance of Cooper's heuristic in solving the ten twenty-point problems discussed above is appraised comparatively in the following table:

Case	Value of ϕ: Optimal solution	Value of ϕ: Cooper's heuristic	*Highest* value of ϕ observed in approximative algorithm
1	417·8	417·8	417·8
2	432·7	432·7	436·7
3	441·6	442·0	441·6
4	446·5	452·0	446·5
5	454·4	455·7	454·4
6	458·2	485·9	458·2
7	514·0	514·0	514·0
8	523·7	523·7	523·7
9	553·6	554·1	554·1
10	579·7	587·5	579·7

It is evident from the table that while Cooper's heuristic is moderately powerful, it still does not match in power the approximative algorithm developed here, which appears as only slightly less reliable than the exact method of backtrack programming. In addition it is evident, at least in the cases considered, that with high probability the approximative algorithm will attain full optimality even from a random start.

CONCLUDING COMMENTS

There remains the problem of finding a specific efficient starting position for the approximative algorithm. For a two-fold partitioning problem a good start is probably obtained by selecting as the opening pair of points the two most distant points in the whole point set. Obviously this method cannot easily be generalized to cases where the required number of partitions is more than two. However, the fact that the algorithm seems to converge on such a limited family of solutions suggests that selection by guess-work of an initial set of points would yield good results. In other cases, the elimination stage of Cooper's heuristic might be used to obtain a starting position. On the other hand, perhaps the most effective use of the algorithm in the solution of any one problem might be to attack the problem repeatedly from several different starting positions and to test for optimality among the resulting solutions by mutual corroboration.

Given the approximative algorithm developed above, it is now possible to process rapidly optimal partitioning problems for spatially distributed point sets and be fairly confident that the final solution will not be far from full optimality. Even so, the standard of performance of the algorithm in solving very large and complex problems remains unknown. The overcoming of whatever difficulties such problems may present remains a task for future research.

References

Balas, E., 1965, "An Additive Algorithm for Solving Linear Programs with Zero-One Variables", *Operations Research,* **13**, 517–539.
Balas, E., 1967, "Discrete Programming by the Filter Method", *Operations Research,* **15**, 915–957.
Balinski, M.L., 1961, "Fixed Cost Transportation Problems", *Naval Research Logistics Quaterly,* **8**, 41–54.
Baumol, W.J., and Wolfe, P., 1958, "A Warehouse Location Problem", *Operations Research,* **6**, 252–263.
Berry, B.J.L., 1961, "A Method for Deriving Multi-Factor Uniform Regions", *Przeglad Geograficzny,* **33**, 263–282.
Cooper, L., 1963, "Location–Allocation Problems", *Operations Research,* **11**, 331–343.
Cooper, L., 1964, "Heuristic Methods for Location–Allocation Problems", *SIAM Review,* **6**, 37–53.
Cooper, L., 1967, "Solutions of Generalized Locational Equilibrium Models", *Journal of Regional Science,* **7**, 1–18.
Golomb, S.W., and Baumert, L.D., 1965, "Backtrack Programming", *Journal of the Association for Computing Machinery,* **12**, 516–524.
Hess, S.W., *et al.,* 1965, "Nonpartisan Political Redistricting by Computer", *Operations Research,* **13**, 998–1006.
Kuehn, A.A., and Hamburger, M., 1963, "A Heuristic Program for Locating Warehouses", *Management Science,* **9**, 643–666.
Kuhn, H.W., and Kuenne, R.E., 1962, "An Efficient Algorithm for the Numerical Solution of the Generalized Weber Problem in Spatial Economics", *Journal of Regional Science,* **4**, 21–34.
Maranzana, F.E., 1964, "On the Location of Supply Points to Minimize Transport Costs", *Operational Research Quarterly,* **15**, 261–270.

Neft, D.S., 1966, *Statistical Analysis for Areal Distributions,* Monograph Series No.2, (Regional Science Research Institute, Philadelphia).

Scott, A.J., 1969, "The Optimal Network Problem: Some Computational Procedures", *Transportation Research,* 3, (forthcoming).

Sokal, R.R., and Sneath, P.H.A., 1963, *Principles of Numerical Taxonomy* (W.H.Freeman and Company, San Francisco).

Ward, J.H., 1963, "Hierarchical Grouping to Optimize an Objective Function", *Journal of the American Statistical Association,* 58, 236–244.

Reducing the Travel Time in a Transport Network

T.M.RIDLEY
Greater London Council

Introduction

One of the most important problems in transportation analysis and planning is that of the allocation of investment to a network. Related to this is the problem of the proper scheduling of investments. Given an existing network, a number of possible links which can be built or improved, and a fixed budget, what is the best combination of links in which to invest? What indeed is the correct level at which the budget should be fixed and in what order should the links be added?

Obviously, these are economic questions which raise problems of discounting over time, rates of return and the like. Quite apart from these questions, however, the problem is complex because of the interrelation between the links in which investment takes place. In this paper the general problem of the best combination of links for investment with a given budget is discussed and a method of solution is illustrated. A restriction on the general problem leads to a solution for the problem of the scheduling of investment. Finally a heuristic method is described which reduces the size of the problem.

Transportation Study Techniques

The mathematical methods which are used in transportation studies, when reduced to their simplest terms have the sequence:
- (i) trip generation   - rate of trip making
- (ii) trip distribution   - trip pattern
- (iii) trip assignment   - routes of trips.

Traffic forecasts are made by first calibrating these models (mathematical descriptions of behaviour) and then using them in conjunction with forecasts of planning data. More recently this sequence has been extended by the addition of an economic analysis stage.

The mathematical technique used in the 'trip generation' stage is regression analysis, by means of which trip rates for traffic zones are defined as a function of measures of person and land use characteristics. In the 'trip distribution' and 'assignment' stages a simplified description of the transport network is necessary. A theoretical network of nodes and links is used. In general, trips are assumed to be generated at, and attracted to, certain nodes and to travel between their origin and destination nodes by means of links for which unit travel times have been assumed.

Budget Allocation

The method of budget allocation which is presented here is directly related to the standard methods of 'trip distribution' and 'assignment', in that it uses a network of nodes and links with unit travel times associated with each link. It represents only one of a number of different ways in which the budget allocation problem can be presented, however.

The problem can be defined as follows—given a network of nodes and links with which unit travel times are associated, what is the optimal manner in which a given sum of money can be invested in the links? In order to calculate this optimum it is necessary to define the criterion which will be used to assess optimality. In the 'trip distribution' and 'assignment' stages it is usual to calculate that route which, between each pair of nodes, has the minimum travel time. When all the trips have been assigned, a given distribution of trips will follow routes such that the total travel time in the network is minimised.

It is not realistic, of course, to assign only with respect to travel time. Operating and other costs also affect the way in which traffic assigns itself to a network. It is perfectly possible to assign traffic by use of some unit measure of travel resistance for each link, expressed as a function of travel time and operating cost, but in this discussion travel time is assumed to be the single measure of travel resistance.

The minimisation of travel time in a network is the criterion used in simple assignment. It is also the criterion which is used here in searching for the optimal allocation of a budget to a transport network. It is assumed that the distribution of traffic is fixed, that is that the pattern of travel is unchanged as investment takes place and only the routes change.

With these assumptions the problem can now be restated as:
given (a) a network of nodes and links,
      (b) unit travel times associated with each link, which vary in a
          specified manner with the amount of investment in the link
and (c) a fixed trip matrix
for any given budget, find an optimal set of links for investment so that the total travel time in the network is minimised.

It might be assumed that a solution would be found by ranking the links in order of their individual returns on investment and then investing in order of the ranking. In fact this is not so, because each time an investment is made in a link the traffic is reassigned and the subsequent ranking is changed. It may be that all of the links, which are included in the optimal set for m units of investment, are not included in the optimal set for $m + 1$ units of investment.

Problems of large networks, that can be expressed in mathematical terms, may very often be solved by modern methods of analysis which are being developed in other fields. It turns out that this problem is particularly intractable because it is non-convex. This is illustrated by means of a trivial two-link example.

Two Link Case

Consider two links, 1 and 2, between the pair of nodes i, j; see Figure 1, and suppose that the unit travel time for each link for 0, 1 and 2 units of investment is as shown in Table 1. If we assume that there is a continuous (not step-wise) relation between investment and unit travel time, then the table can be represented by Figure 2.

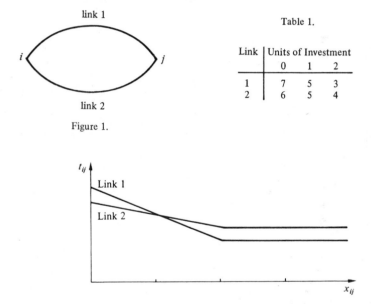

link 1

i j

link 2

Figure 1.

Table 1.

Link	Units of Investment		
	0	1	2
1	7	5	3
2	6	5	4

t_{ij}

Link 1

Link 2

x_{ij}

Figure 2. Unit travel time vs. investment.

In this simple case, the problem is to find the minimum travel time between nodes i and j for each unit of travel time. Clearly for 0 units of investment the minimum travel time equals 6 by link 2. For 1 unit of investment the minimum travel time is 5 regardless of which link receives the investment. For 2 units of investment the minimum travel time equals 3 by link 1.

In Figure 3 the length of the shortest route is shown as a function of investment. It will be seen that the results calculated above correspond to tracing the minima of the two unit travel time curves in Figure 2. Two points will be apparent. The shortest route curve in Figure 3 is non-convex, it is not gradually decreasing. This is a simple illustration of the fact that the more general problem has no convenient mathematical solution.

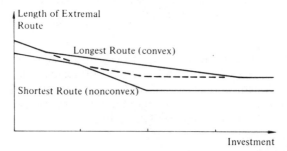

Figure 3. Shortest and longest routes vs. investment.

The second point has the more important practical implication however. It is clear that if there is between 0 and 1 unit of investment available, then the shortest travel time between nodes i and j is obtained if it is invested in link 2. Between 1 and 2 units of investment, however, the best result is obtained for investment in link 1. Thus, perhaps contrary to expectation, the order in which one should start to invest depends on the ultimate amount of investment available. It is clearly not necessarily wise to start investing where there is the greatest immediate return.

The Method of Bounded Subsets

The general combinatorial problem has been presented elsewhere (Ridley, 1965, 1968) its non-convexity discussed and a method of solution proposed. A special case, namely that of reducing the length of the minimum path between an origin and all destinations in a network has also been presented (Ridley, 1967). For this case, a simple extension of the algorithm which finds the shortest route tree in a network was used.

The method proposed for the general problem, the method of bounded subsets, is now described briefly. It is then extended to handle the problem of the sequence of investment. Finally, an alternative heuristic approach is presented. Each case is illustrated by means of a simple example.

The combinatorial method searches among all subsets of arcs in the network in which a total of m units may be invested. For each subset, lower bounds on the value of minimum travel time after investment can be calculated from the results obtained for an investment of $m + 1$ units. These bounds define a restricted number of investment policies among which the optimal policy for m units of investment may be found. The existence of these bounds enables us to find a recursive procedure which first calculates the optimal set and the minimum travel time corresponding to the maximum investment $m = P$, required to reduce the unit travel times of all arcs to their lower bounds. The optimal set and minimum travel time are then calculated for $m = P-1, P-2, P-3, ..., Q+1, Q$, that is, until the optimal set and minimum travel time are calculated for the given budget, Q.

Using the network $G = \{N, A\}$ of nodes and arcs, it is useful to define a set of investment arcs,

$$A_{m+1} = \{(i, j) \in A \mid x_{ij} = 1, \sum_{ij} x_{ij} = m+1 \leqslant P\}$$

as a set of $m + 1$ arcs in which one unit of investment has been made. P is the maximum possible investment in the arcs of the network. Define the unit travel time on arc ij as

$$t_{ij} = t_{ij}(x_{ij}) = t_{ij}(1) \qquad ij \in A_{m+1}$$
$$= t_{ij}(0) \qquad ij \in \overline{A}_{m+1}$$

where

$$A_{m+1} \cup \overline{A}_{m+1} = A; \quad A_{m+1} \cap \overline{A}_{m+1} = \phi$$

Thus, the set A_{m+1} also defines a set of unit travel times.

For a given set A_{m+1}, the minimum travel time in the network may be expressed as the sum of travel times in the arcs of set A_{m+1} and travel times in the remaining arcs $\overline{A}_{m+1}$

$$t(A_{m+1}) = \underset{f_{ij}}{\text{Min}}\left[\sum_{ij \in A_{m+1}} f_{ij}t_{ij} + \sum_{ij \in \overline{A}_{m+1}} f_{ij}t_{ij}\right].$$

This defines nonunique flows $f_{ij}(A_{m+1})$ such that

$$t(A_{m+1}) = \sum_{ij \in A_{m+1}} f_{ij}(A_{m+1})t_{ij} + \sum_{ij \in \overline{A}_{m+1}} f_{ij}(A_{m+1})t_{ij}.$$

In other words, the flows $f_{ij}(A_{m+1})$ and the minimum travel time $t(A_{m+1})$ are the solution to the traffic assignment problem, when investment is made in the set of arcs A_{m+1}. The minimum travel time associated with the investment of $m + 1$ units is the minimum over all sets A_{m+1}, that is

$$T_{m+1} = \underset{A_{m+1} \subset A}{\text{Min}} \ t(A_{m+1}) = t(A^*_{m+1}).$$

Thus, this equation defines a nonunique set of arcs A^*_{m+1}, which we call an optimal set for $m + 1$ units of investment. It is easy to establish that $T_m \geqslant T_{m+1}$, and in so doing to obtain a computational procedure which finds the minimum travel time T_m and an optimal set A^*_m for every value of $m \leqslant P$.

To begin our analysis we define a function

$$s(A_m) = \underset{A_{m+1} \supset A_m}{\text{Max}} \ t(A_{m+1}).$$

It can be shown that $s(A_m) \leqslant t(A_m)$, and that $s(A_m)$ is in fact a lower bound on the value of the minimum travel time associated with the set A_m. Starting with the values $t(A_{m+1})$ for all sets A_{m+1}, all values A_m can be calculated simply. The values of $t(A_m)$ are then calculated for the sets A_m in increasing order of the values $s(A_m)$. This is carried out until the lowest value of $t(A_m)$ found does not exceed the value of all remaining values $s(A_m)$. That particular set is an optimal set A_m^* and its minimum travel time represents the minimum among all possible values for m units of investment,

$$T_m = \text{Min } t(A_{m+1}) = t(A_{m+1}^*).$$

The computation is started with the calculation of the minimum travel time for the set A_P, when all possible investments are made. It then proceeds to the calculation of A_m^* for $m = P-1, ..., Q+1, Q$, until the optimal set A_Q^* is obtained together with its minimum travel time τ_Q for a budget Q. For each value m, the optimal set A_m^* is chosen among the finite number of sets A_m. The use of a procedure by which the optimal sets are calculated in turn, as m is reduced in unit steps from P to Q, leads to the optimal set A_Q^* being found in a finite number of steps.

A Committed Investment Policy

It may be important to consider a special class of investment policies where the subsets of invested arcs for larger budgets strictly contain the subsets of invested arcs for a smaller budget. This may occur, for example, when one considers the way in which budgets are prepared and committed to use. Over two fiscal periods, the total budget may dictate an optimal investment set A_n^* when, for the first period, the optimal set is A_m^* for a known available budget $m < n$. Once budget m is committed in the first period it is not possible for this investment to be recovered and combined with the budget of the next period. Rather, m units are invested in the first period, and $n - m$ in the second period subject to $A_n^* \supset A_m^*, (m < n)$.

We will, therefore, define a committed investment policy as one in which optimal sets are chosen so that

$$A_m^* \subset A_{m+1}^*.$$

This implies that no arc is ever dropped from the optimal set as the total investment increases. Thus a committed investment policy defines an order of investment.

Let us assume that for some total budget Q, an optimal set A_Q^* has been found. The order in which the investments are to be made is now required. Committed investment policies may be calculated in two ways. A_m^* may be chosen among all A_m such that

(i) $$A_m \subset A_{m+1}^* \subset A_Q^*$$

or A^*_{m+1} may be chosen among all A_{m+1} such that

(ii) $A^*_m \subset A_{m+1} \subset A^*_Q.$

If, under these restrictions, we search for the optimal set for each value of m, different orders of investment may result from the two policies.

First consider the policy defined by method (ii). A^*_1 is found, if the first unit of investment is made in that arc, among the set A^*_Q, which gives the greatest return on investment. With the first unit already committed, A^*_2 is obtained by investing in that arc which gives the greatest additional return. At each step only the consequences of a single unit of investment are considered. The concern is to maximize immediate return. With A^*_m and T_m given,

$$A^*_{m+1} = \{A^*_m \subset A_{m+1} \subset A^*_Q \mid (T_m - T_{m+1}) = \underset{A_{m+1}}{\text{Max}}\,[T_m - t(A_{m+1})]\}.$$

Now consider method (i). With A^*_Q and T_Q given, A^*_{Q-1} is that set for which $t(A_{Q-1})$ is minimized. This is equivalent to minimizing the difference $t(A_{Q-1}) - T_Q$. Each successive optimal set is calculated in the same way, by considering the effect of only unit change of investment. In this case, however, the change is a decrease of investment. For policy (i), with A^*_{m+1} and T_{m+1} given

$$A^*_m = \{A_m \subset A^*_{m+1} \subset A^*_Q \mid (T_m - T_{m+1}) = \underset{A_m}{\text{Min}}\,[t(A_m) - T_{m+1}]\}.$$

A consequence of this policy is that if the budget Q falls to $Q-1$, the resultant increase in minimum travel time is minimized.

For method (i) define

$$S_m = \underset{A_m \subset A^*_{m+1}}{\text{Min}}\,t(A_m).$$

The method of bounded subsets may now be used to calculate optimal sets A^*_m, $0 \leqslant m \leqslant Q$, such that

$$A^*_Q \supset A^*_{Q-1} \supset , ..., \supset A^*_0$$

and the relation between minimum travel times is

$$S_0 \geqslant , ..., \geqslant S_{Q-1} \geqslant S_Q.$$

Thus, for a given optimal set A^*_Q, the method obtains an order of investment for that set, such that the effect of a budget decrease is minimized.

For any given value of m

$$S_m = \underset{A_m \subset A^*_{m+1}}{\text{Min}}\,t(A_m) \geqslant \underset{A_m \subset A}{\text{Min}}\,t(A_m) = T_m.$$

Thus for all m, S_m is an upper bound on the value of minimum travel time T_m, the unrestricted minimum.

Application

It is clear that in any real problem both procedures must be combined. It is first necessary to calculate the optimal set for a given budget, which might itself be obtained by means of the procedure. Once the optimal set is obtained the sequence is then calculated for that set.

First choose the set of P investment arcs from which the budget set A_Q^* is to be chosen. This budget set is obtained by calculating the optimal set in turn for $m = P, P-1, ..., Q$. The procedure for calculating the sequence is then followed for $m = Q-1, ..., 2, 1$.

Since the first part of the calculation is the more extensive combinatorially, it is desirable to choose P close to Q. This of course reduces the number of combinations considered and therefore reduces the scope of the analysis. The choice of the value of P is therefore a compromise between the information to be obtained and amount of computation possible.

Example

A simple example is used to demonstrate the calculation of the optimal sets of investment arcs in a network for all values of budget. For a network of four nodes and four arcs one unit of investment reduces the unit travel time in an arc from its maximum value k_{ij} to its minimum l_{ij}. The data are shown in Figure 4 and the calculation in Table 2.

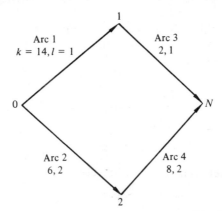

Data						Distribution of Traffic				
Arc	01	02	1N	2N		Node	0	1	2	N
Arc number	1	2	3	4		0	-	1	8	5
Unit rate of return a	13	4	1	6		1	-	-	-	3
Max investment $(k-l)/a$	1	1	1	1		2	-	-	-	5
						N	-	-	-	-

Figure 4. Four-arc example.

Table 2. Optimal sets

Investment \ Sets	1	2	3	4	5	6
$m = 4$	$A_m = \{1,2,3,4\}$ $s\ =\ \ 0$ $t\ =\ \ 40$					
3	$\{1,2,3\}$ 40 70	$\{1,2,4\}$ 40 48	$\{1,3,4\}$ 40 72	$\{2,3,4\}$ 40 63		
2	$\{1,2\}$ 70 –	$\{1,3\}$ 72 –	$\{1,4\}$ 72 –	$\{2,3\}$ 70 –	$\{2,4\}$ 63 66	$\{3,4\}$ 72 –
1	$\{1\}$ 72 110	$\{2\}$ 70 126	$\{3\}$ 72 175	$\{4\}$ 72 118		
0	$\{-\}$ – 178					

First calculate the minimum travel time for $m = P = 4$ and for $m = 3$. The minimum travel time for each case is 40 and 48 respectively. Now calculate the values of $s(A_2)$. The value for arcs $\{1, 2\}$ is the maximum of 70 and 48 and so on.

If all values of $s(A_2)$ are examined, we find that the minimum value is 63 for arcs $\{2, 4\}$. Calculating the value $t(A_2)$ for these arcs we obtain 66. Since this is less than all other lower bounds, it represents the minimum travel time for investment in any two arcs and $\{2, 4\}$ is the optimal set. The procedure continues for $m = 1$. Note that where a value of $t(A_{m+1})$ does not exist for the calculation of $s(A_m)$, the value of $s(A_{m+1})$ may be used in its place. If a committed investment policy is followed, then the calculation is as shown in Table 3.

A Heuristic Solution for the General Problem

In the case of the general problem a simple method of calculation would be to rank all the arcs in the order of their individual returns on investment and then to invest in order of the ranking. This does not lead to an optimum solution, however, because whenever investment is made in an arc the traffic is reassigned and the ranking changes. Nevertheless, this basic approach is used here, combined with a method of searching for new assignments which gradually leads towards an optimum for all levels of investment. The method is heuristic only and optimality is not proved.

Table 3. Committed investments

Investment \ Sets	1	2	3	4
$m = 4$	$A_m = \{1,2,3,4\}$ $s = 0$ $t = 40$			
3	$\{1,2,3\}$ 40 70	$\{1,2,4\}$ 40 48	$\{1,3,4\}$ 40 72	$\{2,3,4\}$ 40 63
2	$\{1,2\}$ 70 –	$\{1,4\}$ 72 –	$\{2,4\}$ 63 66	
1	$\{2\}$ 70 126	$\{4\}$ 72 118		
0	$\{-\}$ – 178			

The procedure starts with the assignment of traffic to the network before any investment has taken place. From the product of the travel time saved in each arc for unit investment and the flow in that arc, the return on the investment of one unit in the arc can be obtained. These returns are then ranked in decreasing order and the mininum travel time, for that assignment at each level of investment, is calculated by subtracting the returns in order from the minimum travel time for zero investment.

The network is then tested at every level of investment in turn, to see whether the new arc travel times produce reassignment with minimum travel times lower than those already obtained. As soon as such a new assignment is found, new rankings are calculated and the process is repeated. At each stage the mininum travel times to date are calculated for each level of investment. When no further reassignment can take place, the most recent values of the minimum travel times represent the optimum values obtained by the method, but not necessarily the overall optimum.

The traffic in the network may be assigned in a large but finite number of different ways. Consider a given assignment B_n and define the flow in arc k, and the minimum travel time in the network before any investment has taken place, as $f_k(B_n)$ and $t(B_n)$ respectively. Next define the unit return for the investment of one unit in arc k as

$$a_k = t_k(0) - t_k(1).$$

The return for investment of one unit in arc k with assignment B_n may be obtained by multiplying the unit return by the flow in the arc and equals $f_k(B_n)a_k$.

The arcs may now be ranked in descending order of return, so that

$$f_k(B_n)a_k \geqslant f_{k+1}(B_n)a_{k+1}; \qquad k = 1, 2, ..., P-1.$$

Define $t(B_{nm})$ as the minimum travel time for assignment B_n when m units have been invested. This value may be obtained by subtracting from $t(B_n)$ the m highest returns thus:

$$t(B_{nm}) = t(B_n) - \sum_{k=1}^{m} f_k(B_n)a_k,$$

which defines an optimal set of m arcs A_{nm} for assignment B_n.

Now consider an ordered series of assignments $B_1, B_2, ..., B_n$. The minimum travel time associated with the investment of m units is the minimum over all assignments B_n; that is

$$R_{nm} = \underset{B_{nm}}{\text{Min}}\ t(B_{nm}),$$

which defines an optimal set of m arcs A_{nm}^{*} among all n assignments.

We seek T_m, the minimum travel time associated with the investment of m units for any assignment. For any m, if there exists a new assignment B_{n+1} with flows $f_k(B_{n+1})$ such that

$$t(B_{n+1, m}) = \underset{f_k}{\text{Min}} \sum_{f_k} f_k t_k(A_{nm}) < R_{nm},$$

then

$$T_m < R_{nm}$$

and we have not found the minimum. The procedure therefore searches for a new assignment by checking the inequality for increasing values of m, and B_{n+1} is defined by the first m for which

$$t(B_{n+1, m}) < R_{nm}.$$

The ranking and calculations may be repeated for this new assignment and new values of $R_{n+1, m}$ are obtained from

$$R_{n+1, m} = \text{Min}[t(B_{n+1, m}), R_{nm}].$$

The method proceeds by alternately finding new assignments and calculating rankings and travel times until a value of $n = N$ is reached, when no further reassignment takes place for any m. We then have for each value m the minimum travel time produced by the method, namely:

$$R_m = R_{Nm} = \text{Min}[t(B_{Nm}), R_{N-1, m}]$$

associated with an optimal set of arcs A_m^{*}.

By the use of this method, R_m successively approaches T_m, the overall optimum, though there is no guarantee that it will reach it in every case. The above discussion leads to the following procedure:

1. Given the set of arc travel times before any investment has taken place and a matrix of flows, then the assignment B_1 defines flows $f_k(B_1)$ and the minimum travel time $t(B_1)$.   Note that these are equivalent, in the notation of the method of bounded subsets to A_0, to flows $f_{ij}(A_0)$ and to minimum travel time $t(A_0)$.

2. The values from step 1 allow the calculation of returns on each arc, which can be ranked in descending order, and lead to the calculation of

$$R_{1m} = t(B_{1m}) = t(B_1) - \sum_{k=1}^{m} f_k(B_1) a_k,$$

which defines set A_{1m} for every m.

3. Now check whether

$$\operatorname*{Min}_{f_k} \sum_{f_k} f_k t_k(A_{1m}) < R_{1m}$$

for each m in increasing order.   For the first value of m for which re-assignment takes place, then

$$t(B_2) = \operatorname*{Min}_{f_k} \sum_{f_k} f_k t_k(A_{1m})$$

defines the new assignment B_2 and flows $f_k(B_2)$.

4. Calculate the new returns and rank them and then calculate values of

$$t(B_{2m}) = t(B_2) - \sum_{k=1}^{m} f_k(B_2) a_k,$$

which defines set A_{2m} for every m.

5. Now calculate
$$R_{2m} = \operatorname{Min}[t(B_{2m}), R_{1m}],$$

which defines A_{2m}^*, an optimal set of arcs for every m for both assignments 1 and 2.

6. Repeat step 3.

7. Repeat step 4.

8. Repeat step 5

and so on.   The procedure terminates when no new assignments can be found.

Example

The same example as before is used to illustrate the heuristic solution. In this case it does lead to an optimal solution.

The first assignment, before any investment, produces arc flows of 1, 13, 3 and 10. These are multiplied by the unit returns to give a ranking of arcs 4, 2, 1, 3, with returns of 60, 52, 13 and 3. Subtracting these from $t(B_1)$, equal to 178, gives the values of $t(B_{1m})$, which for the first assignment equals R_{1m}. Also $A_{1m}^* = A_{1m}$.

Table 4.

m	0	1	2	3	4
R_m	178	110	66	48	40
A_m^*	{-}	{1}	{2,4}	{1,2,4}	{1,2,3,4}
T_m	178	110	66	48	40

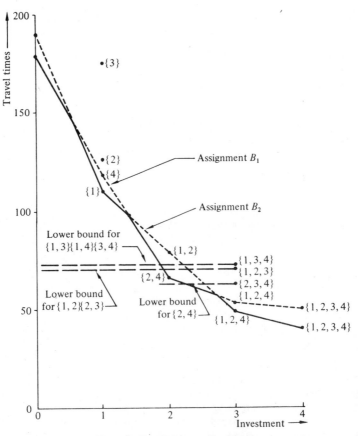

Figure 5. Travel times vs. investments.

Table 5. Assignment B_1.

(a) Calculation of ranking

Arc k	1	2	3	4
Unit return a_k	13	4	1	6
Flow $f_k(B_1)$	1	13	3	10
Return $f_k(B_1)a_k$	13	52	3	60
Ranking	3	2	4	1

$t(B_1) = 178$

(b) Test for reassignment

Investment m	Minimum travel times $t(B_{1m}) = R_{1m}$	$A_{1m} = A_{1m}^*$	Reassignment $\underset{f_k}{\text{Min}} \sum_{f_k} f_k t_k(A_{1m})$	Reassign
0	178	$\{-\}$	178	No
1	118	$\{4\}$	118	No
2	66	$\{2,4\}$	66	No
3	53	$\{1,2,4\}$	48	Yes
4	50	$\{1,2,3,4\}$		

Table 6. Assignment B_2

(a) Calculation of ranking

Arc k	1	2	3	4
Unit return a_k	13	4	1	6
Flow $f_k(B_2)$	6	8	8	5
Return $f_k(B_2)a_k$	78	32	8	30
Ranking	1	2	4	3

$t(B_2) = 188$

(b) Test for reassignment

Investment m	Travel times $t(B_{2m})$	A_{2m}	Minimum travel times R_{1m}	R_{2m}	A_{2m}^*	Reassignment $\underset{f_k}{\text{Min}} \sum_{f_k} f_k t_k(A_{2m})$	Reassign
0	188	$\{-\}$	178	178	$\{-\}$	188	No
1	110	$\{1\}$	118	110	$\{1\}$	110	No
2	78	$\{1,2\}$	66	66	$\{2,4\}$	78	No
3	48	$\{1,2,4\}$	53	48	$\{1,2,4\}$	48	No
4	40	$\{1,2,3,4\}$	50	40	$\{1,2,3,4\}$	40	No

The test for reassignment takes place and it is found that when investment occurs in arcs $\{1, 2, 4\}$ a new assignment is produced with a minimum travel time, 48, lower than that for assignment B_1 which is 53.

For this new assignment the arc flows are 6, 8, 8 and 5 and lead to a
ranking of arcs 1, 2, 4, 3 with returns of 78, 32, 30 and 3. The values
$t(B_{2m})$ are calculated and compared with those of R_{1m} to give new values
R_{2m} with associated A_{2m}^*. In this case there is no reassignment and the
procedure terminates.

The result, as a comparison with T_m from Table 2 is shown in Table 4.

The calculations are given in Tables 5 and 6 and the results are plotted
on Figure 5. The relationships between the minimum travel time for set
$\{2, 4\}$ and the lower bounds for the other pairs of investment are also
shown.

References

Ridley, T.M., 1965, *An Investment Policy to Reduce the Travel Time in a Transportation Network*, Operations Research Centre Report ORC 65-34, University of
California, Berkeley, U.S.A.

Ridley, T.M., 1967, "Investment in a Network to Reduce the Length of the Shortest
Route", *Proceedings of the Third International Symposium on the Theory of
Traffic Flow, June 1965* (Elsevier, New York) pp.235-236.

Ridley, T.M., 1968, "An Investment Policy to Reduce the Travel Time in a Transportation Network", *Transportation Research* **2**, 409-424.

The Integration of Accounting and Location Theory Frameworks in Urban Modelling

A.G.WILSON
Centre for Environmental Studies

THE USE OF AN ACCOUNTING FRAMEWORK IN URBAN MODELLING

To build a set of accounts as a basis for an urban model is to describe systematically stocks and flows of all the quantities of interest. These quantities can be summed in various ways, and some of the sums obtained may themselves play an important role in models. The value of having a set of accounts to underpin a model is that important interactions between variables are not easily missed. For example, it is common to build a model of a single urban activity; it is then difficult to represent in such a model the competition for land between all such activities. With an accounting framework, this interaction is immediately apparent and solutions to the problem of representing the interaction and competition suggest themselves within the framework. The objective of this paper is to illustrate with a simplified account-based model of a city or a region, just how fruitful this approach can be when linked with other approaches to urban modelling.

Accounts are usually set up in money units, and this practice will be followed here, although it is not essential, and other measures, such as employment, could be used. At the outset, two main types of aggregation problem can be distinguished: spatial and sectoral. In the urban and regional accounting literature, the spatial system is usually rather coarsely zoned; in this paper, it will be assumed that a fine zoned system is adopted—at least as fine as any which would be used in a location model. The basic sector classification should also be as fine as possible. Artle (1959), in his work on Stockholm, characterised the urban economy with over sixty sectors for example. In this paper, where the model is simple and illustrative, only five sectors will be used. There will be a short discussion at the end of the paper on how the assumptions could be generalised.

Earlier work on accounting has been based mainly in economic analysis at the national and regional levels, and is well illustrated in two books edited by Hirsch (1962 and 1964) and in a book by Stone (1965). When sets of accounts are built, simple transformations can be made on them (such as dividing by row or column totals) and simple hypotheses about the accounts then enable models to be developed. The development of input–output models has proceeded in this way and has been very fruit-ful.

In the next section, an illustrative urban economy built on an account-ing framework will be set up and discussed; in the third section this will be related to some urban location models; in the fourth section the resulting model will be related to the analysis of urban development; and in the final fifth section, some possible future directions of this kind of work will be studied.

AN ILLUSTRATIVE URBAN ECONOMY

We shall illustrate with a rudimentary, but hopefully not entirely trivial, example how an accounts framework can be used to describe an urban system, and can be used to underpin urban models. (The term "urban" is used in the usual way as a shorthand for "urban and regional"). It will then be possible to show how submodels of different sectors interact, and to build a model which exhibits and explains some interesting real world characteristics.

It will be assumed, as mentioned earlier, that a fine zoning system has been adopted, and subscripts i and j will be used to label zones. There will be five sectors: population (or labour), consumer goods, retail, trans-port, and capital. A finer sector classification is obviously desirable, but even this example will exhibit the following phenomenon: people reside and work and consume goods bought through the retail sector. The only primary commodity will be land. Consumer goods are produced in firms using labour, capital, and land. Capital goods are produced similarly, and the existence of a capital goods sector enables us to exhibit a growing economy, and its associated problems (such as the competition for land). The retail sector simply sells consumer goods, and the transport sector simply maintains and charges for all necessary linkages. Broadly speaking, a finer sector breakdown would simply involve disaggregation within the five sectors which have been defined, though in such a case the retail and transport sectors should be renamed service and communications sectors respectively.

How would this kind of economy work? Firstly, assume a very simple family structure: that all people work and have the same skills. Then it will be assumed that we know the technical production functions for con-sumer goods and capital goods, as functions of labour, capital, and land. All transport costs are assumed to be known (as unit rates for people, c_{ij}^p, consumer (retail) goods, c_{ij}^{rg}, and for capital goods, c_{ij}^{cg}). A capital stock exists and does not depreciate; that is, assume the cost of depreciation is somehow included in the cost of capital, and also assume that capital is transferable between sectors. We shall assume an annual growth of population (additions to the labour force, needing a residence), and of capital, this being determined by the propensity to save. Alternative growth models are possible but this will suffice for illustrative purposes, and for studying the character of the spatial consequences of economic growth.

It is assumed that all capital and land is owned in the population sector, and that the users of capital pay r per cent per annum, and the users of land pay l_j per unit in zone j.

The above considerations, and more detailed mechanisms, are implicit in the following list of the principal variables, and their place in a set of accounts:

(i)   *Variables associated with population receipts:*

T_{ij}^k = number of people resident in i working in sector k in j.
ΔT_{ij}^k = increment in year under consideration.
w_j = wage rate in j.
U_{ij}^k = rent paid to residents of i by sector k land users in j.
a_{ij} = proportion of j zone land owned by residents of i.
l_j = unit price of land in j.
L_j^k = amount of land used by sector k in j.
r = rate of interest on capital.
K_{ij}^k = amount of capital in sector k in j owned by residents of i.
ΔK_{ij}^k = increment in year under consideration.

(ii)   *Variables associated with receipts in the consumer goods sector:*

q_{ij} = quantity of consumer goods made in i and bought by retailers in j for resale.
p_i = price per unit for these goods in i.

(iii)   *Variables associated with receipts in the retail sector:*

r_{ij} = quantity of consumer goods purchased by residents of i in retail centres in j.
P_j = the retail price per unit of such goods in j.

(iv)   *Variables associated with receipts in the transport sector:*

c_{ij}^p = "cost" of a person trip from i to j.
c_{ij}^{rg} = "cost" of sending a unit of consumer (retail) good from i to j.
c_{ij}^{cg} = "cost" of sending a unit of capital good from i to j.
ρ_{ij} = number of trips made by a person from i to j per unit purchase of consumer goods.
$\Delta \hat{K}_{ij}^k$ = capital goods manufactured in i and sent for use in sector k in j.

(v)   *Variables associated with receipts in the capital goods sector:*

S_{ij} = savings by residents of i paid into the capital goods sector in j.
π_i = selling price of capital goods manufactured in i.

These descriptions of variables associated with receipts facilitate the construction of the set of accounts which describe this simple urban system. In the accounts, receipts will be recorded in rows, and payments in columns. The structure of the accounting framework is shown in Table 1.

Table 1.

		↓ Payments		
		Zone 1 (1) (2) (3) (4) (5)	Zone 2 (1) (2) (3) (4) (5)	. . . .
Zone 1 → Receipts	(1) (2) (3) (4) (5)	. . . .	 X	
Zone 2	(1) (2) (3) (4) (5)			

There is a row for each of the five sectors, for each zone in which receipts to that sector in that zone are recorded, and five columns for each zone in which payments are recorded. As an example, the element marked as X will be the receipts of the consumer goods sector (2) in zone 1 from the the retail sector (3) in zone 2. It will represent what these retailers of zone 2 pay for goods (to resell) made in zone 1.

The structure of the accounts, using the variables defined in the previous paragraph, can be shown more finely if we exhibit the detail for a particular pair of zones, say the ith and the jth zones. This is done in Table 2. The rows of accounts, using the variables in the different sections above, are constructed using the variables listed earlier; the receipts of the various sectors in i are as follows:

(i) the population sector:
  (a) wages: $(T_{ij}^k + \Delta T_{ij}^k)w_j$ from sector k in j.
  (b) land rent: U_{ij}^k from sector k in j.
  (c) capital interest: $r(K_{ij}^k + \Delta K_{ij}^k)$ from sector k in j.

(ii) the consumer goods sector: $q_{ij}p_i$ from retailers in j.

(iii) the retail sector: $r_{ji}P_i$ from the public, resident in j.

(iv) the transport sector:

  (a) $(T_{ji}^* + \Delta T_{ji}^*)c_{ji}^p$ from the population sector of j.[1] (Transport receipts thus being deemed to be received at the destination end of person trips; all c_{ij}'s include the costs of the return journey.)

  (b) $c_{ij}^{rg}q_{ij}$ from retailers in j paying to have consumer goods carried from manufacturers in i. (Note the convention here, that retailers pay for the carriage of the consumer goods.)

  (c) $\Delta \hat{K}_{ij}^k c_{ij}^{cg}$ from sector k in j for the carriage of capital goods manufactured in i. (The convention here is that users of capital goods pay their transport charges.)

(v) the capital sector:

  (a) S_{ji}, the part of the savings of the residents of j channelled into capital goods manufacturing in i.

  (b) $\pi_i \Delta \hat{K}_{ij}^k$ from sector k in j as the purchase price of capital goods made in i.

These can all be represented on the zone i–zone j part of Table 1, and this is done in Table 2.

Table 2.

		(1)	(2)	(3)	(4)	(5)
				Payments ↓ Zone j		
	(1)	$(T_{ij}^1+\Delta T_{ij}^1)w_j$ $+U_{ij}^1$ $+r(K_{ij}^k+\Delta K_{ij}^k)$	$(T_{ij}^2+\Delta T_{ij}^2)w_j$ $+U_{ij}^2$ $+r(K_{ij}^2+\Delta K_{ij}^2)$	$(T_{ij}^3+\Delta T_{ij}^3)w_j$ $+U_{ij}^3$ $+r(K_{ij}^3+\Delta K_{ij}^3)$	$(T_{ij}^4+\Delta T_{ij}^4)w_j$ $+U_{ij}^4$ $+r(K_{ij}^4+\Delta K_{ij}^4)$	$(T_{ij}^5+\Delta T_{ij}^5)w_j$ $+U_{ij}^5$ $+r(K_{ij}^5+\Delta K_{ij}^5)$
	(2)			$q_{ij}p_i$		
Receipts → Zone i	(3)	$r_{ji}P_i$				
	(4)	$(T_{ji}^*+\Delta T_{ji}^*)c_{ji}^p$ $+r_{ji}\rho_{ji}c_{ji}^p$ $+\Delta \hat{K}_{ij}^1 c_{ij}^{cg}$	$\Delta \hat{K}_{ij}^2 c_{ij}^{cg}$	$q_{ji}c_{ji}^{rg}$ $\Delta \hat{K}_{ij}^3 c_{ij}^{cg}$	$\Delta \hat{K}_{ij}^4 c_{ij}^{cg}$	$\Delta \hat{K}_{ij}^5 c_{ij}^{cg}$
	(5)	$S_{ji}+\pi_i\Delta \hat{K}_{ij}^1$	$\pi_i\Delta \hat{K}_{ij}^2$	$\pi_i\Delta \hat{K}_{ij}^3$	$\pi_i\Delta \hat{K}_{ij}^4$	$\pi_i\Delta \hat{K}_{ij}^5$

Note. In row 4, $T_{ij}^* = \sum_k T_{ij}^k$; the asterisk is used to denote summation over an index.

[1] An asterisk is used to denote summation over an index throughout the paper.

Of the variables introduced, T_{ij}^k and ΔT_{ij}^k are the person flows, which become income flows when multiplied by w_j; various aggregates are of
interest: for example, T_{i*}^* and T_{*j}^* give the distribution of resident population and of employment respectively. (The accounting framework facilitates the study of such aggregates, about which it may be possible to
build useful models, while continually relating them to the more basic
variables.) U_{ij}^k, rK_{ij}^k, $r\Delta K_{ij}^k$, and S_{ij} are money flows. q_{ij}, r_{ij}, and $\Delta \hat{K}_{ij}^k$ are
flows of goods. l_j, w_j, r, p_j, P_j, and π_i are prices, and we shall study the
processes which determine these later. Note that it is implicitly assumed
that the market operates in a particular way, so that wage rates and land
prices in zones are independent of sector. l_j, the unit price of land, has
not been explicitly represented in the accounts, but note that U_{ij}^k can be
represented as $a_{ij}l_jL_j^k$ using variables defined above. It will be the task
of location models to estimate the various flow variables above, in terms
of aggregates whose behaviour we assume we know. The location models
will be introduced in the next section, and as a preliminary, we can study
some of the aggregates. Firstly, the technical production functions for
consumer and capital goods respectively can be written as:

$$q_{i*} = q_{i*}(K_{*i}^2, T_{*i}^2, L_i^2),\tag{1}$$

$$\Delta\hat{K}_{i*}^* = \Delta\hat{K}_{i*}^*(K_{*i}^5, T_{*i}^5, L_i^5).\tag{2}$$

For the year being studied, K and T should be replaced by $K+\Delta K$,
$T+\Delta T$ in Equations (1) and (2). The effect of the shapes of these functions on urban development will be studied later.

Define R_i^k to be the total receipts of sector k in zone i (that is, a row
sum) and P_i^k to be the total payments of sector k in i (that is, a column
sum). Then, if N is the total number of zones, since we have 5 sectors,
we have $5N$ equations of the form

$$R_i^k = P_i^k\tag{3}$$

to ensure that receipts equal payments. The interpretation of each of
these equations is obvious from an examination of Tables 1 and 2. There
are also other equations relating various aggregates of flow variables, such
as

$$q_{*i} = r_{*i},\tag{4}$$

but these will be discussed in the next section on the location models
themselves. It may be possible to make progress by counting equations
and unknowns, but in this paper, we shall study each variable in turn and
make hypotheses about its determination.

The essence of the economic analysis of this model would be an investigation of how prices are determined in the model. However, this discussion
will be postponed until later when mechanisms of urban development are
explored. It will be assumed for the present that a set of prices l_j, w_j, p_j,
P_j, π_j, and r, is given and we shall investigate some possible location models.

Some possible location models

The main purpose of this section will be to estimate all the flow variables. The traditional "location" variables, the distribution of population and economic activities will then be aggregates of these. The use of the accounting framework in effect insists that location variables should be modelled through flow variables and this forces a better explanation of spatial interaction than would be possible if location variables were estimated directly. Various methods can be used for constructing models of the flow variables. The one which will be used in this paper is the maximum entropy method discussed and outlined in earlier papers by the author (Wilson, 1967a, 1967b, 1968a), though a final paragraph of this section will be devoted to a discussion of alternative methods. The method is briefly outlined in an Appendix. Models for the three main groups of flow variables—money, people, and goods—will be discussed.

If we assume, as has been done implicitly in the accounts, that money flows in a costless way, we can make very simple assumptions about K_{ij}^k, ΔK_{ij}^k, U_{ij}^k, and S_{ij}. We need to be more explicit than hitherto about the working of the capital market. The capital goods sector channels savings to users of capital. The users pay interest on this new capital and the price, π_i, paid for capital goods covers only the costs of the capital goods sector in converting savings into goods and passing them on. Further, since the rate of interest in each sector is the known constant r, investors will not care which sector they invest in, and so we can aggregate over k. These assumptions imply that

$$S_{ij} = \Delta K_{ij}^*, \tag{5}$$

and so further

$$S_{i*} = \Delta K_{i*}^*, \tag{6}$$

$$S_{*j} = \Delta K_{*j}^*. \tag{7}$$

We can then assume that

$$S_{i*} = \gamma R_i^1, \tag{8}$$

where γ is the propensity to save. In Equation (5), savings are assumed to flow direct to users of capital. In Table 2, they are shown as flowing to the capital goods sector. This can be reconciled by the additional assumption that manufacturers of capital goods issue bonds to savers, and they pass on the debt to the *users* of capital, who pay the interest as shown in the accounts. We shall assume that ΔK_{*j}^* is determined by employers in zone j, and we shall discuss how later. Then the zero flow-cost gravity model which maximises entropy subject to known values of S_{i*}, from Equation (8), and S_{*j} (which is K_{*j}^*, and is assumed known) would be

$$S_{ij} = \Delta K_{ij}^* = \frac{S_{i*}\Delta K_{*j}^*}{S_{**}}, \tag{9}$$

where S_{**} is known because S_{i*} is known from Equation (8). K_{ij}^* can be estimated similarly as

$$K_{ij}^* = \frac{K_{i*}^* K_{*j}^*}{K_{**}^*}, \tag{10}$$

where K_{i*} and K_{*j} are known stocks. Similarly, land owners will be indifferent to the use to which land is put, as rents are equal in different uses, and so the best estimate of U_{ij}^* is

$$U_{ij}^* = \frac{U_{i*}^* U_{*j}^*}{U_{**}^*}, \tag{11}$$

where the terms on the right-hand side are known stocks. Since

$$U_{ij}^k = a_{ij} l_j L_j^k \tag{12}$$

this expression can be used to estimate a_{ij}, by summing over k and substituting in Equation (11). Equation (12) can then be used to disaggregate U_{ij}^* into U_{ij}^k. ΔK_{ij}^* in Equation (9) and K_{ij}^* in Equation (10) can be disaggregated sectorally by taking ΔK_{ij}^k and K_{ij}^k as follows:

$$\Delta K_{ij}^k = \frac{\Delta K_{*j}^k}{\Delta K_{*j}^*}\,\Delta K_{ij}^* \tag{13}$$

and

$$K_{ij}^k = \frac{K_{*j}^k}{K_{*j}^*}\,K_{ij}^* \tag{14}$$

where all the terms on the right-hand side are known because employers in sector k in j will have determined ΔK_{*j}^k and K_{*j}^k will be known from the past history of such decisions.

Suppose that the city being modelled has a strong planning system, and that ΔT_{i*}^*, the incremental distribution of population and ΔT_{*j}^k, the incremental distribution of employment by sector, are determined by the planning authority. This supposition means, in effect, that the total distribution can be fixed by the planning authority, as the stocks will be known. The assumption is not really as restrictive as it sounds: the resulting model can be used to explore alternative sets of distributions, or the restriction can be dropped altogether. Write $\hat{T}_{ij}^k = T_{ij}^k + \Delta T_{ij}^k$, when the above assumptions can be represented as follows:

$$\sum_{jk} \hat{T}_{ij}^k = \hat{T}_{i*}^* \quad (15) \qquad\qquad \sum_{i} \hat{T}_{ij}^k = \hat{T}_{*j}^k \quad (16)$$

$$\sum_{ijk} \hat{T}_{ij}^k w_j = W \quad (17) \qquad\qquad \sum_{ijk} \hat{T}_{ij}^k c_{ij}^p = C^{(1)}. \quad (18)$$

The last two equations represent the facts, that the population has a certain total income, and a total expenditure on transport. The corresponding maximum entropy model is

$$\hat{T}_{ij}^k = \lambda_i^{(1)}\lambda_j^{(2)k}\,\hat{T}_{i*}^*\hat{T}_{*j}^k \exp(\sigma_1 w_j - \mu_1 c_{ij}^p) \tag{19}$$

where

$$\lambda_i^{(1)} = 1\bigg/\sum_{jk}\lambda_j^{(2)k}\hat{T}_{*j}^k \exp(\sigma_1 w_j - \mu_1 c_{ij}^p) \tag{20}$$

$$\lambda_j^{(2)k} = 1\bigg/\sum_{i}\lambda_i^{(1)}T_{i*}^*\exp(\sigma_1 w_j - \mu_1 c_{ij}^p) \tag{21}$$

Suppose the restrictive assumptions, that $\hat{T}_{i*}^*$ and $\hat{T}_{i*}^k$ are fixed by the planning authority, are dropped. Then the constraints of Equations (15) and (16) disappear, and the model becomes:

$$\frac{\hat{T}_{ij}^*}{\hat{T}_{**}^*} = \frac{\exp(\sigma_1 w_j - \mu_1 c_{ij}^p)}{\displaystyle\sum_{ij}\exp(\sigma_1 w_j - \mu_1 c_{ij}^p)} \quad . \tag{22}$$

In practice, this tends to be rather unstable, as it does not take account of the inertia of the existing workforce, who may not relocate as quickly as 'equilibrium' forces appear to demand. It may be better to locate only the incremental population, which would give:

$$\frac{\Delta T_{ij}^*}{\Delta T_{**}^*} = \frac{\exp(\sigma_1 w_j - \mu_1 c_{ij}^p)}{\displaystyle\sum_{ij}\exp(\sigma_1 w_j - \mu_1 c_{ij}^p)} \quad . \tag{23}$$

and $\hat{T}_{ij}^*$ would then be determined from $\hat{T}_{ij}^* = T_{ij}^* + \Delta T_{ij}^*$. It may be possible to refine such a model even further by defining ΔT_{**}^* to include not only the increment of population but some part of T_{**}^* (which would then itself have to be redefined) as a pool of 'potential movers'. $\hat{T}_{ij}^*$ in Equation (22), or ΔT_{ij}^* in Equation (23), would have to be multiplied by a coefficient e_j^k which would represent the proportion of jobs in j in sector k. In this simple model, e_j^k is assumed to be supplied exogenously. In a better model, the behaviour of firms would be understood, and the knowledge could be represented in an equation similar in form to (16), and another form of maximum entropy model could be written down. Similarly, deeper analysis at the residential end would enable the model to be related to house prices and land prices. The particular models given here are some only of the possible ones (cf. Wilson, 1968b). There is a further comment on this issue below.

One final note on incremental population: people use capital for housing, and so it would seem reasonable to determine ΔK_{*i}^1 by

$$\Delta K_{*i}^1 = b\Delta T_{i*}^*, \tag{24}$$

where b is some coefficient. We shall return to the other ΔK_{*j}^k's, as stated previously, later.

Page proofs: London Papers. Wilson

Let us now study $\Delta\hat{K}_{ij}^k$ as the first of the three goods sectors. The first assumption to make is that the manufacturers of capital goods will be indifferent to which sectors use their products in this model. If we assume for the present that $\Delta\hat{K}_{i*}^*$ and $\Delta\hat{K}_{*j}^k$ are known, then we will obtain, in the usual way from the implied constraint equations together with a transport equation, that

$$\Delta\hat{K}_{ij}^k = \epsilon_i^{(1)}\epsilon_j^{(2)k}\Delta\hat{K}_{i*}^*\Delta K_{*j}^k \exp(-\mu_2 c_{ij}^{cg}),\tag{25}$$

where

$$\epsilon_i^{(1)} = 1/\sum_{jk}\epsilon_j^{(2)}\Delta K_{*j}^k \exp(-\mu_2 c_{ij}^{cg})\tag{26}$$

and

$$\epsilon_j^{(2)k} = 1/\sum_i\epsilon_i^{(1)}\Delta K_{i*}^* \exp(-\mu_2 c_{ij}^{cg}).\tag{27}$$

Note that this flow of goods is proportional to the amount of capital goods manufactured in i, but the amount of capital (money, not goods) used in j.

In an exactly similar way, if we assume for the present that q_{i*} and q_{*j} are known, then the maximum entropy model for the flows of consumer goods between manufacturers and retailers is

$$q_{ij} = \alpha_i^{(1)}\alpha_j^{(2)}q_{i*}q_{*j}\exp(-\mu_3 c_{ij}^{rg}).\tag{28}$$

where

$$\alpha_i^{(1)} = 1/\sum_j\alpha_j^{(2)}q_{*j}\exp(-\mu_3 c_{ij}^{rg}).\tag{29}$$

and

$$\alpha_j^{(2)} = 1/\sum_i\alpha_i^{(1)}q_{i*}\exp(-\mu_3 c_{ij}^{rg}).\tag{30}$$

A similar procedure gives r_{ij}. In this case, however, we know that

$$r_{i*} = fT_{i*}^*,\tag{31}$$

where f is some constant, since in this simple model retail expenditure will be proportional to population, and

$$r_{*j} = q_{*j}\tag{32}$$

as all consumer goods bought by retailers are assumed to be resold. Thus,

$$r_{ij} = \beta_i^{(1)}\beta_j^{(2)}fT_{i*}^*q_{*j}\exp(-\mu_4 c_{ij}^p),\tag{33}$$

where

$$\beta_i^{(1)} = 1/\sum_j\beta_j^{(2)}q_{*j}\exp(-\mu_4 c_{ij}^p).\tag{34}$$

and

$$\beta_j^{(2)} = 1/\sum_i\beta_i^{(1)}fT_{i*}^*\exp(-\mu_4 c_{ij}^p).\tag{35}$$

The next step is to bring together our untidy assumption about what is known on the right-hand sides of these equations and to explore more deeply how they may be determined by the various market processes. The loose ends are the problems of determining q_{i*}, q_{*j}, ΔK_{*j}^k (except for $k = 1$, where Equation (24) gives an appropriate assumption), ΔK_{i*}^*, L_j^k, and possibly ΔT_{*j}^k and ΔT_{i*}^*. q_{i*} and $\Delta \hat{K}_{i*}^*$ are production functions whose functional form is given by Equations (1) and (2). q_{*j} is really the output function of the retail sector, but in gravity models of the forms shown in Equations (28) and (33) it will usually be some measure of size of a retail centre, used as an index for attractiveness. ΔK_{*j}^k, L_j^k, and possibly ΔT_{*j}^k are all variables whose value has to be determined by the decision-making employers in j, and the values found will then fix the amount of production. ΔT_{i*}^* is a similar variable for the incremental population: where to live? It has been pointed out that ΔT_{*j}^k and ΔT_{i*}^* may be determined by a local planning authority *Thus the process could be made explicit as a function of the goals of these different decision makers.* This amount of clarification will suffice for the present, though we shall return to these behavioural modelling problems later.

It should be noted that the urban model presented in this paper represents a different, and probably better, method of handling the land use accounting problem in activity location models than that implicit in an earlier paper by the author (Wilson, 1967b).

The following section will now analyse the urban development process using the models and machinery which have been introduced, and will explore more deeply the determination of prices. This will give an indication of how much explanation could be achieved by such a model. However, as a preliminary, we can briefly study an alternative method of constructing location models which may itself help in the determination of prices. It has already been stated, that we need a more explicit representation of goals before we can build models to predict certain aggregate quantities. A similar argument could be used even for the flow variables; for example, that we should represent our knowledge of goals in some objective function and use a programming method to find the set of flows which maximise or minimise this function. Such a procedure would be similar to that used by Stevens (1961). The advantage of this type of method is that the dual of the linear program (if it is linear) can be used to estimate what Stevens calls 'location rent', and this will be closely related to the j-variation in our prices l_j, w_j, p_j, P_j, and π_j. However, it is doubtful whether the time is ripe for the development of such location models, as compared to the gravity type of maximum entropy model of this paper. The main-reason for this statement is that our knowledge probably does not sustain the development of either objective functions or constraints for sufficiently finely categorised population groups to give good answers. The gravity type of model gives much

more robust estimates of flow variables, as the underlying hypotheses
are weaker: we get the best unbiased estimate *subject to what we know,
and no more* (cf. Wilson, 1968a). This particular argument is, in any
case, peripheral to this paper, where the main intention is to *illustrate* the
use of accounting principles in conjunction with location models, rather
than to proselytise.

THE ANALYSIS OF URBAN DEVELOPMENT

A remark should be made at the outset to emphasise the reservations
expressed above, that although the spatially aggregated urban economy
will grow (given any reasonable assumption about the production functions) this particular model, at the aggregate level, is a very traditional
one with a multiplier relying on the propensity to save and the rate of
growth of the labour force, and could be replaced by alternative underlying models without destroying the spirit of the approach. The main
task of this section is to examine the kind of behaviour which will result
from the type of urban model that has been outlined in this paper. This
analysis will throw more light on the potentialities of such models and on
the mechanisms, such as the determination of prices, which have not been
fully discussed. The behavioural characteristics of each sector will be
examined in turn, followed by their interactions (although some study of
interaction will be needed before this), and finally how certain urban
development patterns can occur.

The location behaviour of the population is characterised by Equation (19) [with Equations (22) or (23) as alternatives] and partly by
Equation (24) in relation to housing (capital) provision. Within the
accounting framework, and this will be true for each sector, we should
expect behaviour to be such as to try to increase receipts (or income) and
to decrease payments (or expenditure). Thus, by studying the accounts
and the above equations (*which are actually almost entirely implied by
the accounts—the main point of the paper*) we can study likely behaviour.
The principal receipts are wages. We can discount the importance of
capital and land owners in this behavioural analysis; if behaviour is to
maximise wages, it will enable more saving to take place but will not have
any other special characteristics. The main locational trade-offs are between wage rates on the one hand, and the cost of transport to work and
of housing on the other. The 'difference' will be maximised, probably
not in a simple way but through some utility function, which will also
measure the benefits of purchasing consumer goods. Thus, as one would
expect, there will be a higher demand to live near zones with high wage
rates and this (as well as competing land uses) will tend to force up land
prices in and near such zones. (Note that in this model, people pay for
land and housing superstructure separately, in rows 1 and 5 respectively.)

The behaviour of manufacturers of goods can be considered together. Let us assume that they know their production functions, given by Equations (1) and (2). Also, assume that the manufacturers of consumer goods have good estimates of what people will buy, through good contacts with the retail sector. Then, these manufacturers will estimate their capital goods requirements, and in this model, the interest rate r will adjust itself to give correct aggregate results. Thus, $\Delta \hat{K}^2_{*j}$ will be estimated. It is easy to envisage that these estimates will 'lead' the economy, and the other $\Delta \hat{K}^k_{ij}$'s can be estimated on the basis of 'need'. The manufacturers' behaviour will probably determine the main components of w_j and p_j. The locational behaviour (and the main locational components of w_j and p_j) will be determined by the various transport costs and the mix of inputs (this being determined partly by decisions and partly by the production functions). It is easy to see that clustering is likely to occur: manufacturers of consumer and capital goods being close together to minimise inter-industry transport costs. It will be possible for employers in larger (more dense) clusters to offer higher wage rates w_j because of the external economies of such a location; they may wish to do this to attract more skilled labour, for obvious reasons. Finally, land prices will be forced up in more dense areas, in the clusters, because of the competition for land.

The retail and transport sectors can be considered, in this simple model, very much as service sectors. Retail outlets will tend to be in the clusters, both to reduce the costs of obtaining goods from the manufacturers and to get access to the biggest propulation markets. In this model, the price difference, $P_j - p_j$ will be determined principally by the costs of supplying the retail service. All the transport costs will be determined on a similar basis.

We can now consider how quite complex urban development patterns can occur, even with this simple illustrative model. It is easy to see, for example, how clustering can occur. Consider a small settlement and locate a firm which manufactures consumer goods. Suppose it is the major employer. Then the wage rate w_j and the wholesale price of the goods p_j will be determined by this employer (in relation to regional and national economies). It follows that people will want to live in nearby zones to reduce costs of travel to work. The service and capital goods centres will also want to locate near the original firm, and this location becomes the *centre* of a free standing town. As we have seen, in the early stages of urban development, employment will be concentrated in a small number of firms in the centre, and the population spread around the centre, with the 'outer' population living at lower densities than the 'inner' because land would be cheaper and more could be consumed. The nature of the transport costs in the accounting system and the resulting gravity models implies that each sector tries to maximise its accessibility to other activities. The accessibility of zone i to activity X, with amount X_j in zone j would be

$$A_i = \sum_j X_j \exp(-\mu c_{ij}) \qquad (36)$$

where c_{ij} is the appropriate transport cost and μ a suitable constant. The importance of such terms can be seen by looking at any of the gravity model equations, and is in any case well known in the literature. It would then seem to be a good assumption to make land prices, l_j, a function, say a linear sum, of various accessibilities. This provides a mechanism for resolving competition for land from different sectors and for the determination of a common price. It is easy to see, in the small centre-dominated free standing town, whose development was discussed above, that accessibilities, and therefore land prices, decrease continually from the centre.

It is worth asking the question: why, in any urban development, does everything not collapse into the centre? The answer lies in the nature of the production functions and the price of land. As the central density becomes higher, a user has to pay a very high amount for land, or use a smaller amount and pay extra capital for higher buildings. The behaviour of the residential population can be analysed in a similar way. Thus, it begins to pay people to move out of the centre and to trade off higher transport costs against lower land costs and probably lower wage costs. The worker can accept lower wages because his journey to work is shorter and cheaper.

We have begun to see, in the previous paragraph, how more complex urban development patterns can arise. Let us be more explicit and see what happens when the settlement described above grows. Initially, employment will grow in the central area and population, at continually decreasing densities, away from the centre. Overall densities would increase due to infilling and redevelopment. Land prices and rents would rise continually because accessibilities would be increasing continually, and these increases would reflect the externalities which should benefit the whole community. It is clear, however, that the time will come when it will pay a firm, say a new one, to locate out of the central area for the reasons explained earlier. There will probably be some optimum distance from the centre, which a good manager will be able to calculate. However, this location could be anywhere on a ring around the centre, but once the firm has moved, all the accessibility patterns will change and the symmetry is removed. Thus, dynamically, our models need to have Markovian properties: locations will depend on decisions made in the previous time period, though not earlier ones, except through accessibility indices. The interaction of pressures, for decentralisation of firms, increasing population and rising real incomes would mean that quite complicated urban development patterns would occur even with this simple model. These could be heavily influenced by the way transport patterns develop, perhaps as planned by a government agency: partly to meet demand and partly to influence future land use by changing accessibility patterns. Even more complicated interactions could occur when previously distinct urban settlements grow into each other.

Conclusions and the need for further developments

It is hoped that this simple illustrative model contains most of the elements of a real urban system, and that it shows just how fruitful the 'accounts' approach can be in the early stages of setting up a model. In this example, it has been demonstrated what a maximum entropy gravity model world might look like. It is also clear that the use of an accounts framework greatly facilitates aggregation or disaggregation of models. The directions of refinement of such models are in many cases obvious: a finer sector classification is needed, together with a deeper study of the interactions between sectors using more disaggregated accounts; a more realistic representation of the various prices involved is needed together with a systematic study of the processes which determine them; we also need a more explicitly dynamic model. Some steps in the last named direction may be possible by linking the ideas of this paper with the use of some concepts in social physics described in another paper by the author (Wilson, 1968a).

References

Artle, R., 1959, *Studies in the Structure of the Stockholm Economy*, The Business Research Institute of the Stockholm School of Economics.

Hirsch, W., 1962, *Elements of Regional Accounts*, Ed. Hirsch, W. (The Johns Hopkins Press, Baltimore).

Hirsch, W., 1964, *Regional Accounts for Policy Decisions*, Ed. Hirsch, W. (The Johns Hopkins Press, Baltimore).

Stevens, B.H., 1961, "Linear Programming and Location Rent", *Journal of Regional Science*, 3, 15–26.

Stone, R., 1965, *Mathematics in the Social Sciences and Other Essays* (Chapman and Hall, London).

Wilson, A.G., 1967a, "A Statistical Theory of Spatial Distribution Models", *Transportation Research*, 1, 253.

Wilson, A.G., 1967b, *Towards Comprehensive Planning Models*, Presented to the Annual Meeting of the British Section of the Regional Science Association, London, 1967.

Wilson, A.G., 1968a, *Notes on Some Concepts in Social Physics*, Centre for Environmental Studies Working Paper No.4, to be Presented to the Annual Conference of the Regional Science Association, Budapest, 1968.

Wilson, A.G., 1968b, "*Some Possible Developments of Elementary Residential Location Models*" (Centre for Environmental Studies, London), Working Note No.31.

APPENDIX

THE RULES FOR DERIVING ENTROPY MAXIMISING MODELS

This method is described in detail in earlier papers by the author (see, for example, Wilson, 1968a) and so only the barest outline will be given here. The method applies in situations where a 'state' of a system is characterised by variables giving the number of entities in individual states. Thus, as shown earlier, $\hat{T}_{ij}^k$ gives the number of individuals who live in zone i and work in sector k in zone j. The array $\hat{T}_{ij}^k$ specifies the state of the system. The entropy of the system is defined by

$$S = -\sum_{ijk} \hat{T}_{ij}^k \log \hat{T}_{ij}^k$$

in this example. It has been shown in the earlier papers, that the best unbiased estimate of $\hat{T}_{ij}^k$ is that which maximises the entropy S subject to any constraints which represent our knowledge of the situation and which reduce the randomness of possible occurrences. In this example, the constraints are Equations (15)–(18). It can easily be shown that if S is maximised subject to these constraints, then the $\hat{T}_{ij}^k$ given in Equation (19) is the result. $\lambda_i^{(1)}$ and $\lambda_j^{(2)k}$ are closely related to the Lagrangian multipliers associated with Equations (15) and (16) respectively, and σ_1 and μ_1 are the Lagrangian multipliers associated with Equations (17) and (18) respectively.

Alternate Urban Population Density Models: An Analytical Comparison of Their Validity Range

E.CASETTI
Ohio State University

Introduction

A variety of mathematical formulations of the relationship between urban population densities and distance from city centres have been proposed and tested, and an extensive though somewhat abstract discussion of these formulations has been given by Gurevich and Saushkin (1966). The best known of these uses negative exponential functions of first degree (Equation 1):

$$D(s) = \exp(a - bs), \tag{1}$$

where s and $D(s)$ indicate respectively a distance of s from a city centre, and the population density at distance s.

These functions were first applied to data for Frankfurt by Bleicher (1892). Recently they were reproposed and used extensively by Clark (1951), (1958), followed subsequently by many others. A comprehensive review of the application of first degree negative exponential functions can be found in Berry, Simmons, and Tennant (1963).

Negative exponential functions of second degree (Equation 2) have been suggested by Tanner (1961) and by Sherrat (1960), who successfully tested them on data for Sydney:

$$D(s) = \exp(a - cs^2). \tag{2}$$

Square root negative exponential functions (Equation 3) were found by Ajo (1965) to give good fits to density data for the rural periphery of London

$$D(s) = \exp(a - m\sqrt{s}). \tag{3}$$

The trends identified by Equations (1), (2), and (3) are characterized by a monotonic decline of population densities away from city centres. However, it is widely believed that in large cities the population density at first increases with distance from the centre and only later declines. Families of curves corresponding to these "density craters" were used by

Reinhardt, Ajo, and Newling.   Reinhardt (1950), tried Laguerre functions of the type identified by Equation (4):

$$D(s) = (1 + vs) \exp(a - bs). \tag{4}$$

Ajo applied Equation (5) to data for the central portion of the city of
London

$$D(s) = s^n \exp(a - bs). \tag{5}$$

Newling (1967), (1968) has fitted quadratic exponential functions (Equation 6) to data for Pittsburgh and Montreal and to most of the series on
which Clark used negative exponentials:

$$D(s) = \exp(a + bs + cs^2). \tag{6}$$

   The number and variety of these formulations poses a problem of
choice that is not solved by relating families of density distance functions to particular theoretical frameworks (Wingo, 1961; Muth, 1961;
Alonso, 1964, and Casetti, 1966).   Alternative theoretical formulations
may point toward different functions, so that ultimately the problem
remains one of determining which function is better suited to given
empirical data.

   This paper suggests procedures for determining which one among
alternative families of functions is more suited to given data.   The
procedures are then applied to testing the hypotheses (a) that functions
allowing for density craters are better suited to data for large cities than
functions involving only a density decline, and (b) that in large cities
different families of functions are better suited to data for different
distance bands surrounding the city centres.

The Procedure

   A direct method for determining which one, out of several classes of
functions, yields the best fit to a set of empirical data can be based
on a comparison of the results obtained by using all the functions in
sequence.   The member of each class of functions is chosen that gives an
optimal fit to the data, and a measure of the fit, such as a correlation
coefficient or a coefficient of determination, is calculated.   The functions are then ranked according to their performance and the one with
the best fit is selected.   Hansen (1961) provides an example of the application of this procedure to the selection of the best regression function
for predicting residential extensions.   However, the method is meaningful
only when the parameters of the functions compared are significantly
different from zero at the same significance level, and it has the short-
coming that it requires the computation of as many regressions as there
are functions.

   A more effective method is applicable whenever several functions can
be subsumed as special cases of one function.   Take for instance Equations (1), (2), and (6).   Equations (1) and (2) are special cases of

Equation (6) from which they may be obtained respectively by setting c or b to zero. Suppose that the parameters of Equation (6) are estimated for given data by a stepwise regression procedure as discussed by Draper and Smith (1966). Select the step which yields the regression with the highest correlation and in which all the coefficients are significantly different from zero on the basis of the t-test at a given significance level. If both the coefficients b and c appear in this regression, then Equation (6) gives a better fit than Equations (1) and (2). If, instead, either b or c does not appear in the regression, respectively Equation (2) or Equation (1) is best suited to the data.

The Analysis

An exploratory analysis was carried out in order to ascertain whether some functions are consistently better suited to certain density distance data. Two hypotheses were investigated. The first corresponds to the widespread belief, that density crater trends are better suited to data for large cities than trends involving a simple density decline. The second hypothesis develops the suggestion put forward by Ajo (1965), that in large cities different functions are better suited to density data for different distance bands surrounding the city centre (see also Newling, 1968).

The data used are population densities for circular rings of increasing distance from the city centres for the following cities and years: Montreal (1941), Montreal (1961), Philadelphia (1900), Philadephia (1950), Los Angeles (1940), Detroit (1940), Houston (1940), London (1960). A table of data with the respective sources is given in Appendix I.

For each city and time period the investigation was carried out (a) on the complete sets of data, (b) on the data that refer to the central portion of the city, and (c) on the data referring to the outskirts and rural fringe. The complete set of data, the data for the central area, and the data for the fringe will be referred to as the A, B, and C data respectively. Definition of the content of the B and C sets for each city and time period can be found in Appendix II. The B and C data for the cities of Detroit and Houston were not employed, because they do not contain enough observations.

For each set of data the following regressions were estimated:

$$D(s) = (1+s)^n \exp(h+as+bs^2+cs^3); \tag{7}$$

$$D(s) = \exp(h+as); \tag{8}$$

$$D(s) = \exp(h+bs^2); \tag{9}$$

$$D(s) = \exp(h+cs^3); \tag{10}$$

$$D(s) = H(1+s)^n; \tag{11}$$

$$D(s) = \exp(h+m\sqrt{s}). \tag{12}$$

The expression $(1+s)^n$ in Equations (7) and (11) is related to the similar expression $(1+vs)$ appearing in the Reinhardt function, given in Equation (4), and is also related to the term s^n in the Ajo function, given in Equation (5). The expression $(1+vs)$ was avoided because it leads to equations in which the parameters cannot be estimated by linear regression. $(1+s)^n$ was preferred to s^n because it does not tend to infinity or zero when the distance from the city centres s tends to zero. The expression $(1+s)^n$ corresponds to a potential function and actually Equation (13) can be considered as a simple potential model (Stewart and Warntz, 1958; Warntz, 1967). The functions of Equations (8) through (11) plus six three-parameter and four four-parameter families of functions are special cases of Equation (7) obtained by setting appropriate coefficients to zero. Any one of the three- and four-parameter functions, as well as the function corresponding to Equation (7) itself, may correspond to a density crater trend for suitable values of the non-zero coefficients.

A regression using Equation (7) can determine which one of the fifteen families of functions subsumed in that equation is best suited to given data. The actual analysis was carried out using the Ohio State University stepwise regression computer program. Equation (7) was fitted to all the data sets. Those steps were selected which gave regression equations with the highest correlation and with coefficients significantly different from zero on the basis of a t-test at the 5 per cent significance level. The results of this phase of the analysis are shown in Table 1. Later, Equations (8) through (12) were fitted, and Table 2 shows the correlation coefficients measuring their performance. In Table 3 averages of these correlation coefficients are given for the A, B, and C data and for the different functions.

Results

The results in Table 1 support rather weakly the hypothesis, that trends of the density crater type are better suited to density distance data for large cities than trends involving a simple density decline. For most of the data, two-parameter equations were obtained that correspond to a monotonic density decline. Only in four cases on fourteen A and B sets of data (Detroit 1940 A, Philadelphia 1950 B, London 1960 A, and London 1960 B) density crater equations were obtained in which D(s) has a maximum for some positive value of s. Evidently the density crater, although perceptible in most of the A and B data generally, produces only a minor deviation from a trend, the basic feature of which is the decline of urban population densities with distance from the city centres. This deviation is so slight that the regression often does not incorporate it as a major trend feature, not even in the B data that refer to densities in the central areas of cities. Probably more disaggregated data for a smaller central area would yield different results. However, the outcome of this analysis suggests that more often than not density craters are quantitatively of minor importance, while the density distance decline is the main fact to be reckoned with, even when urban population distributions of large cities are studied.

Table 1. Regression Fits of the Function $D(s) = (1+s)^n \exp(h+as+bs^2+cs^3)$

					Correlation coefficient, R
Montreal 1941	A	$\ln(D) =$	$10 \cdot 800 - 2 \cdot 747 \ln(1+s)$		$0 \cdot 953$
			$(17 \cdot 46)$ $(-8 \cdot 90)$		
Montreal 1941	B	$\ln(D) =$	$8 \cdot 570 - 0 \cdot 021 s^3$		$0 \cdot 978$
			$(47 \cdot 55)$ $(-9 \cdot 306)$		
Montreal 1941	C	$\ln(D) =$	$10 \cdot 240 - 2 \cdot 601 \ln(1+s)$		$0 \cdot 959$
		'	$(10 \cdot 99)$ $(-6 \cdot 79)$		
Montreal 1961	A	$\ln(D) =$	$8 \cdot 568 - 0 \cdot 270 s$		$0 \cdot 963$
			$(31 \cdot 77)$ $(-10 \cdot 08)$		
Montreal 1961	B	$\ln(D) =$	$8 \cdot 345 - 0 \cdot 008 s^3$		$0 \cdot 875$
			$(47 \cdot 22)$ $(-3 \cdot 62)$		
Montreal 1961	C	$\ln(D) =$	$12 \cdot 47 - 2 \cdot 993 \ln(1+s)$		$0 \cdot 992$
			$(27 \cdot 67)$ $(-16 \cdot 12)$		
Philadelphia 1900	A	$\ln(D) =$	$13 \cdot 16 - 2 \cdot 695 \ln(1+s)$		$0 \cdot 966$
			$(30 \cdot 58)$ $(-13 \cdot 47)$		
Philadelphia 1900	B	$\ln(D) =$	$12 \cdot 06 - 0 \cdot 705 s$		$0 \cdot 981$
			$(47 \cdot 65)$ $(-11 \cdot 24)$		
Philadelphia 1900	C	$\ln(D) =$	$12 \cdot 09 - 2 \cdot 294 \ln(1+s)$		$0 \cdot 923$
			$(15 \cdot 66)$ $(-7 \cdot 19)$		
Philadelphia 1950	A	$\ln(D) =$	$11 \cdot 57 - 0 \cdot 391 s$	$+ 0 \cdot 0003 s^3$	$0 \cdot 984$
			$(60 \cdot 90)$ $(-12 \cdot 67)$	$(4 \cdot 31)$	
*Philadelphia 1950	B	$\ln(D) =$	$9 \cdot 87 - 3 \cdot 297 s$	$+ 6.392 \ln(1+s)$	
			$(68 \cdot 21)$ $(-10 \cdot 69)$	$(10 \cdot 23)$	
				$+ 0 \cdot 192 s^2$	$0 \cdot 998$
				$(8 \cdot 91)$	
Philadelphia 1950	C	$\ln(D) =$	$14 \cdot 89 - 2 \cdot 901 \ln(1+s)$		$0 \cdot 973$
			$(27 \cdot 33)$ $(-12 \cdot 90)$		
Los Angeles 1940	A	$\ln(D) =$	$9 \cdot 80 - 0 \cdot 184 s$		$0 \cdot 945$
			$(52 \cdot 22)$ $(-14 \cdot 14)$		
Los Angeles 1940	B	$\ln(D) =$	$9 \cdot 57 - 0 \cdot 018 s^2$		$0 \cdot 974$
			$(114 \cdot 3)$ $(-13 \cdot 58)$		
Los Angeles 1940	C	$\ln(D) =$	$14 \cdot 34 - 2 \cdot 705 \ln(1+s)$		$0 \cdot 906$
			$(16 \cdot 94)$ $(-8 \cdot 83)$		
*Detroit 1940	A	$\ln(D) =$	$9 \cdot 603 + 0 \cdot 338 s$	$- 0 \cdot 086 s^2$	
			$(104 \cdot 6)$ $(5 \cdot 92)$	$(-9 \cdot 10)$	
				$+ 0 \cdot 0035 s^3$	$0 \cdot 998$
				$(7 \cdot 85)$	
Houston 1940	A	$\ln(D) =$	$9 \cdot 64 - 0 \cdot 324 s$		$0 \cdot 985$
			$(91 \cdot 07)$ $(14 \cdot 28)$		
*London 1960	A	$\ln(D) =$	$8 \cdot 709 + 2 \cdot 000 \ln(1+s) - 0 \cdot 402 s$		
			$(24 \cdot 17)$ $(5 \cdot 39)$ $(-6 \cdot 36)$		
			$+ 0 \cdot 0064 s^2 - 0 \cdot 00004 s^3$		$0 \cdot 993$
			$(4 \cdot 77)$ $(-3 \cdot 90)$		
*London 1960	B	$\ln(D) =$	$5 \cdot 398 + 9 \cdot 044 \ln(1+s) - 2 \cdot 828 s$		
			$(9 \cdot 60)$ $(7 \cdot 54)$ $(-6 \cdot 57)$		
			$+ 0 \cdot 141 s^2 - 0 \cdot 003 s^3$		$0 \cdot 994$
			$(5 \cdot 47)$ $(-4 \cdot 90)$		
London 1960	C	$\ln(D) =$	$14 \cdot 19 - 1 \cdot 1711 \ln(1+s)$		$0 \cdot 998$
			$(150 \cdot 8)$ $(-63 \cdot 99)$		

The asterisks identify density crater functions.

Table 2. Correlation Coefficients Measuring the Degree of Fit of Two-Parameter
Functions

		Potential Function	Exponential Functions of Degree			
			1/2	1	2	3
Montreal 1941	A	**0·953**	0·950	0·907	0·780	0·682
Montreal 1941	B	0·819	0·846	0·916	0·975	**0·978**
Montreal 1941	C	**0·959**	0·935	0·897	0·807	0·721
Montreal 1961	A	0·917	0·953	**0·962**	0·891	0·814
Montreal 1961	B	0·570	0·607	0·715	0·835	**0·875**
Montreal 1961	C	**0·992**	0·982	0·961	0·899	0·834
Philadelphia 1900	A	**0·966**	0·947	0·881	0·721	0·600
Philadelphia 1900	B	0·931	0·949	**0·980**	0·968	0·922
Philadelphia 1900	C	**0·923**	0·896	0·856	0·764	0·677
Philadelphia 1950	A	0·948	**0·971**	0·961	0·860	0·755
Philadelphia 1950	B	0·876	0·898	**0·943**	0·941	0·893
Philadelphia 1950	C	**0·974**	0·964	0·942	0·872	0·794
Los Angeles 1940	A	0·909	0·941	**0·947**	0·894	0·828
Los Angeles 1940	B	0·876	0·912	0·954	**0·974**	0·960
Los Angeles 1940	C	**0·906**	0·898	0·884	0·843	0·798
Detroit 1940	A	0·860	0·911	0·968	**0·982**	0·947
Houston 1940	A	0·975	0·984	**0·986**	0·935	0·872
London 1960	A	0·916	**0·964**	0·961	0·880	0·795
London 1960	B	0·611	0·689	0·772	0·835	**0·837**
London 1960	C	**0·998**	0·990	0·970	0·907	0·839

Potential function $D(s) = H(1+s)^n$
Exponential functions of ith degree $D(s) = \exp(h - ws^i)$
The highest correlation coefficient for each set of data is set bold

Table 3. Average Correlation Coefficients by Function and by Type of Data

	Potential Function	Exponential Functions of Degree			
		1/2	1	2	3
A data	0·930	0·952	0·946	0·805	0·786
B data	0·780	0·816	0·880	0·921	0·909
C data	0·958	0·944	0·918	0·848	0·777
A, B, and C data	0·890	0·909	0·918	0·878	0·821

The second hypothesis, however, that the families of functions best
suited to density distance data differ for different distance bands, is
strongly supported. Table 1 shows that the functions of best fit for the
C data (peripheral areas) are potential functions, as in Equation (11),
which is consistent with the finding that rural population densities are
proportional to a function of population potentials (Stewart and Warntz,
1958; Warntz, 1967). However, negative exponential functions of first,

second, or third degree, as in Equations (8), (9), and (10), give the best fit for the B data (central areas). These results are consistently confirmed by the measures of fit for different two-parameter functions in Table 2. In this table the highest measures of fit are always given by the potential function for the C data, and by exponential functions of first degree or higher for the B data. Furthermore, in Table 3, which shows average measures of fit for each function and for each type of data, the best results for the C data are given by the potential function with the exponential functions performing the worse the higher their degree; for the B data second degree exponentials are best, with the performance of other exponential functions declining for degrees larger and smaller than the second.

Conclusion

This paper discusses alternative procedures for determining which one of several families of functions is best suited to describe the relationship between population densities and distance from city centres for specific data. The procedures are used for testing the hypothesis that (a) density crater functions are better suited to density distance data for large cities, than functions involving only a density decline, and that (b) in large cities different functions are suited to different distance bands. The results obtained support weakly the first hypothesis and strongly the second one. The investigation has shown that the strikingly dominant feature of urban population distributions is the decline of densities with distance from city centres, and that negative exponential functions of degree from 1 to 3 are better suited to represent the density decline in central urban areas, while potential functions are best suited to outskirts and rural fringes. However, all the functions investigated give excellent fits, so that good results obtained with one particular family of functions is, in itself, not a good enough reason for preference. Perhaps the negative exponential of first degree, that lies somewhere between exponential functions of higher degree, better suited to central areas, and functions of lower degree, suited to peripheral areas, deserves its popularity because it is a compromise solution. Its widespread use has provided a variety of interpretable and roughly comparable measures of formal city structure. On the other hand, the functions corresponding to density craters do have a relevance that reflects the qualitative relevance of the density craters in the morphology of cities. Even though the decline of densities near city centres may have the same magnitude as random variations of density occurring in other areas, we do know that this decline is not random but is related to processes that have been changing the structure of cities. Consequently, the repeated application of some density crater function (the quadratic exponential perhaps) to data for city cores, would possibly perform the same positive role that the applications of the negative exponential has had.

References

Alonso, W., 1964, *Location and Land Use* (Harvard University Press, Cambridge, Mass.).

Ajo, Reino., 1965, "On the Structure of Population Density in London's Field", *Acta Geographica*, **18**, 1–17.

Berry, B.J.L., Simmons, J.W., and Tennant, R.J., 1963, "Urban Population Densities: Structures and Change", *Geographical Review*, **53**, 389–405.

Bleicher, H., 1892, *Statistiche Beschreibung der Stadt Frankfurt am Main und Ihrer Bevölkerung*, Frankfurt am Main.

Blumenfeld, H., 1954, "The Tidal Wave of Metropolitan Expansion", *Journal of the American Institute of Planners*, **20**, 3–14.

Blumenfeld, H., 1959, "Are Land Use Patterns Predictable?", *Journal of the American Institute of Planners*, **25**, 61–66.

Casetti, E., 1967, "Urban Population Density Patterns: An Alternate Explanation", *Canadian Geographer*, **11**, 96–100.

Clark, C., 1951, "Urban Population Densities", *Journal of the Royal Statistical Society*, Ser.A, **114**, 490–496.

Clark, C., 1957–58, "Transport—Maker and Breaker of Cities", *Town Planning Review*, **28**, 237–250.

Clark, C., 1958, "Urban Population Densities", *Bulletin de l'Institute International de Statistique*, **36**, Part 4, 60–68.

Draper, N., and Smith, H., *Applied Regression Analysis* (Wiley, New York).

Gurevich, B.L., and Saushkin, Yu.G., 1966, "The Mathematical Method in Geography", *Soviet Geography: Reviews and Translations*, **7** (4), 3–35.

Hansen, W.B., 1961, "An Approach to the Analysis of Metropolitan Residential Expansion", *Journal of Regional Science*, **3**, 37–56.

Muth, R.F., 1961, "The Spatial Structure of the Housing Market", *Papers and Proceedings of the Regional Science Association*, **7**, 207–220.

Newling, B.E., 1966, "Urban Growth and Spatial Structure: Mathematical Models and Empirical Evidence", *Geographic Review*, **56**, 213–225.

Newling, B.E., 1966, "A Partial Theory of Urban Growth: Mathematical Structure and Planning Implications". Paper presented at the Latin American Regional Conference of the IGU, Mexico City.

Newling, B.E., 1967, "Urban Population: The Mathematics of Structure and Processes". Paper presented at the St.Louis Meeting of the Association of American Geographers.

Newling, B.E., 1968, "The Spatial Variation of Urban Population Densities". Mimeographed paper prepared for the 21st International Geographical Union Congress, New Delhi.

Service d'Urbanism, Ville de Montreal, 1964, "The Wave of Metropolitan Expansion", Technical Bulletin No.1.

Sherratt, G.G., 1960, "A Model for General Urban Growth", *Management Sciences: Models and Techniques. Proceedings of the Sixth International Meeting of the Institute of Management Science.* Eds. Churchman, O.W., and Verhulst, M. (Pergamon Press, New York), **2**, 147–159.

Stewart, J.Q., and Warntz, W., 1958, "Physics of Population Distribution", *Journal of Regional Science*, **1**, 99–123.

Tanner, J.C., 1961, "Factors Affecting the Amount of Travel", *Road Research Technical Paper No.1, Department of Scientific and Industrial Research*, London.

Warntz, W., 1967, "Macroscopic Analysis and Some Patterns of the Geographical Distribution of Population in the United States, 1790-1950", *Quantitative Geography*, Part 1, Eds. Garrison, W.L., and Marble, D.F.,(*Northwestern University Studies in Geography*, No.13, Evanston, Illinois), pp.191-218.

Weiss, H.K., 1961, "The Distribution of Urban Population and an Application to a Servicing Problem", *Operation Research*, 9, 860-876.

Wingo, L.Jr., 1961, *Transportation and Urban Land* (Resources for the Future, Inc. Washington, D.C.).

Winsborough, H.H., 1961, *A Comparative Study of Urban Population Densities*. Unpublished Ph.D. dissertation, Department of Sociology, The University of Chicago.

APPENDIX I

Urban Population Densities Data for Selected Cities

The density measures given in the tables below are average figures referring to concentric rings around the city centres. The distance measures are averages of the distances of the outer and inner boundary of each ring. For the methods and operational definitions used in order to obtain these data, see the sources.

| | Philadelphia *a* | | Montreal *b* | |
| | 1900 | 1950 | 1941 | 1961 |
Distance (miles)		Density (persons per acre)		
0·5	79·50	52·40	47·60	28·60
1·5	84·00	75·10	61·70	51·00
2·5	42·70	52·70	36·20	37·80
3·5	13·60	28·40	26·30	43·40
4·5	5·30	18·10	4·60	15·40
5·5	4·10	14·40	2·00	11·60
6·5	1·65	12·10		
7·5	0·77	5·80	1·20	4·50
8·5	0·93	6·30		
9·5	0·38	1·64		
11·0	0·50	1·61		
11·5			0·20	0·92
13·0	0·54	1·45		
15·0	0·41	0·95		
16·5			0·13	0·51
17·0	0·17	0·65		
21·5	0·22	0·43		
22·0			0·14	0·26

a source: Blumenfeld (1954)
b source: Service d'Urbanisme (1964)

Los Angeles 1940 *c*   Houston 1940 *c*   Detroit 1940 *c*

Distance (miles)	Density (persons per square mile)		
0·5	19216	13941	16793
1·5	13186	10104	22645
2·5	10734	6779	19517
3·5	9562	4007	17694
4·5	8806	3199	17781
5·5	8776	2952	12471
6·5	8498	1545	9913
7·5	6023	1537	6070
8·5	4461		4487
9·5	2157		2681
10·5	1838		2170
11·5	1582		1758
12·5	2678		1309
13·5	1553		1104
14·5	789		
15·5	532		
16·5	362		
17·5	515		
18·5	667		
19·5	449		
20·5	350		
21·5	1122		
22·5	642		
23·5	356		
24·5	113		

London 1950 *d*

Distance (miles)	(persons per square mile)
1·4	14500
2·5	40600
3·9	41000
6·3	32100
8·6	22900
11·2	19300
14·2	14800
17·6	10900
19·1	8000
22·7	6100
26·6	4600
30·9	3800
35·4	3200
40·3	2500
45·5	2000
51·0	1700
56·8	1400
63·0	1200
69·4	1000

c source: Reinhardt (1950)
d source: Ajo (1965)

APPENDIX II

Definition of the B and C Data Sets

The B and C sets include data referring to concentric rings at distances hereafter indicated. Distances (in moles) are denoted by s.

			Number of observations
Philadelphia 1900	B	$s \leqslant 6 \cdot 5$	7
Philadelphia 1900	C	$s \geqslant 4 \cdot 5$	11
Philadelphia 1950	B	$s \leqslant 6 \cdot 5$	7
Philadelphia 1950	C	$s \geqslant 4 \cdot 5$	11
Montreal 1941	B	$s \leqslant 5 \cdot 5$	6
Montreal 1941	C	$s \geqslant 4 \cdot 5$	6
Montreal 1961	B	$s \leqslant 5 \cdot 5$	6
Montreal 1961	C	$s \geqslant 4 \cdot 5$	6
Los Angeles 1940	B	$s \leqslant 11 \cdot 5$	12
Los Angeles 1940	C	$s \geqslant 7 \cdot 5$	19
London 1960	B	$s \leqslant 19 \cdot 1$	9
London 1960	C	$s \geqslant 11 \cdot 2$	14

Some Factors Influencing the Income Distribution of Households within a City Region

M.J.H.MOGRIDGE
Centre for Environmental Studies

Introduction

In this paper, an attempt is made to show how the concept of maximum entropy can be applied to the problems of income distribution and residential and employment location in a large city. The paper is an exploratory discussion of the theory, limitations and usefulness of the concept, drawing on evidence obtained for London as an illustration.

The concept enables measurements of average behaviour over the city as a whole to be converted into probabilistic measurements of individual behaviour, and provides a strong framework to which these measurements can be related. The measurements of average behaviour here are made in economic terms, that is, costs of journeys and of accommodation.

For clarity this demonstration of the usefulness of the concept of maximum entropy is limited to a few types of behaviour. Once its use has been justified for the skeletal framework of the city, then more complex behavioural assumptions can be incorporated into the analysis.

Definition and Requirements of a Homogeneous City

For the purpose of the analyses of city structure which follow certain simplifying assumptions are made. It is to be understood that these assumptions are introduced for the sole purpose of aiding clarity. A more rigorous treatment, in which the full extent of the city's complexity is comprehended, can be gradually built up step by step on the present skeleton.

To this end, then, the following assumptions about the city will be made. Because it has a highly complex development, no one element (such as a single firm) plays a significant part in the structure of the city as a whole. Moreover, the city has a highly complex structure in each of its sub-systems such as population, firms, employment, factories, offices, services, transport networks, etc. It will be realised that these sub-systems form interlocking partial descriptions of the city; they are not mutually exclusive. Under these highly complex structural conditions, then, the mathematical function describing the density of any of these sub-systems throughout the city's spatial extent can be represented approximately by continuous, smooth functions, and will be so represented in this paper.

Although real cities consist of discrete components in each sub-system, such as people, houses, jobs, etc., the mathematical techniques of handling such continuous, smooth functions enable a much simpler exposition of some of the interactions within a city, whilst maintaining the identities of the individual components by using the concepts of probability distributions. The mathematical techniques can be generally described under the heading of the laws of large numbers.

Interlocking Effects Giving Dynamic Equilibrium

The major difficulty in laying bare the skeletal structure of a complex city is to know what comes first. The components are so inextricably interconnected, that disentangling the web of relationships presents considerable problems. Moreover, any living city is a dynamic, evolving organism in which the relationships can change continuously.

Nevertheless, it is obviously possible to determine, although only probabilistically, the future movement of an organism once the present structural skeleton has been determined together with those tensions or forces acting on the structure. The accuracy of prediction depends on the correctness of the structural determination and of the measurement of the forces now acting and likely to act in the future. The very size and complexity of the city organism is our chief aid in its analysis, because it is possible to use powerful mathematical techniques derived from physics to quantify the forces acting on the city's structure, without becoming involved in individual detail.

Moreover, if the city is large enough, so that external influences on it are small in relation to internal influences, then the changing equilibrium can be neglected if we take all our measurements of behaviour at one moment. This is equivalent to saying that the city is a closed system at the moment of measurement.

The problem then becomes one of choosing those sub-systems of the city which are the most influential on its spatial distribution pattern, and of determining the forces acting between them.

Simplifications Necessary for Progress in Understanding

For the purposes of clarity in this study, it is proposed to simplify the structure of the city in the following manner: all individuals will live in households, whilst one and only one individual from each household will work in a firm. Each separate place of employment is taken as a separate firm, whether part of a larger group or not—e.g. a railway station is defined as a firm, although it is part of a railway network. These assumptions are not critical, but they are a considerable aid to clarity.

Each household, then, has a total income which will be dependent solely on the wages received by the one employed member. Expressed as a rate over time, this income will be equal to the expenditure of the household, provided taxation, state benefits, investments and the income from them are included correctly. These additional sources of income will be neglected as a first approximation; they are discussed more fully in a paper by Wilson (1968b). The assumption here is that total wage income equals total expenditure, so that household expenditures on various commodities and services depend solely on total wage income.

Each firm will also be assumed to have a total income equal to its total expenditure, but, for purposes of comparison with households, it must be expressed as a rate per employee. This raises many practical problems, particularly in groups of firms and in the definition of employees. All people, who receive money from the firm for services rendered to it over a given period of time, must be considered as employees, even if they are actually owners of the firm. The place of capital investment and income from this investment in the form of rent will not be investigated here. However, a more complete view of city structure must obviously include this latter form of income, whether the rent is from investments in firms or in land (see Wilson, 1968b).

Households and firms, then, will both have income expressed per employee. This will be assumed to give rise to an income distribution within the city as a whole for both households and firms, although there are, of course, far fewer firms in a city than there are households.

Both households and firms will spend their income on many things; those that are of concern here are: (a) the cost of the journey to work per household; (b) the transport cost on goods bought by each firm, expressed per employee; (c) the transport cost on goods purchased from firms by members of households; (d) the cost of housing per household; (e) the cost of accommodation per employee in each firm.

These costs are constrained by all the other purchases of the household or firm and, at a given moment in time, are fairly stable if the city structure is changing slowly. It will be assumed that they can be expressed for a typical household or firm as a set of Engel curves[1]. These Engel curves, although themselves dependent on the existing structure because they are derived from an examination of the behaviour of individuals within the city at present, are expressed in terms of typical individuals at given income levels over the city as a whole. The present technique aims to show how these Engel curves for the city as a whole can be used to derive the skeletal structure of the spatial distribution functions of individuals within the city. Knowing only typical behaviour in the city, it is aimed to demonstrate probable individual behaviour—as far as location is concerned.

---

[1] An Engel curve is the graphical plot of typical expenditure on a commodity or service versus the corresponding total income. It is usually plotted on double logarithmic scales so that the slope of the curve at any point is then equal to the elasticity of demand for the commodity or service with respect to income.

The treatment, being limited in scope to the five Engel curves described above, can thus be regarded as an attempt to establish a residen-
tial-employment location model, where all households are located
according to travel costs from work and all firms are similarly located
according to transport costs. All land values in any area will be determined by the number of firms and households desiring to establish themselves in that area and the price they are prepared to pay, this latter being
constrained by their other expenditures. This limitation, it is asserted,
is sufficient to demonstrate the skeletal structure. Further complexities
such as retail location can be incorporated in a similar manner to the
present technique, but would add confusion in this initial demonstration.

The Use of the Probability Model

The derivation of the probability model is discussed in the Appendix.
The basic assumption is that the distribution, which is most probable, is
that which has the maximum entropy subject to the given information
about the system. The resulting equation for the probability distribution in the continuous case as used here is the negative exponential. This
equation, however, is derived by an analogy with a physical distribution
of entities among the energy levels of a closed system. Before its application to an economic system is made, the interpretation of the analogy
must be carefully delineated, so that the advantages and limitations of
the approach are clear.

Discussion of the Analogy

Firstly, the energy analogue will be money. Both energy and money
have the necessary property of conservation during contacts, (or transactions in economics). Both can be commuted, energy to matter, money
into capital investment or wealth; such commutation does not, however,
concern us at the moment. Money, it must be emphasised, does not
have the absolute fixed value that energy has: monetary units, whether
cash or kind, vary in relativity. Within a city system, however, one does
not expect these relative values to change rapidly if the city is stable.

Secondly, in this treatment it is asserted that the expenditures on each
commodity or service, once determined by the constraints on total expenditure, are then fixed and independent, and the expenditures can be
considered as if they were to become different forms of energy.

Thirdly, and of paramount importance to this approach, is the asser-
tion that all the households or firms with a given total income form an
undifferentiated set. The expenditure on a given commodity by the
typical individual at this given income level will be given by the corresponding point on the Engel curve relating expenditure to income. This
is the expectation value of expenditure and will be called the buying
power of the typical individual at that income level. It may be noted
that, strictly speaking, both expenditure and income are measured as

rates over time, which gives justification to the use of the term "buying power" for the expenditure rate of typical individuals.

This buying power will then be used to determine the probability distribution of the expenditures on the given commodity at that income level, assuming that there is no interaction between buyers competing for the same commodity. This is more reasonable than it seems at first sight, if it is remembered that the Engel curves must be measured to find how individuals are behaving in relation to all the constraints acting on them; they cannot be predicted *a priori*. Nevertheless, because the constraints are stable this assumption of independence becomes workable, although it only remains valid over a highly complex city as a whole, and not for small areas contained within it.

Fourthly, for simplicity of working, it is necessary to assume that each expenditure on a commodity or service buys one unit only, e.g. a dwelling, a one-way journey to work. In practice, the real situation is far more complicated.

Fifthly, as already stated at the beginning, continuous functions will be used for mathematical simplicity, implying that all prices of the commodities or services are available from zero to infinity. It is asserted that the error this contributes does not affect the overall pattern.

The Price vs. Buying-power Equation

The negative exponential equation derived from the maximum entropy treatment will now be defined in the following way: let e be the typical expenditure on a given commodity by individuals of given income, E. e is thus the buying power of these individuals for this commodity. Let p be the prices of the commodity (available at all values from zero to infinity). Let n be the number of individuals at the income-level E buying at price p. Let N be the total number of individuals at income E. Then

$$n = N\exp(-p/e)$$

and

$$\int_0^\infty n\mathrm{d}p = Ne$$

which is the total expenditure by the N individuals at income level E on the given commodity.

The Price Distribution over a Population

Extending the treatment now to include the whole population at all income levels, there are both different buying powers at different income levels, and different numbers of individuals at each income level. For simplicity, the analysis will be carried out in terms of the number of individuals at each buying power level, e, rather than that at each income level E.

For each buying power, there is a corresponding probability distribution for the prices paid given by the appropriate negative exponential.

If a three-dimensional solid is constructed with n, p, and e as axes, and using an appropriate income distribution, then a shape will be obtained as represented in Figure 1.

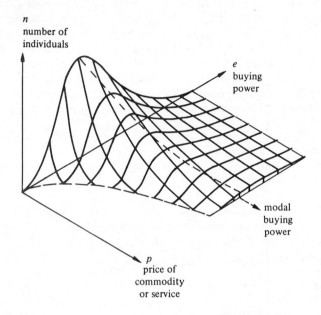

Figure 1. The "purchasing solid". An isometric representation.

The following points about this solid are noteworthy:
(a) The amount spent by individuals at a given buying power is

$$\int_0^\infty \mathrm{n}(p)\mathrm{d}p = \mathrm{N}(e)e$$

where $\mathrm{N}(e)$ is the number of individuals at the given buying power,
(b) the number of individuals buying at a given price p is

$$\int_0^\infty \mathrm{n}(e)\mathrm{d}e = \mathrm{N}(p)$$

where $\mathrm{N}(p)$ is the number of individuals buying at the given price. It may be seen that $\mathrm{N}(p)$ is a function that falls as p increases, the rapidity of falling depending on the total income distribution—it does not, however, fall as fast as an exponential function, as shown in Figure 2. This fact will be returned to later.
(c) The total amount spent by the whole population on the given commodity is the volume of the solid

$$\int_0^\infty \int_0^\infty \mathrm{n}(p, e)\mathrm{d}p \, \mathrm{d}e.$$

(d) The modal buying power, i.e. that buying power at any given price, p, at which the highest number of individuals will buy, is not constant but increases with price p. The rate of increase of the modal buying power with price depends on the shape of the income distribution, and is greatest for positively-skewed distributions such as the logarithmic normal. More simply, the higher the tail of the income distribution, the more people will buy at higher prices. Moreover, the higher the price of the good, the fewer the people that will buy it and the more they will tend to be people of high buying power.

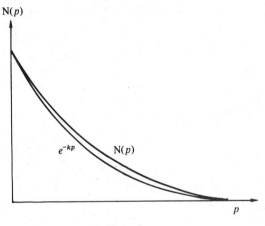

Figure 2.

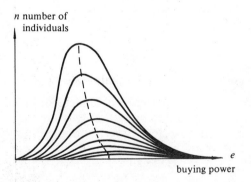

Figure 3. Constant Price Sections through the "Purchasing Solid".

(e) Sections through the solid represented by Figure 1, (the purchasing solid), taken at constant price, show that the form of the distribution of the number of individuals of given buying power buying at a given price changes smoothly. This is shown in Figure 3. If the functional form of the buying power distribution is known, then the functional form of the individuals buying at each price, p, can be calculated. Precise statements about individual behaviour can be made, knowing only the averages.

These curves will be unlikely to occur in real life exactly as shown because of the simplifying assumptions made and the necessity for continuous variation in all variables, but the general trends that the treatment shows and the way that the distributions change is certainly apparent in real life as will be shown.

The Distribution of Households about a Point Source of Employment

The first step to be taken in using this probabilistic or maximum entropy approach is to determine the spatial distribution of households about a point source of employment. All households will be located by distance from this point source of employment according to their travel purchasing power and the cost of the journey to work to this point.

Again the argument will be simplified even further by assuming that all journeys cost the same per mile travelled. The price, p, of travel bought then represents a distance to work. The number of households at a given distance, p, from the point source origin is then given by

$$N(p) = \int_0^\infty n(e)de.$$

The indications from this very simple example are: (a) The number of households located at increasing distance from the origin falls off less slowly than exponentially, (b) the modal buying power and thus the modal and mean incomes of households increase slowly as distance from the origin increases.

Having obtained this first approximation to the spatial distribution of households about a point source of employment, it is now possible to describe the kind of changes that this method would suggest when employment is spread over the city, and the travel buying power of firms is used to locate them within the city structure.

The Distribution of Firms within the Simplified City Structure

The location of firms is rather more complicated than the location of households, even using the assumption that location is determined by travel costs alone. This is because firms not only sell to and perhaps buy from residents of households, but they also buy from and sell to other firms. Moreover, there is usually a large number of different commodities or services involved. It may also be noted that purchasers of goods from a firm will be assumed to pay a price which includes the cost of travel to the firm. This cost of travel is the relevant travel cost of those goods sold by the firm, even though the firm does not pay them itself.

It is necessary to simplify this complexity by taking two functions, the travel buying power of households buying goods from firms and the travel buying power of firms who purchase goods from other firms. The latter is expressed as a travel buying power per employee of the buying firm.

These travel buying powers are often far smaller than those associated with the journey to work by employees, because the commodities and services that they are associated with are usually considerably less in value than the income from employment; there are, however, certain commodities whose value is considerably more, so the travel buying power will tend to be larger. In other words the range of the distribution of travel buying powers is much greater for firms than for households, so that in extreme cases firms can be many miles from their markets on the one hand, or only walking distance on the other.

There will therefore be a continuum of location decisions based on these travel buying powers.

Consider the case of households buying goods from firms for (a) e small. The distribution will be identical to that for households. (b) e medium and large. The distribution will be gradually biased more and more towards the centre of the city as e increases, so that the number of households reached within a given distance p is maximised.

This may be shown most simply by taking the cost of reaching all households from various radial distances from the origin, as shown in Figure 4. Obviously the costs of selling to all, or rather, randomly scattered households, increase considerably, where total cost, P, is given by

$$P = \int N(p)p\,\mathrm{d}p$$

as firms are located further from the centre.

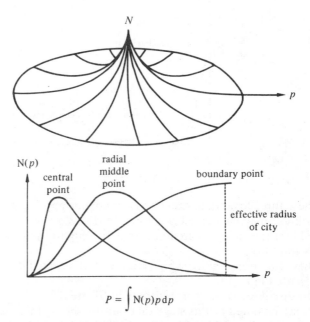

Figure 4. Total Distribution Costs to Households.

Depending on the form of the distribution of travel buying powers by households buying from firms, we have a locational structure for firms from these functions which is biased more towards the centre of the city as shown in Figure 5.

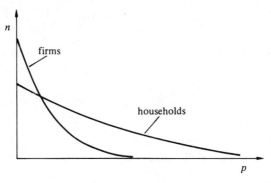

Figure 5.

The effect of the second travel buying power, namely firms who buy goods from other firms, is shown in Figure 6 as an accentuation of the dependence of firms on the centre of the city.

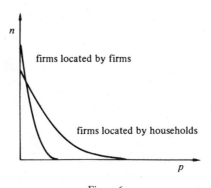

Figure 6.

These three locational functions can now be applied iteratively so that households may be located according to the source of employment, followed by firms being located in turn according to the location of households and of other firms.

These functions will converge rapidly to the spatial distributions represented in Figure 7.

The distribution of firms is shown in Figure 8.

It may be noted at this stage that our household income distributions will also have been altered by the addition of lower income households to those households occurring at some distance from the centre. Moreover, the directions of flow of the journey to work, being symmetrical about each source of employment, have now become complex. Nevertheless, the initial conclusion, that high income households are situated on the outskirts of the city, will still be valid.

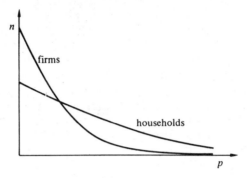

Figure 7.

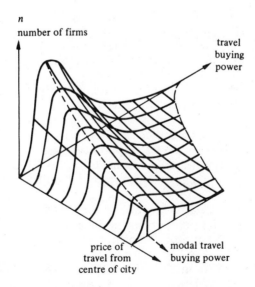

Figure 8. Location of Firms Relative to City Centre and Travel Buying Power. An isometric representation.

The constraints on these distributions imposed by accommodation costs will be dealt with shortly. Firstly, however, some conclusions that can be drawn about the wage rates of firms situated in the different areas of the city will be adduced.

The Dependence upon Location of the Wage Rates of Firms

The income of employees of firms can be derived in precisely the same way as above by assuming that firms have a wage buying power per employee. Employees' income is then treated as a commodity or service, which is being bought by firms. This wage buying power is expected to increase monotonically as the travel buying power of firms increases; i.e. those firms with the highest travel buying power will tend also to have the highest wage buying power. As these firms have already, by the above treatment, been found to be located centrally, it follows that the highest wages will be paid by firms located in the centre of the city.

There is, however, a distinct difference in the maximum entropy distribution, obtained with these wage buying powers, from that discussed above. In this case, employees can bargain, individually and collectively, over wage rates. This bargaining is taken to be a function of the wage offered in relation to all other wages. In other words, each individual in a population interacts with other individuals of like kind in such a way, that random changes in *relative* incomes occur. In the Appendix, the resulting maximum entropy distribution is derived; it is shown to be the logarithmic normal distribution. The statement of this distribution in terms of income E is

$$n = \frac{1}{[2\pi(\log\sigma)^2]^{\frac{1}{2}}} \exp\left[-\frac{(\log E - \log\mu)^2}{2(\log\sigma)^2}\right]$$

where μ is the median income and $(\log\sigma^2)$ is the variance expressed logarithmically.

It will be noted that the wage distribution is in reality far more complex. Factors which have to be considered include:
(a) the progression of employees through the income distribution during a working lifetime. A 'birth and death' process must be included, whereby individuals tend to enter the distribution towards the lower end of the income range, progress upwards in income throughout life and leave towards the top end of the range. This probably has little effect in a complex city.
(b) The notion of a bargaining function means, in part, that employees compare themselves with other people in the same firm, with other people in the same job but at different firms and probably with other people in the neighbourhood of their residence. The first two also probably have little effect in a complex city, but the third may influence residential location considerably.

As a result of this interaction of individuals at a given place, whereby a logarithmic normal distribution of income for the households in a given area is established, it may be possible to develop an *a priori* justification of the amount of money individuals spend on travel. This is not attempted here, but the additional constraints that this interaction imposes on the travel buying powers for a city in equilibrium are worth noting for later examination.

A further difficulty is that so far the discussion has concerned wage rate buying powers per employee; the number of employees in the firm has not been considered. It must be assumed, therefore, that each firm of each type belongs to the same size distribution (by number of employees); the bias caused by this assumption is unknown. However, with this assumption, it is then possible to factor all location probabilities upwards by identical amounts to give total employees at each position of the distribution. It would, none the less, appear to be probable, that the higher wage rate buying power firms tend to have a higher number of employees, thus further enhancing the centralising forces already discussed.

To sum up the discussion so far, it has been shown how it is possible for (a) households to be located such that those of higher income tend to be on the periphery of the city together with an income distribution of similar kind throughout the city but with a large increase in modal value of household income towards the periphery; (b) firms to be located predominantly centrally with the highest wages given in the centre but with a small difference in the modal value between the centre and the periphery.

The Effect of the Constraints on Accommodation Costs

The next step is to examine how the constraints produced by accommodation costs affect the patterns so far obtained. It is obvious that all the households and firms located at a particular distance from the city centre must share out the available land between them. It will be assumed that firms and households between them take all, or rather, a constant proportion, of the available land.

The basic assumption necessary is that all land at a particular distance from the centre will have a certain price, (determined only by the total cost that firms and households are able to pay) and that this price is constant at a given distance. As households and firms vary in their ability to pay, they may occupy a greater or lesser area of land.

The area of land available at any given distance from the centre of the city, r, is

$$A = 2\pi r \, dr$$

As mentioned above, this will be occupied by firms and households in the proportions denoted respectively by $f(r)$ and $h(r)$ and shown in Figure 9. The number occupying a given area at r is thus:

$$\frac{1}{2\pi r} [f(r) + h(r)].$$

This is discontinuous at the origin, being infinite. It will also be noted that, assuming that firms of higher wage rate buying power have a higher accommodation buying power and likewise households with a higher income have a higher housing buying power, then the buying power of $f(r)$

firms near the centre will be proportionately higher than for the h(*r*) households, and vice versa at the periphery.

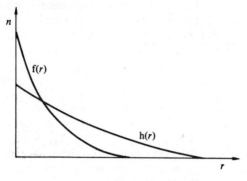

Figure 9.

It is therefore apparent that, if the constraints are sufficiently high then they affect only the distributions at the origin, and the density of occupation of the city will fall off approximately as

$$\text{density} \approx \frac{1}{r}[f(r)+h(r)]$$

where density is measured over all land. In the centre, the constraints on accommodation buying power will force the otherwise infinite peak to saturate at a maximum value, pushing other firms and households out from the centre as depicted in Figure 10.

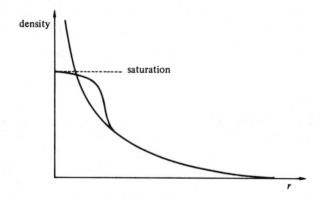

Figure 10.

These constraints should be financial in nature. Governmental re-straints on densities are not calculable by these methods although it is obviously possible to observe and even predict governmental restraints.

It is also probable that households will be pushed out the furthest, as there is a considerable peak in the distribution of firms' buying power in the centre which is not matched by a corresponding peak in the household distributions. Both firms and households will otherwise be able to exist in or near the centre at all levels of buying power. Only their space will be reduced proportionately to their buying power, if necessary by multiple-storey occupation.

Limitations of the Approach

The approach outlined above has been largely concerned with the elements of a predominantly travel-determined location model, where land has no value except for its proximity to the city. Obviously, even apart from topographical features which can have a strong influence on land value, this is a simplification which becomes justifiable only as the city's development becomes so complex, that agricultural or extractive uses of the land are negligible and also that the geological structure has negligible influence.

In other words, in the basic model, any piece of land is equally as good as any other for a potential buyer or renter, and its value will be determined merely by the demand for it. The demand will be as calculated by a maximum entropy approach.

In real cities, we find, of course, that outside the centre, industry and commerce are not spread evenly as this approach suggests. There is a great deal of geographical descriptive work on the problem of threshold sizes for the establishment of industrial and retail centres, but this problem is outside the scope of the present study. Far more information would be required before a maximum entropy approach could begin to demonstrate some of these clustering effects, and the problem is probably better dealt with in other ways.

If other factors apart from work are to be taken into account, then again the analysis could usefully proceed by basing them on travel costs. Most of the households' purchases of goods and services have already been implicitly included in the above discussion by incorporating the cost of travel in the travel buying power of firms with respect to households. The only major item that should now be included as the next step is the social travel between households, or from households to a common meeting ground such as church, public meeting, etc. This will obviously introduce a function which has the same characteristics as the firms' location distribution function. We therefore have, superimposed upon the previously defined household location function, a function which tends to increase the number of high income, particularly very high income, households towards the centre. The resultant household distribution becomes rather complex; in particular, as total income is fixed, there would be a lowering of income elsewhere to compensate for the increase at the centre.

Another factor of significance in the distribution is the cost of travel for different purposes and in different places. There will be considerable differences between travel costs by different modes. This has two major effects. In the first place, households with one or more cars may regard the cost of travel by car as running costs alone, whereas other modes are costed by total costs. Whether or not the modes are costed in a similar manner, it is still likely that each will have a different price per mile, so that costs of travel will vary from household to household depending on their mix of transport uses. The effect is expected to lower costs of travel for high income households, thus causing a relative spread of the outer parts of the city. It is also obvious that firms moving goods will pay costs of transport which are quite different from the costs of moving people.

The second major effect is that the cost of land use is not incorporated in transport systems (except indirectly via construction costs). This means that it is as cheap to use central transport networks as it is to use peripheral networks whereas this is not in conformity with our other assumptions about land costs. If transport were more expensive in central areas, then obviously the centre would be spread out more relative to the rest of the city. There is, rather, a congestion effect on costs which arises where transport space allocation does not equal transport demand, and this has the same effect but probably to a lesser degree.

The most fundamental problem of this whole approach is to determine the average behaviour of the individuals in the city. From this, individual behaviour is determined by the maximum entropy principle. If this average behaviour is not stable over time, then any prediction based on the method would be invalid.

Preliminary empirical work by the author (Mogridge, 1966) has shown that most commodity groups have very slowly changing Engel functions, but that housing is changing fairly rapidly, although steadily. This work is for the country as a whole; data on spending patterns for cities is much sparser and unreliable as yet. Some years will therefore elapse before these basic spending patterns are known in enough detail to allow speculation on the relative proportions of income spent on different commodities and the cross-elasticities between groups. Until then, this treatment, while promising, remains tentative.

The Evidence for this Treatment

Available published evidence does confirm the conclusion that household density falls less rapidly than exponentially, (see, for example, Casetti, 1968, and references cited therein). Some evidence for this treatment has also been published separately by the author (Mogridge, 1968), in an examination of data produced by the London Transportation Study (L.T.S.).

The L.T.S. evidence was made available for consultation by the Greater London Council, and seems to substantiate to some degree the treatment proposed here. Using this evidence, a simple model was constructed, assuming a single-pole employment centre. As a first approximation this is reasonably valid for London, where 50% of the total travel mileage by internal residents, (and thus approximately 50% of travel cost), is directed to the 1% of the L.T.S. area forming the conurbation centre. It may be noted that 1·4% of employed residents of the L.T.S. area work outside the area, whereas 12·8% of internal employees are resident outside the area.

This single-pole employment model was calculated using the journey to work travel buying powers (converted to distance) measured over the whole L.T.S. area for given household income levels. The maximum entropy negative exponential distribution of distance travelled by all the households in each income level was calculated. The resulting number of households and the income distribution of households locating at given distances from the centre were calculated.

The results showed that the single-pole employment model gave a 35% increase in average income for households located on the periphery of London, (i.e. 12½ miles out from the centre), compared to those near the centre; this is very close to the actual increase. Moreover, the total population locating at this distance would be one-tenth of that locating at the centre if the firms occupied no space; direct comparison of the population figures, although difficult to interpret, looks encouraging, therefore.

Modifications were then made in this simple model to illustrate the kinds of changes occurring in the income distribution: (a) with different distributions of non-central employment; (b) with identical wage distributions to those of the centre, and (c) with a modified, lower wage distribution. The resulting calculations were very complex but indications are hopeful that some of the features of real income distributions could be reproduced.

Conclusion

It has been shown how a simple probabilistic model may be developed to reproduce some of the major variables in city structure, namely:
(a) the household location and income distribution patterns; (b) the firm location and income distribution patterns; (c) city density of development.

The conclusion from this examination is that the probabilistic model of maximum entropy produces distribution patterns which bear a strong resemblance in some areas to actual patterns, but are an insufficient description, given the amount of information presently available. More data are needed to constrain the model before major industrial and geographical differences can be explained.

This preliminary examination is encouraging, however, and it is hoped that further work will demonstrate the effectiveness of this probabilistic approach.

References

Aitchison, J., and Brown, J.A.C., 1957, *The Lognormal Distribution* (Cambridge University Press).

Berry, B.J.L., and Schwind, P.J., 1968, *Information and Entropy in Migrant Flows* (Centre for Urban Studies, University of Chicago).

Casetti, E., 1968, *Alternate Urban Population Density Models: An Analytical Comparison of their Validity Range*, in this volume.

Chisholm, M., 1967, "General Systems Theory and Geography", *Transactions of the Institute of British Geographers,* **42**, p.45.

Curry, L., 1964, "The Random Spatial Economy: An Exploration in Settlement Theory", *Annals of the Association of American Geographers*, pp.138–146.

Gibbs, J.W., 1902, *Elementary Principles of Statistical Mechanics* (Yale University Press).

Goldman, S., 1953, *Information Theory* (Prentice-Hall, Englewood Cliffs).

Greater London Council, 1964, 1966, *London Transportation Study,* Vol.1 and Vol.2.

Jaynes, E.T., 1957, "Information Theory and Statistical Mechanics", *Physical Review*, **106**, 620–630.

Kinchin, A.I., 1957, *Mathematical Foundations of Information Theory* (Dover, New York).

Mogridge, M.J.H., 1966, *The Stability of Household Expenditure: An Examination of the Family Expenditure Survey*, Greater London Council, Report No.HT/RM14.

Mogridge, M.J.H., 1967, *Theory of Demand for Durable Goods Applied to Car Price Structure*, Greater London Council, Report No.HT/RM52.

Mogridge, M.J.H., 1968, *A Discussion of Some of the Factors Influencing the Income Distribution of Households within a City Region*, Centre for Environmental Studies, London, Report No.CES-WP-7.

Ollson, G., 1967, "Central Place Systems, Spatial Interaction, and Stochastic Processes", *Papers of the Regional Science Association*, p.18.

Shannon, C., and Weaver, W., 1949, *The Mathematical Theory of Communication* (University of Illinois Press).

ter Haar, D., 1954, *Elements of Statistical Mechanics* (Constable, London).

Theil, H., *Economics and Information Theory* (North-Holland Publishing Company, Amsterdam).

Tolman, R.C., 1938, *The Principles of Statistical Mechanics* (Oxford University Press).

Wilson, A.G., 1968a, *The Use of Entropy Maximising Models in the Theory of Trip Distribution, Mode Split, and Route Split*, Centre for Environmental Studies, London, Report No.CES-WP-1. Also presented to the Annual Meeting of the Highway Research Board, Washington D.C., January 1968.

Wilson, A.G., 1968b, *The Integration of Accounting and Location Theory Frameworks in Urban Modelling*, in this volume.

APPENDIX

THE PROBABILISTIC MODEL

The basic assumption of the model developed here has a long history in statistical mechanics, (Jaynes, 1957; ter Haar, 1954; Tolman, 1938; Gibbs, 1902), and in communications theory, (Shannon and Weaver, 1949; Goldman, 1953; Kinchin, 1957; Theil, 1967); it has been used recently, in a tentative and descriptive fashion, in applications of location theory by geographers, (Berry and Schwind, 1968; Curry, 1964; Ollson, 1967; Chisholm, 1967), but only recently has its application to economic variables been discussed, by Wilson (1968a, 1968b), on trip distribution and implicitly by the author (Mogridge, 1967) on car population structure.

The model arises from a consideration of the equilibrium properties of a closed system of entities which are free to move from one energy level, or its analogue, to another in the system, each entity being at some energy level. The problem is to define the probability distribution which describes the number of entities that will occupy each separate energy level in the system.

The definition of the probability distribution is achieved in the following manner. If all the entities are undifferentiated, but distinguishable, then each and every entity has an equal probability of existing at any given energy level (provided there are no constraints on the number of entities which may occupy a given energy level). The key assumption is that the opportunity for contact between entities is limited, although there is no restriction as to which entities may come into contact. This will be the case if the entities are separated in space and time, with no permanent bonds between them. As it is only by contact that an entity may exchange energy with another, and thus change its own and the other's energy level, each entity thus exists at an energy level determined on the basis of a limited number of contacts with other entities, and thus in a state of partial information.

This definition of information is crucial. Information exchange and energy change are used synonymously. An entity will only be able to discover the state of the system by a very large number of contacts with other entities in the system and thus by the exchange of information with them. Inevitably, however, the more contacts the entity has with other entities, the more information it has about the system, but the more difficult it becomes to determine the energy level the entity is at at any given moment. The probability distribution describing such an entity and system of entities becomes therefore more uncertain.

It will be realised that this discussion is about the internal characteristics of the system, namely how the entities themselves form the distribution. The problem of the outside observer sampling the behaviour of
the system to determine its characteristics is quite separate and is not
relevant here at all.

It is now asserted that the most probable distribution of the entities
among the energy levels is that where the entities make the maximum use
of the information available to them via the exchange of energy during
contacts.

These concepts will now be expressed mathematically, in conventional
notation for a continuous distribution. Define a system of entities
which have the probabilities p of existing at an energy level x, where

$$\int_0^\infty p(x)\mathrm{d}x = 1. \tag{A1}$$

As shown by Shannon in communications theory, and discussed by
Jaynes in relating this to statistical mechanics, it is useful to consider the
quantity "uncertainty" which describes the type of probability distribution obtained for different amounts of contact between the entities in
the system. A high degree of uncertainty results from many contacts
and exchanges of energy, and thus represents a broad distribution.

These authors have demonstrated that there is a unique, unambiguous
criterion for the degree of uncertainty in a discrete probability distribution. This quantity is defined uniquely by the following requirements:
that it shall be positive, increase with increasing contacts, and be additive for independent sources of uncertainty. In other words, the same
total transfer of energy to a given entity, however many contacts were
made to achieve this, must result in the same ultimate degree of uncertainty. The only expression which satisfies these simple requirements
for the continuous case, can be shown to be

$$\mathrm{H}(x) = -k\int_0^\infty p\log p\,\mathrm{d}x$$

where k is a positive constant depending on the units of measurement of
H, and H is measured over all possibilities p. Since this expression for H
is simply the expression for entropy found in statistical mechanics, then
this use of uncertainty is synonymous with entropy.

The probability distribution which makes the maximum use of available information, whilst being most non-committal with regard to missing information, is thus the distribution which has the maximum entropy,
subject to whatever is known about the constraints on the system. It
has the important property that no possibility is ignored; every energy
level is assigned positive weight unless specifically excluded.

Hence this concept supplies a reasonable and logical criterion for generation of the probability distribution, and removes the arbitrariness of

other assumptions. As additional information is used to constrain the probability distribution, so the concept of maximum entropy shows how this new information may be integrated with existing information. Whilst each entity in the system is only partially aware, through intermittent contact with other entities, of the total energy of the system, then the probability distribution of entities will be given by the distribution with maximum entropy. Any other probability distribution of lower entropy and thus lower uncertainty could have been achieved with a lower degree of contact between the entities, and thus does not make maximum use of the contacts. As long as each entity has no choice as to which other entity or entities it is brought into contact with, and as long as these contacts are small in relation to the total number of contacts, (i.e. a large number of free entities), then the probability distribution of maximum entropy is the most likely.

It is also noteworthy, that this probability distribution of maximum entropy can be shown by the techniques of statistical mechanics to be that distribution which would occur in the maximum possible number of ways with the given entities, in support of the contention that it is the most probable distribution.

For the simplest possible closed system where we know the normalisation condition, Equation (A1), and also the average energy per entity, called the expectation value of energy (given by the total energy of the system divided by the number of entities),

$$\langle E(\vec{x}) \rangle = \int_0^\infty p(x) E(x) \, dx \qquad (A2)$$

where $E(x)$ is the energy of level x, and $\vec{x}$ represents all the entities in the system, then we have to maximise the entropy

$$H(\vec{x}) = - \int_0^\infty p(x) \log p(x) \, dx,$$

where the units of H have been chosen such that $k = 1$.

It is usual to introduce Lagrangian, or indeterminate, multipliers, λ, β, such that

$$H(\vec{p}) = - \int_0^\infty p \log p \, dx + \int_0^\infty \lambda \left(1 - \int_0^\infty p \, dx\right) + \int_0^\infty \beta \left[\langle E(\vec{x}) \rangle - \int_0^\infty p E(x) \, dx\right] dx$$

where $\vec{p}$ represents the probability distribution.

$$\frac{\partial H(\vec{p})}{\partial p} = -\log p - 1 - \lambda - \beta E(x)$$

$$= 0 \text{ at the maximum.}$$

Incorporating $\lambda + 1 \to \lambda$, then

$$p = \exp[-\lambda - \beta E(x)].$$

It may be shown that:

$$\log \lambda = \int_0^\infty \exp[-\beta E(x)]dx.$$

Therefore

$$p = \frac{\exp[-\beta E(x)]}{\displaystyle\int_0^\infty \exp[-\beta E(x)]\, dx}$$

Finally from Equation (A2) we have

$$E(\vec{x}) = \int_0^\infty \frac{\exp[-\beta E(x)]}{\displaystyle\int_0^\infty \exp[-\beta E(x)]\, dx} E(x)\, dx$$

The rest of this Appendix deals with a more complex system of entities, for which there is a further constraint upon them, namely, the expectation value of the variance is constant. The processes by which this constraint is generated are mainly, but not exclusively, biological and arise whenever a distribution is generated by a stimulus which tends to produce a constant result, the mean. Deviations from this mean occur by random stochastic processes as before, but the spread of the distribution is governed by the number of these processes, so that a given distribution will have a constant expectation value of the variance.

Mathematically, the constraints are:

$$\int_{-\infty}^\infty p(x)\,dx = 1 \tag{A3}$$

and

$$\int_{-\infty}^\infty p(x)\,[E(x)-\mu]^2\,dx = \langle\sigma^2\rangle, \tag{A4}$$

where μ is the mean, and σ^2 is the variance.

It will be noted that integration must be taken over all energy levels from $-\infty$ to $+\infty$, as the origin is no longer a bound. Normally, of course, values will be positive.

We have to maximise the entropy

$$H(\vec{p}) = -\int_{-\infty}^\infty p\log p\,dx + \int_{-\infty}^\infty \lambda\left(1 - \int_{-\infty}^\infty p\,dx\right)dx$$
$$+ \int_{-\infty}^\infty \gamma\left\{\langle\sigma^2\rangle - \int_{-\infty}^\infty [E(x)-\mu]^2 p\,dx\right\}dx,$$

where λ, γ are Lagrangian multipliers.

Therefore:

$$\frac{\partial H(\vec{p})}{\partial p} = -\log p - 1 - \lambda - \gamma[E(x)-\mu]^2$$

$$= 0 \text{ at the maximum.}$$

Incorporating $\lambda + 1 \to \lambda$, then

$$p = \exp\{-\lambda - \gamma [E(x) - \mu]^2\}.$$

From Equation (A3)

$$\int_{-\infty}^{\infty} p\, dx = \int_{-\infty}^{\infty} \exp\{-\lambda - \gamma [E(x) - \mu]^2\}\, dx$$

$$= \exp(-\lambda) \int_{-\infty}^{\infty} \exp\{-\gamma [E(x) - \mu]^2\}\, dx$$

$$= \exp(-\lambda)\left(\frac{\pi}{\gamma}\right)^{\frac{1}{2}} = 1$$

Hence

$$p = \left(\frac{\gamma}{\pi}\right)^{\frac{1}{2}} \exp\{-\gamma [E(x) - \mu]^2\}.$$

From Equation (A4)

$$\int_{-\infty}^{\infty} [E(x) - \mu]^2 \left(\frac{\gamma}{\pi}\right)^{\frac{1}{2}} \exp\{-\gamma [E(x) - \mu]^2\}\, dx = \left(\frac{\gamma}{\pi}\right)^{\frac{1}{2}} \frac{1}{2}\left(\frac{\pi}{\gamma^3}\right)^{\frac{1}{2}} = \frac{1}{2\gamma}.$$

Whence

$$p(x) = \left(\frac{1}{2\pi\langle\sigma^2\rangle}\right)^{\frac{1}{2}} \exp\left(-\frac{[E(x) - \mu]^2}{2\langle\sigma^2\rangle}\right).$$

This is the equation of the normal distribution with mean μ and variance σ^2. The normal distribution is thus the distribution with the maximum entropy subject to the constraint of a fixed variance.

It may be noted that the constraint

$$\int_{-\infty}^{\infty} E(x)p(x)\, dx = \langle E(\vec{x})\rangle = \mu \qquad (A5)$$

is a redundant constraint, being automatically satisfied.

The entropy of the normal distribution is thus:

$$H = -\int_{-\infty}^{\infty} p \log p\, dx \qquad (A6)$$

where

$$\log p = -\log(2\pi\langle\sigma^2\rangle)^{\frac{1}{2}} - \frac{[E(x) - \mu]^2}{2\langle\sigma^2\rangle}.$$

Therefore:

$$H = \int_{-\infty}^{\infty} \frac{\log(2\pi\langle\sigma^2\rangle)^{\frac{1}{2}}}{(2\pi\langle\sigma^2\rangle)^{\frac{1}{2}}} \exp\left\{-\frac{[E(x) - \mu]^2}{2\langle\sigma^2\rangle}\right\} dx$$

$$+ \int_{-\infty}^{\infty} \frac{1}{(2\pi\langle\sigma^2\rangle)^{\frac{1}{2}}} \frac{[E(x) - \mu]^2}{2\langle\sigma^2\rangle} \exp\left\{-\frac{[E(x) - \mu]^2}{2\langle\sigma^2\rangle}\right\} dx$$

$$= \log(2\pi\langle\sigma^2\rangle)^{\frac{1}{2}} + \tfrac{1}{2} = \log(2\pi e\langle\sigma^2\rangle)^{\frac{1}{2}}. \qquad (A7)$$

It is interesting to show that for a constant entropy, the normal distribution is the one with the smallest variance. This is done in the following way. Our constraints are now Equations (A3) and (A6) so that:

$$\langle\sigma^2\rangle = \int_{-\infty}^{\infty} [E(x)-\mu]^2 p\,dx + \int_{-\infty}^{\infty}\lambda\left(1-\int_{-\infty}^{\infty}p\,dx\right)dx$$
$$+ \int_{-\infty}^{\infty}\gamma\left(H+\int_{-\infty}^{\infty}p\log p\,dx\right)dx,$$

where λ, γ are Lagrangian multipliers.

Hence
$$\frac{\partial\langle\sigma^2\rangle}{\partial p} = [E(x)-\mu]^2 - \lambda + \gamma\log p + \gamma$$

$$= 0 \text{ at the minimum}$$

and
$$p = \exp\left\{\frac{\lambda-\gamma-[E(x)-\mu]^2}{\gamma}\right\}.$$

From Equation (A3):
$$\int_{-\infty}^{\infty}p\,dx = \int_{-\infty}^{\infty}\exp\left\{\frac{\lambda-\gamma-[E(x)-\mu]^2}{\gamma}\right\}dx$$

$$= (\pi\gamma)^{\frac{1}{2}}\exp[(\lambda-\gamma)/\gamma]$$

whence
$$p = (\pi\gamma)^{-\frac{1}{2}}\exp\{[E(x)-\mu]^2/\gamma\}.$$

From Equation (A6)
$$\int_{-\infty}^{\infty}p\log p\,dx = -H$$

where
$$\log p = -\log(\pi\gamma)^{\frac{1}{2}} - \{[E(x)-\mu]^2/\gamma\}$$
and
$$\int_{-\infty}^{\infty}p\log p\,dx = -\left(\frac{1}{\pi\gamma}\right)^{\frac{1}{2}}\log(\pi\gamma)^{\frac{1}{2}}\int_{-\infty}^{\infty}\exp\{-[E(x)-\mu]^2/\gamma\}dx$$

$$= -\left(\frac{1}{\pi\gamma}\right)^{\frac{1}{2}}\frac{1}{\gamma}\int_{-\infty}^{\infty}[E(x)-\mu]^2\exp\{-[E(x)-\mu]^2/\gamma\}dx$$

$$= -\log(\pi\gamma)^{\frac{1}{2}} - \frac{1}{2}$$

$$= -\log(\pi e\gamma)^{\frac{1}{2}} = H$$

The parallel between Equation (A7) and the last equation is obvious with $\gamma = 2\langle\sigma^2\rangle$.

(As a distinction, it may also be noted that the negative exponential is the distribution which has the maximum variance for constant entropy and the constraints given by Equations (A1) and (A2), whilst the normal distribution has the minimum variance for constant entropy and the parallel constraints of Equations (A3) and (A5). The conclusion from this is that the negative exponential distribution has the maximum disorder whilst the normal distribution has the minimum disorder or maximum organisation.)

A further system of entities may also be described in which the same constraints are applied but in which the generating process produces a random stochastic deviation from the mean, not as a linear progression but as a relative or geometrical progression. In other words, the size of the change in energy levels depends on the magnitude of the energy level from which the change takes place. By an analogous argument, the distribution which has the maximum entropy will be the geometric normal distribution, more commonly called the logarithmic normal. In contrast to the usual formulation, as given by Aitchison and Brown (1957) the analogy suggests that the formulation must be independent of the base of logarithms chosen, and must be invariant in form when all values are changed multiplicatively, i.e. if all values double, the relative position of every individual is unchanged, the variance must be unchanged, but the mean will double in value. The formulation will be therefore:

$$p(x) = \frac{1}{(2\pi \langle (\log \sigma)^2 \rangle} \exp \left\{ -\frac{[\log E(x) - \log \mu]^2}{2 \langle (\log \sigma)^2 \rangle} \right\}.$$

Systems which are generated by this geometric random stochastic process are usually biological growth processes, but various decay processes satisfy the same conditions. The growth process will often be associated with a birth and death process for particular individuals in the population, and this will substantially complicate the mathematics.

The following conclusions are drawn:

1) For a system of entities existing over all positive energy values, and with a fixed mean value, the negative exponential distribution has the maximum entropy and is the most probable distribution.

2) For a system of entities existing over all energy values, and with a fixed variance, the normal distribution has the maximum entropy, and is the most probable distribution if the generating process is random stochastic, whereas the logarithmic normal distribution has the maximum entropy and is the most probable distribution if the generating process is geometric random stochastic.

Regional Econometric Models: A Case[†] Study of Nova Scotia

S.CZAMANSKI
Cornell University

INTRODUCTION

There has been recently a surge of interest in the application of econometric methods to regional planning. It is perhaps natural that most regional models which have been so far constructed, as well as those which are being currently developed in ever increasing numbers, follow more or less the pattern and format of national models. Yet it should not be overlooked that there exist some fundamental differences between national and regional economic problems, which are bound to affect the structure of regional econometric models.

These differences may be categorized as follows:

(a) *Scope and objectives*

National planning has to encompass the economic aspects of all policies carried out by the federal government and its agencies. Many of these, like defence or foreign policy, are not tackled below the national level.

Until recently, the cyclical stability of the national economy has been the main focus of attention. Such problems as growth, equalization of differences in development between various parts of the nation, and distribution of wealth and income have received serious attention only latterly. At the regional level, on the other hand, considerations of growth, welfare, and provision of various amenities and services are paramount.

Another and perhaps more fundamental difference stems from the fact that regional socio-economic planning is much nearer to, and often serves as a framework for, purely physical planning. This aspect of regional planning is further underscored by the disaggregated level at which it operates. A single investment, such as the construction of a dam or of a factory, is rarely important enough to be incorporated as a separate element in a national economic plan but very often becomes the central issue, and indeed the very reason, for preparing a regional plan.

† The study presented in this paper is based on work carried out by the author at the Institute of Public Affairs, Dalhousie University, during the summers of 1967 and 1968. The author is grateful for permission to use material prepared for the Institute.

(b) Policy instruments

Differences in the tools with which to influence economic phenomena are equally pronounced.   The national government can make use of various powerful tools of fiscal, monetary, and commerical policy such as taxation, supply of money, measures influencing the interest rate, import duties or even import quotas, exchange controls, export premiums, or price controls.

At the sub-national level, on the other hand, even in the case of study regions corresponding to provinces, the tools at the disposal of the regional government are relatively modest both because of the political limitations of the provincial government and, more importantly, because basic national economic measures cannot usually be adapted to the needs of a single region.

An important limitation stems from the inability of regional governments to control the movements of factors of production over their boundaries by placing restrictions on migrations or inter-regional money flows.   This is further aggravated by their inability to control exports and imports, money supply, and the general economic climate which essentially depends upon national development.

(c) Availability of data

A major difficulty often encountered in regional studies is paucity of data stemming largely from the fact that inter-regional flows are not subject to any controls.   Not only are attempts at direct controls absent, but the phenomena are hardly ever measured.   This often results in serious gaps in basic knowledge, with important consequences as far as construction of models and estimating techniques are concerned.

(d) Elements of regional growth

An open region can hardly be thought of as a replica of the national economy.   Many of the time-honoured theories and hypotheses concerning economic growth are not applicable at the sub-national level.   It is here, perhaps, that the most important differences between national and regional econometric growth models come to the fore.

Speaking in broad terms, national growth models may be grouped into those dealing primarily with advanced industrialized nations and focussing mainly on effective demand, and those addressing themselves largely to under-developed nations and focussing mainly on problems of balance of payments and foreign aid.   The first group has its roots in the Keynesian model, the second in the Harrod–Domar and Mahalanobis type models. In both types, investments are treated as important exogenous variables, but, in the first, the act of investment and the balance between savings and investments is of prime interest, while in the second, the effects of investments upon capacity, and their relation to the rate of growth are investigated.

It appears, however, and it has been claimed that both approaches are quite inadequate for dealing with open economies (Czamanski, 1964). A small region faces an essentially perfectly elastic demand curve for most of its products. In other words, it can sell all it produces as long as it is able to produce at competitive prices. Hence, fluctuations in demand for exports should not be treated as the main exogenous variable of regional model—not, at any rate, in the long run.

Secondly, because of the high inter-regional mobility of financial capital, local investments do not depend, as a rule, upon local savings. In other words, in an open region savings and investments may be permanently imbalanced.

The above can be restated perhaps in the following way. It is postulated that under modern conditions, friction of space does not affect in an important way inter-regional movements of factors of production, and especially those of financial capital and labour. Fixed investment and natural resources on the other hand are immobile. It follows that the most important and permanent characteristics of an open region have to do with natural resources and the accumulation of fixed investments. Generally speaking, certain stock variables assume crucial importance as far as regional growth is concerned.

The phenomena dealt with in regional models and the conclusions derived from their study are concerned with the long run. Now, long run, both in macro- and micro-economics, is defined as that period after which existing stocks are used up, and installations are sufficiently obsolete for resources to be capable of redeployment. Therefore, growth of economic activity in the sense discussed here can take place only through new productive investment, or, less rigorously stated, new job creating investments. Increases in economic activity through a fuller use of existing equipment, increases in productivity, etc. need not be considered. The core of a regional model, therefore, is based on investment functions which try to determine the effects of various locational factors upon the attractiveness of a region for investments in new productive facilities[1].

A corollary of the view that regional growth is concerned mainly with the increase in fixed capital, while population flows and changes in the level and composition of output simply follow changes in invested productive capacity, is that location theory substitutes for a study of flow phenomena taking place in the regional economy. An open region is thus viewed primarily as a place competing with all other places in the nation in order to attract new investments, especially new productive investments. These new investments take place on the basis of individual location decisions of entrepreneurs who often may not be residents of the region[2]. Hence, an open region does not grow because local residents

[1] For details and early development of this hypothesis see Czamanski (1965).
[2] Czamanski (1965); and for an evaluation: Isard and Czamanski (1965).

save and invest part of their income[3]. More generally, because of high
inter-regional mobility of financial capital, savings or balance of foreign
trade seem relatively less important as determinants of investments.

THE PROBLEM OF NOVA SCOTIA

Before proceeding to an examination of a model embodying the above
hypotheses it may be worthwhile to review briefly the major features of
the regional economy which it analyses.

The total land area of Nova Scotia is 21 064 square miles. The population was estimated in the 1961 Census to be 730 000. The degree of
urbanization of the province may be judged from the fact that Halifax,
the capital and largest city, accounted for just over 92 000 persons;
Dartmouth for almost 47 000; and Sydney for over 33 000.

Two of the principal industries of Nova Scotia, coal mining and primary iron and steel industry, are at present facing serious problems.
By now the easily accessible deposits of coal are almost exhausted, and
the industry can survive only with the help of heavy government subsidies, both direct and in the form of cheaper freight rates. At present
the cost of coal in Nova Scotia at the pithead is about three times higher
than in the United States. According to recent plans, the coal mines are
to be bought up by the government and the operation is to be phased out
over a period of fourteen years. The seriousness of this decision is under-
lined by the fact that in 1961 coal mining accounted for 3·75 per cent of
total employment, and together with primary ion and steel production
provided the basis for the economy of Sydney and of the cluster of towns
around it.

The iron and steel industry is suffering from a lack of nearby markets.
The long distance to the markets in Central Canada as well as the high
cost and low quality of local coal puts the industry at a great disadvantage
in relation to its competitors. More importantly, it failed to attract iron
and steel processing industries to Nova Scotia and thus to trigger the
development of a local industrial complex. The industry itself has
reached the minimum efficient size as far as total capacity is concerned,
but its equipment is obsolete. Late in 1967, its owners decided to close
the plant. Ownership is now being taken over by the Nova Scotia

---

[3] To take an extreme example, the development of the oil industry in Western Canada resulted
from considerations of availability of a natural resource (location theory) and not of local capital
formation or capital accumulation. A study of flow phenomena taking place in the local economy
prior to the establishment of the oil industry, of inter-industry relations and input–output coefficients or of the national or world oil demand would not be particularly relevant and would not
have contributed to our ability to forecast the imminent development of the oil industry. The
study of past saving patterns of local residents would be in this case equally irrelevant, because
investments in the new oil industry might have easily exceeded savings of the residents of the
county or even of the province.

government in order to prevent serious dislocations to the economy of the Sydney area which would follow a sudden closure, but its future is uncertain.

Other manufacturing activities of Nova Scotia include many small and rather inefficient plants, mainly in the food industry, and oriented towards the needs of the local market or engaged in fish processing.

The rather weak industrial base of the regional economy provides employment to only about one third of the employed labour force. The heavy concentration of activities in the service sectors, typical of under-developed economies, is partly explained in Nova Scotia by the presence of the defence establishment. Here again, however, the future is uncertain.

The plight of Nova Scotia is by no means an isolated phenomenon. The existence of declining regions and of pockets of unemployment and poverty in the highly industrialized nations of North America and Western Europe has attracted attention recently. Their problems are very different from those of the underdeveloped countries of Africa, Asia, and Latin America.

There are numerous criteria according to which Nova Scotia may be classified as a declining region. The per capita personal income is considerably lower than the Canadian average. Unemployment rate is high, while labour force participation rates are low. The result is a net out-migration from the province. As a rule this type of out-migration is a highly selective process producing unfavourable changes in the age and sex structure of the remaining population, and affecting the quality of the remaining labour force from the point of view of training and education.

In addition, over a number of years personal income in Nova Scotia has been consistently greater than net regional income. This is rather typical of declining regions, where personal spending often exceeds the earnings accruing to the factors of production owned by local residents. As a result, if one does not count the federal government expenditures, the balance of payments of the region with the outside world has been, over many years, persistently unfavourable.

Structure of the model

The model of Nova Scotia is comprised of 104 variables of which 54 are endogenous. The endogenous variables are further subdivided into target and intermediate variables. Among the 50 predetermined variables the following categories have been singled out: instruments or variables which can be affected by government, data variables, and lagged endogenous variables. The number of target variables equals the number of instrument variables, as otherwise some of the instrument variables would be redundant and left at zero level.

The system consists of 54 equations which exactly equals the number of endogenous variables. This is summarized in Table 1. The full system of equations and variables is as follows:

Table 1. Structure of the model.

(1) Target variables	8	Structural equations	31
(2) Intermediate variables	46	Balance equations	5
		Definitional equations	18
Total endogenous variables	**54**	Total equations	**54**
(3) Instrument variables	8		
(4) Data variables			
Unlagged 29			
Lagged 7	36		
(5) Lagged endogenous variables	6		
Total predetermined variables	**50**		
Predetermined parameters	8		

Structural equations

$$X_{IS(t)} = \begin{matrix} 7\cdot827 & + & 0\cdot6497K_{IS(t)}; \\ (4\cdot7040) & & (6\cdot5531) \end{matrix} \qquad \begin{matrix} R^2 = 0\cdot7922 \\ d = 1\cdot6505 \end{matrix} \qquad (S.1)$$

$$Q_{IS(t)} = \begin{matrix} 2\cdot49X_{IS(t)}; \\ (12\cdot5) \end{matrix} \qquad R^2 = 0\cdot9176 \qquad (S.2)$$

$$e_{IS(t)} = \begin{matrix} 0\cdot9848Q_{IS(t)}; \\ (752\cdot2053) \end{matrix} \qquad \begin{matrix} R^2 = 0\cdot9994 \\ d = 1\cdot8549 \end{matrix} \qquad (S.3)$$

$$E_{1(t)} = \begin{matrix} 2\cdot643 & + & 1\cdot1029FZ_{(t)}; \\ (0\cdot1790) & & (1\cdot9040) \end{matrix} \qquad \begin{matrix} R^2 = 0\cdot1338 \\ d = 0\cdot2597 \end{matrix} \qquad (S.4)$$

$$E_{4(t)} = \begin{matrix} -80\cdot696 & + & 0\cdot4708P_{u(t)}; \\ (-3\cdot6023) & & (8\cdot4261) \end{matrix} \qquad \begin{matrix} R^2 = 0\cdot8333 \\ d = 0\cdot3193 \end{matrix} \qquad (S.5)$$

$$E_{5(t)} = \begin{matrix} 24\cdot061 & + & 0\cdot6741DF_{s(t)} & - & 2\cdot0454t; \\ (11\cdot9162) & & (7\cdot7784) & & (-7\cdot7027) \end{matrix} \qquad \begin{matrix} R^2 = 0\cdot8207 \\ d = 1\cdot7141 \end{matrix} \qquad (S.6)$$

$$I_{m(t)} = \begin{matrix} 1\cdot1488(GI_G + GS_m)_{(t-4)} & + & 0\cdot0186Z_{1(t-4)}; \\ (2\cdot6590) & & (1\cdot1821) \end{matrix} \quad \begin{matrix} R^2 = 0\cdot6404 \\ d = 1\cdot7254 \end{matrix} \quad (S.7)$$

$$Z_1 = 0\cdot5483U_Y + 0\cdot5767U_{E3} + 0\cdot6056H_H;$$

$$e_{m(t)} = \begin{matrix} 26\cdot185 & + & 1\cdot2436GNP_{(t)} & + & 0\cdot6672(\bar{p}_m^C - \bar{p}_m^{NS})_{(t)}; \\ (2\cdot9136) & & (3\cdot1628) & & (2\cdot3635) \end{matrix}$$

$$\begin{matrix} R^2 = 0\cdot3932 \\ d = 1\cdot9141 \end{matrix} \qquad (S.8)$$

$$X_{m(t)} = \begin{matrix} -239\cdot599 & + & 1\cdot2005K_{m(t)}; \\ (-10\cdot7214) & & (19\cdot8214) \end{matrix} \qquad \begin{matrix} R^2 = 0\cdot9727 \\ d = 1\cdot5105 \end{matrix} \qquad (S.9)$$

$$E_{3(t)} = \begin{array}{cc} 0 \cdot 0304 X_{m(t)} + & 0 \cdot 3795 SZ_{(t)}; \\ (2 \cdot 8514) & (17 \cdot 7193) \end{array} \qquad \begin{array}{l} R^2 = 0 \cdot 6261 \\ d = 1 \cdot 3214 \end{array} \qquad \text{(S.10)}$$

$$X_{CS(t)} = \begin{array}{cc} -629 \cdot 923 + & 9 \cdot 2050 E_{4(t)}; \\ (-8 \cdot 0764) & (12 \cdot 2848) \end{array} \qquad \begin{array}{l} R^2 = 0 \cdot 9448 \\ d = 1 \cdot 9770 \\ \rho = 0 \cdot 1221 \end{array} \qquad \text{(S.11)}$$

$$I_{CS(t)} = \begin{array}{cc} 0 \cdot 1079 X_{CS(t)} + & 6 \cdot 2032 i_{(t)}; \\ (2 \cdot 7744) & (2 \cdot 4635) \end{array} \qquad \begin{array}{l} R^2 = 0 \cdot 8024 \\ d = 1 \cdot 6936 \end{array} \qquad \text{(S.12)}$$

$$I_{H(t)} = \begin{array}{ccc} 14 \cdot 714 + & 0 \cdot 1450 \Delta GRP + & 1 \cdot 6289 GS_{H(t)}; \\ (2 \cdot 5542) & (1 \cdot 8159) & (4 \cdot 2178) \end{array} \qquad \begin{array}{l} R^2 = 0 \cdot 6099 \\ d = 1 \cdot 7120 \end{array} \qquad \text{(S.13)}$$

$$\lg W_{(t)} = \begin{array}{ccc} -2 \cdot 1494 + & 0 \cdot 7742 \lg GRP_{(t)} + & 0 \cdot 6382 \lg \bar{p}_{(t)}^{NS}; \\ (-1 \cdot 8830) & (8 \cdot 4429) & (1 \cdot 8587) \end{array} \quad \begin{array}{l} R^2 = 0 \cdot 9916 \\ d = 1 \cdot 0947 \\ \rho = 0 \cdot 4583 \end{array} \qquad \text{(S.14)}$$

$$F_{a(t)} = \begin{array}{ccc} -22 \cdot 245 + & 0 \cdot 0428 A_{L(t)} + & 0 \cdot 5177 FZ_{(t)}; \\ (-9 \cdot 1337) & (8 \cdot 2933) & (4 \cdot 5502) \end{array} \qquad \begin{array}{l} R^2 = 0 \cdot 9430 \\ d = 2 \cdot 0261 \end{array} \qquad \text{(S.15)}$$

$$F_{m(t)} = \begin{array}{c} 1 \cdot 869 + 0 \cdot 0156 X_m; \\ (3 \cdot 0689) \end{array} \qquad R^2 = 0 \cdot 4022 \qquad \text{(S.16)}$$

$$F_{s(t)} = \begin{array}{cc} 0 \cdot 0835 X_{CS(t)} + & 0 \cdot 3509 \bar{p}_{(t)}^{NS}; \\ (3 \cdot 7470) & (5 \cdot 4255) \end{array} \qquad \begin{array}{l} R^2 = 0 \cdot 9285 \\ d = 1 \cdot 7623 \\ \rho = 0 \cdot 5307 \end{array} \qquad \text{(S.17)}$$

$$i_{p(t)} = \begin{array}{c} -66 \cdot 060 + 1 \cdot 5133 NH_{(t)}; \\ (27 \cdot 9972) \end{array} \qquad R^2 = 0 \cdot 9801 \qquad \text{(S.18)}$$

$$SIP_{(t)} = \begin{array}{cc} -4 \cdot 022 + & 0 \cdot 0525 W_{(t)}; \\ (-1 \cdot 9578) & (12 \cdot 5468) \end{array} \qquad \begin{array}{l} R^2 = 0 \cdot 9125 \\ d = 1 \cdot 3600 \end{array} \qquad \text{(S.19)}$$

$$T_{(t)} = \begin{array}{ccc} -31 \cdot 933 + & 0 \cdot 0494 Y_{p(t)} + & 293 \cdot 944 t_{r(t)}; \\ (-3 \cdot 5966) & (6 \cdot 7526) & (1 \cdot 7762) \end{array} \qquad \begin{array}{l} R^2 = 0 \cdot 9669 \\ d = 1 \cdot 8360 \end{array} \qquad \text{(S.20)}$$

$$C_{1(t)} = \begin{array}{ccc} -225 \cdot 407 + & 2 \cdot 1035 H_{(t-1)} + & 0 \cdot 4197 Y_{DP}; \\ (-2 \cdot 3577) & (2 \cdot 6386) & (8 \cdot 3267) \end{array} \qquad \begin{array}{l} R^2 = 0 \cdot 9966 \\ d = 2 \cdot 0583 \end{array} \qquad \text{(S.21)}$$

$$C_{4(t)} = \begin{array}{cc} -45 \cdot 236 + & 0 \cdot 1682 Y_{DP} + & 0 \cdot 2461 P_u; \\ & (17 \cdot 4463) & (3 \cdot 5707) \end{array} \qquad R^2 = 0 \cdot 9970 \qquad \text{(S.22)}$$

$$C_{5(t)} = \begin{array}{ccc} -66 \cdot 924 + & 0 \cdot 7370 NH_{(t)} + & 0 \cdot 1291 Y_{DP}; \\ (-7 \cdot 5404) & (2 \cdot 4088) & (5 \cdot 3614) \end{array} \qquad \begin{array}{l} R^2 = 0 \cdot 9982 \\ d = 2 \cdot 1316 \end{array} \qquad \text{(S.23)}$$

$$T_{c(t)} = \begin{array}{cc} 12 \cdot 624 + & 0 \cdot 0126 GRP_{(t)}; \\ (4 \cdot 6854) & (4 \cdot 0166) \end{array} \qquad \begin{array}{l} R^2 = 0 \cdot 5022 \\ d = 1 \cdot 4026 \end{array} \qquad \text{(S.24)}$$

$$T_{IN(t)} = \begin{array}{cc} -35 \cdot 363 + & 0 \cdot 2469 Y_E; \\ (-5 \cdot 5414) & (29 \cdot 0736) \end{array} \qquad \begin{array}{l} R^2 = 0 \cdot 9837 \\ d = 2 \cdot 1292 \end{array} \qquad \text{(S.25)}$$

$$e_{L(t)} = \begin{array}{cc} 25 \cdot 989 + & 0 \cdot 2184 GNP_{(t)}; \\ (13 \cdot 7460) & (3 \cdot 8913) \end{array} \qquad \begin{array}{l} R^2 = 0 \cdot 4853 \\ d = 0 \cdot 9704 \end{array} \qquad \text{(S.26)}$$

$$\lg e_{A(t)} = \begin{array}{cc} 1 \cdot 5110 \lg F_B + & 0 \cdot 3954 \lg \sum_{t=-1}^{-4} GS_{A(t)}; \\ (22 \cdot 5825) & (4 \cdot 5464) \end{array} \qquad \begin{array}{l} R^2 = 0 \cdot 8114 \\ d = 1 \cdot 4292 \end{array} \qquad \text{(S.27)}$$

$$m_{(t)} = \begin{array}{l} 0 \cdot 3969\,Y_{E(t)} + 0 \cdot 2860[X_L + X_{IS} + X_m]_{(t)} \\ (12 \cdot 0557) \qquad (4 \cdot 8400) \end{array}$$

$$\begin{array}{ll} + \; 0 \cdot 3377 I_{(t)} + 0 \cdot 9173 DF_{s(t)}; & R^2 = 0 \cdot 9977 \qquad \text{(S.28)} \\ \quad (2 \cdot 8554) \quad (4 \cdot 7760) & d \; = 2 \cdot 8846 \end{array}$$

$$\begin{array}{ll} M_{(t)} = \begin{array}{l} -3 \cdot 007 + 0 \cdot 3718 D^L_{(t-1)}; \\ (2 \cdot 5349) \end{array} & R^2 = 0 \cdot 3687 \qquad \text{(S.29)} \end{array}$$

$$\begin{array}{ll} q_{e(t)} = \begin{array}{l} 24 \cdot 920 \; + \; 0 \cdot 2603 GI_{ED(t)}; \\ (50 \cdot 4639)\;(4 \cdot 1680) \end{array} & \begin{array}{l} R^2 = 0 \cdot 6208 \qquad \text{(S.30)} \\ d \; = 2 \cdot 3583 \end{array} \end{array}$$

$$\begin{array}{ll} q_{v(t)} = \begin{array}{l} 220 \cdot 858 \; + 17 \cdot 8200 GI_{V(t)}; \\ (14 \cdot 2888)\;(3 \cdot 5096) \end{array} & \begin{array}{l} R^2 = \;\; 0 \cdot 3947 \qquad \text{(S.31)} \\ d \; = \;\; 0 \cdot 4443 \\ \rho \; = -0 \cdot 0925 \end{array} \end{array}$$

Definitional equations

$$K_{IS(t)} = K_{IS(t-1)} + I_{IS(t)}; \tag{D.1}$$

$$K_{m(t)} = K_{m(t-1)} + I_{m(t)}; \tag{D.2}$$

$$X_{G(t)} = \overline{w}^{NS}_{G(t)} E_{5(t)}; \tag{D.3}$$

$$GRP_{(t)} = X_{A(t)} + X_{L(t)} + X_{IS(t)} + X_{m(t)} + X_{CS(t)} + X_{G(t)}; \tag{D.4}$$

$$I_{(t)} = I_{L(t)} + I_{IS(t)} + I_{m(t)} + I_{CS(t)} + I_{H(t)}; \tag{D.5}$$

$$MPA_{(t)} = 0 \cdot 5 DF_{s(t)}; \tag{D.6}$$

$$Y_{p(t)} = W_{(t)} + F_{a(t)} + F_{m(t)} + F_{s(t)} + i_{p(t)} + F^G_{(t)} + F^{nr}_{(t)} - SIP_{(t)} + MPA_{(t)}; \tag{D.7}$$

$$tr_{(t)} = T^c_{(t)} / Y^c_{p(t)}; \tag{D.8}$$

$$Y_{DP(t)} = Y_{p(t)} - (T_{(t)} + T_{s(t)}); \tag{D.9}$$

$$Y_{E(t)} = C_{1(t)} + C_{4(t)} + C_{5(t)} + S_{(t)}; \tag{D.10}$$

$$\hat{N}_{(t)} = \tilde{\lambda}\hat{P}_{(t-1)}; \tag{D.11}$$

$$L_{(t)} = \overline{R}\hat{N}_{(t)}; \tag{D.12}$$

$$D^L_{(t)} = E_{(t)} - (1-h)L_{(t)}; \tag{D.13}$$

$$\hat{M}_{(t)} = \hat{\pi} M_{(t)}; \tag{D.14}$$

$$P_{(t)} = \overline{\delta}\hat{P}_{(t)}; \tag{D.15}$$

$$q_{H(t)} = N H_{(t)} / P_{(t)}; \tag{D.16}$$

$$\overline{y}_{DP(t)} = Y_{DP(t)} / P_{(t)}; \tag{D.17}$$

$$\overline{y}_{A(t)} = (\eta W_{(t)} + F_{a(t)} + \alpha F^G_{(t)} + \beta F^{nr}_{(t)}) / (P - P_u)_{(t)}; \tag{D.18}$$

Balance equations

$$E_{(t)} = E_{1(t)} + E_{2(t)} + E_{3(t)} + E_{4(t)} + E_{5(t)} + E_{6(t)}; \tag{B.1}$$

$$Y_{DP(t)} = Y_{E(t)}; \tag{B.2}$$

$$T_{(t)} + T_{c(t)} + T_{s(t)} + T_{IN(t)} + SIP_{(t)} + GD_{(t)}$$
$$= DF_{s(t)} + (GI_{G(t)} + GI_{ED(t)} + GI_{V(t)} + GS_{A(t)} + GS_{L(t)} + GS_{m(t)} + GS_{H(t)})$$
$$+ GS_{c(t)} + F^G_{(t)}; \tag{B.3}$$

$$W_{(t)}+F_{a(t)}+F_{m(t)}+F_{s(t)}+i_{p(t)}+C_{rp(t)}+D_{p(t)}+T_{IN(t)}+MPA_{(t)}+REA_{(t)}$$
$$= C_{1(t)}+C_{4(t)}+C_{5(t)}+[DF_{s(t)}+(GI_{G(t)}+GI_{ED(t)}+GI_{V(t)}+GS_{A(t)}$$
$$+GS_{L(t)}+GS_{m(t)}+GS_{H(t)})+GS_{c(t)}+F_{(t)}^{G}]+(I_{L(t)}+I_{IS(t)}+I_{m(t)}$$
$$+I_{CS(t)}+I_{H(t)})+(e_{A(t)}+e_{L(t)}+e_{IS(t)}+e_{m(t)}+e_{s(t)})-m_{(t)}$$
$$+F_{(t)}^{nr}-BRW_{(t)}-GD; \tag{B.4}$$
$$\hat{P}_{(t)}+ = \hat{N}_{(t)}+\hat{M}_{(t-1)}. \tag{B.5}$$

Target variables

E = total employment (thousands)

GRP = Gross Regional Product (millions of dollars)

M_t = balance of migrations during (t) (thousands)

q_e = index of educational standards

q_v = index of health standards

q_H = index of housing standards

$\bar{y}_{DP}$ = per capita disposable income (dollars)

$\bar{y}_A$ = per capita disposable income in agriculture (dollars)

Intermediate variables

K_{IS} = total capital invested in iron and steel industry (millions of dollars)

X_{IS} = value added in iron and steel industry (millions of dollars)

Q_{IS} = value of shipments in iron and steel industry (millions of dollars)

e_{IS} = exports of iron and steel industry (millions of dollars)

E_1 = employment in agriculture, forestry, and fisheries (thousands)

E_4 = employment in commercial services (thousands)

E_5 = government employment, including military (thousands)

I_m = investments in manufacturing (millions of dollars)

K_m = total capital invested in manufacturing (millions of dollars)

e_m = exports of manufactured products (millions of dollars)

X_m = value added by manufacturing (millions of dollars)

E_3 = employment in manufacturing (thousands)

X_{CS} = value added in commercial services (millions of dollars)

X_G = value added in government services (millions of dollars)

I_{CS} = investments in commercial services (millions of dollars)

I_H = investments in housing (millions of dollars)

I = total investments (millions of dollars)

W = total wage income (millions of dollars)

F_a = net income of farm operators (millions of dollars)

F_m = net income of unincorporated manufacturing (millions of dollars)

F_s = net income of unincorporated service enterprises (millions of dollars)

i_p = interest, dividends, and rental income of persons (millions of dollars)

SIP = employers' and employees' contributions to social insurance (millions of dollars)

MPA = payments to military personnel resident in Nova Scotia (millions of dollars)

Y_p = total personal income (millions of dollars)

t_r = average rate of direct personal taxes

T = total personal income taxes (millions of dollars)

Y_{DP} = total personal disposable income (millions of dollars)

Y_E = total personal expenditures (millions of dollars)

C_1 = consumption of goods by households (millions of dollars)

C_4 = consumption of services and travel expenditures by households (millions of dollars)

C_5 = rents and interest payments by households (millions of dollars)

S = personal net savings (millions of dollars)

T_c = corporate profit taxes (millions of dollars)

T_{IN} = total indirect taxes (millions of dollars)

GS_c = current government expenditures (millions of dollars)

e_L = exports of mining products (millions of dollars)

e_A = exports of agricultural, forestry, and fishing products (millions of dollars)

m = total imports (millions of dollars)

BRW = surplus or deficit on current account with the rest of the world (millions of dollars)

$\hat{N}$ = column vector, the elements of which are various age-sex population cohorts, excluding migrations (thousands)

L = potential labour force (thousands)

D^L = unsatisfied demand for labour, or labour surplus (thousands)

$\hat{M}$ = column vector, the elements of which are net migrations in each age-sex cohort (thousands)

$\hat{P}$ = column vector, the elements of which are various age-sex population cohorts (thousands)

P = total population (thousands)

Instrument variables

DF_s = payments to military personnel (millions of dollars)

GS_H = government subsidies and investments in housing and commercial services (millions of dollars)

GI_G = direct general government investments in transportation, communication, power, and technical facilities, etc. (millions of dollars)

GI_{ED} = direct government investments in education and training (millions of dollars)

GI_V = direct government investments in health, welfare, and administration (millions of dollars)

GS_A = government subsidies and investments in agriculture, forestry, and fisheries (millions of dollars)

GS_m = government subsidies and investments in manufacturing (millions of dollars)

GD = aggregate surplus or deficit of all governments relating to Nova Scotia income and product transactions (millions of dollars)

Data variables

I_{IS} = investments in iron and steel (millions of dollars)

FZ = number of commercial farms as a proportion of all farms

P_u = total urban population (thousands)

t = time

GNP = Canadian Gross National Product (billions of dollars)

$\bar{p}_m^C$ = price index of manufactured goods in Canada (1949 = 100)

$\bar{p}_m^{NS}$ = price index of manufactured goods in Nova Scotia (1949 = 100)

SZ = index of average size of plant

E_2 = employment in mining (thousands)

E_6 = employment in iron and steel (thousands)

$\bar{w}_G^{NS}$ = average yearly wage-income of government employees (dollars)

X_A = value added in agriculture, forestry, and fisheries (millions of dollars)

X_L = value added by mining (millions of dollars)

i = rate of interest on loans

I_L = investments in mining (millions of dollars)

$\bar{p}^{NS}$ = consumer price index for Nova Scotia (1949 = 100)

A_L = amount of cultivated land (thousands of acres)

NH = number of housing units constructed after 1920

F^G = Federal and Provincial Government transfer payments to households (millions of dollars)

F^{nr} = transfer payments from non-residents to households (millions of dollars)

T^C = total direct personal taxes in Canada (billions of dollars)

Y_p^C = total personal income in Canada (billions of dollars)

T_s = estate and miscellaneous personal taxes (millions of dollars)

GS_L = government subsidies and investments in mining (millions of dollars)

F_B = number of fishing boats

C_{rp} = retained corporate earnings (millions of dollars)

D_p = capital consumption allowances (millions of dollars)

REA = unpaid corporate profits other than C_{rp}, federal government investment income, subsidies not accounted for elsewhere, and residual statistical discrepancy (millions of dollars)

e_s = exports of services (millions of dollars)

$GI_{G(t-4)}$ = direct government investments in general facilities with a lag of four years (millions of dollars)

$GS_{m(t-4)}$ = government subsidies and investments in manufacturing with a lag of four years (millions of dollars)

$U_{E3(t-4)}$ = index of relative accessibility with respect to manufacturing employment with a lag of four years

$U_{Y(t-4)}$ = index of relative accessibility with respect to total personal income with a lag of four years

$H_{H(t-4)}$ = tonnage handled in Halifax harbour with a lag of four years (thousands)

$H_{(t-1)}$ = number of households in the previous period (thousands)

$\sum_{t=-1}^{-4} GS_{A(t)}$ = government subsidies and investments in agriculture, forestry, and fisheries cumulated over four years (millions of dollars)

Lagged endogeneous variables

$K_{IS(t-1)}$ = total capital invested in iron and steel in the previous period (millions of dollars)

$K_{m(t-1)}$ = total capital invested in manufacturing in the previous period (millions of dollars)

$GRP_{(t-1)}$ = Gross Regional Product in the previous period (millions of dollars)

$\hat{P}_{(t-1)}$ = column vector whose elements are population in the previous period in different age-sex cohorts (thousands)

$D_{(t-1)}^l$ = unsatisfied demand for labour or real unemployment in the previous period (thousands)

$\hat{M}_{(t-1)}$ = column vector whose elements give net migrations in each age-sex cohort in the previous period (thousands)

Predetermined parameters

$\tilde{\lambda}$ = square matrix of order equal to the number of age-sex cohorts. The elements of the matrix are probabilities of survival of individuals from different age-sex cohorts, and age specific birth rates. The form of the matrix is

$$
\begin{array}{cccccccccccc}
0 & 0 & \cdot & \cdot & \cdot & 0 & b_1^M & 0 & b_2^M & \cdot & \cdot & 0 \\
0 & 0 & & & & & b_1^F & 0 & b_2^F & & & \\
d_1^M & 0 & 0 & \cdot & \cdot & \cdot & \cdot & \cdot & \cdot & \cdot & \cdot & 0 \\
0 & d_1^F & 0 & 0 & \cdot & \cdot & \cdot & \cdot & \cdot & \cdot & \cdot & 0 \\
0 & 0 & d_2^M & 0 & 0 & & & & & & & \\
0 & 0 & 0 & d_2^F & 0 & 0 & \cdot & \cdot & \cdot & \cdot & \cdot & 0 \\
\cdot & \cdot & \cdot & \cdot & \cdot & \cdot & \cdot & \cdot & \cdot & \cdot & \cdot & 0 \\
\cdot & \cdot & \cdot & \cdot & \cdot & \cdot & \cdot & \cdot & \cdot & \cdot & \cdot & 0 \\
\cdot & \cdot & \cdot & \cdot & \cdot & \cdot & \cdot & \cdot & \cdot & \cdot & \cdot & 0 \\
0 & \cdot & \cdot & \cdot & \cdot & \cdot & \cdot & \cdot & \cdot & \cdot & \cdot & \cdot \\
\end{array}
$$

d_i = the probability that an individual selected at random from the ith age-sex group will survive another unit of time

b_i = age specific fertility rate in the ith child-bearing age group

$\overline{R}$ = row vector, the elements of which are the labour force participation rates of different age-sex cohorts in Canada

h = structural unemployment rate

$\hat{\pi}$ = a column vector whose elements are the percentage of total migrations in each age-sex cohort

$\overline{\delta}$ = unit row vector

η = share of agricultural employees in total wage bill

α = share of government transfers going to agricultural population

β = share of transfers from non-residents going to agricultural population[4]

---

[4] In the final version of the model four of the predetermined parameters, namely h, η, α, and β change slightly from year to year. As they do not appear in any regression equation their classification has been left unchanged.

BASIC PROPERTIES

The model may be described as relatively open. Although the number of exogenous variables is substantially smaller than the number of endogenous variables, the ratio of unlagged predetermined variables to endogenous variables is not so small as to make the model unstable[5]. This relative stability of the model, however, is bought at a price, because it makes more difficult the use of the model for purposes of forecasting or exploring the implications of alternative courses of action. Each time the model is used, the future values of all exogenous variables have to be estimated outside of the model.

Another feature of the model is that it contains relatively few lagged variables. This is often the case in one-year models. There are not many economic relationships which occur with a lag of one year's duration. More importantly, lagged relationships lead to a loss of additional degrees of freedom, and this has to be avoided in view of the limited number of observations available.

Among the twenty-nine data variables, five relate to the national economy. While this is not much, it definitely ties the model to developments in the national economy.

The model represents a consistent structure in the sense that each equation in the model has at least one variable which appears in at least one other equation of the model.

The thirty-one structural equations of which the model is comprised are linear in parameters. Two of them describe exponential relationships and are introduced in logarithmic form. In five of the eighteen definitional equations the explanatory variables appear in multiplicative form or as quotients.

The model is balanced at the level of the whole economy only. Balance equations for individual sectors could not be derived, mainly because profits accruing to business could not be apportioned by sector. The significant exceptions are households, for which personal disposable income balances personal expenditures, and governments. The balance of receipts and expenditures has been established, however, for all levels of government combined.

The total performance of the regional economy, or GRP, has been calculated in three ways: as the sum of value added in all sectors of the economy; as the sum of incomes or claims against the product accruing to factors of production, and as the sum of components of product by type of use to which put.

An important feature of the model of Nova Scotia is that it is recursive.

---

[5] It is fairly obvious that a model with a high number of endogenous variables relative to the number of exogenous variables will be generally more sensitive to changes in the values of the exogenous variables. The term *stability* as used here is not to be confused with its use in connection with economic equilibrium.

This refers to the fact that during each time period causal connections run in one direction only. More formally, in a strictly recursive system the following two conditions hold (Malinvaud, 1966):

(a) The matrix of endogenous variables is triangular or

$$Y_{ij} = 0 \text{ for all } j > i,$$

and (b) the co-variance matrix of residuals is diagonal or, in other words,

$$E(\epsilon_{it}\epsilon_{jt}) = 0 \text{ for all } j \neq i.$$

With these two constraints satisfied, each structural equation can be considered as representing the causal determination of the ith endogenous variable. Consequently, a multiple regression of the dependent variable on all other variables occurring in the same structural equation provides a consistent estimator of this equation[6]. In each equation all endogenous variables except one have been determined before and hence can be treated exactly in the same way as predetermined variables. This enables one to estimate the model by using nothing more sophisticated than ordinary least squares or the auto-regressive Cochrane–Orcutt model.

The regional model of Nova Scotia is diagonally recursive (Goldberger, 1964). Not only is the matrix of endogenous variables triangular but all dependent variables are on the main diagonal. Furthermore, the balance equations also have each one variable on the main diagonal. In effect they are definitions establishing the value of one of their variables without imposing additional constraints upon the system.

The reason why the model had to be developed as a recursive and not interdependent system—even at the risk of over-simplifying some of the relationships or violating some preconceived notions concerning the behaviour of the economy—lies with the data. The model has been estimated on the basis of time series data covering the period of fifteen to sixteen years. Hence, estimating the model, even on an equation by equation basis, leaves very few degrees of freedom and introduces some awkward small sample problems. With an interdependent system one would have to resort, however, to simultaneous estimating procedures such as two-stage least squares or limited information maximum likelihood methods. The number of variables involved even in a small interdependent sub-system, would easily exhaust the available degrees of freedom. There could never be any question, of course, of estimating the whole system simultaneously, as it contains many more variables than observations. It appears that this limitation may apply to all regional models which have to be estimated on the basis of time series data.

---

[6] This has been abundantly proven by Malinvaud (1966), while Fox (1958) has shown, that in a fully identified system under certain rather stringent restrictions, ordinary least squares applied to the reduced equations yield virtually identical results with those obtained by indirect least squares.

The synoptic chart given by Table 2 illustrates the main features of the model.

A less obvious condition which the model satisfies is that of identification. The idea of identifiability refers to the issue of whether or not the model is sufficiently restrictive, so that when confronted with data just one hypothesis is consistent with both model and data. In short, in a fully identified system there should be a one to one correspondence between the structural and reduced form coefficients. This is an important problem and in a very real sense has to be examined prior to statistical estimation (Klein, 1953; Malinvaud, 1966; Goldberger, 1964; Tintner, 1952; Johnston, 1963).

Sectoral analysis

In its final version the model can be decomposed neatly into seven sub-models, namely:
1. Iron and Steel Industry
2. Manufacturing and Employment
3. Output and Investments
4. Households
5. Governments and Trade Deficit
6. Population and Migrations
7. Welfare.

With only seven sectors the structure of the regional economy is presented in a rather aggregate way. A fair amount of disaggregation will probably be required at later stages in order to make the results obtainable with help of the model more sharply focussed and hence more useful for policy purposes.

Three of the seven sectors, namely, iron and steel industry, manufacturing and employment, and output and investments, deal in a broad sense with the productivity and efficiency of the Nova Scotia economy. Three others, namely, households, governments and trade deficit, and welfare, are concerned mainly with consumption, welfare, and the means of satisfying and raising their levels. Finally, the sub-model dealing with population and migrations summarizes, in a way, the outcome of the operation of the other sectors in terms of migrations and population changes.

The seven sub-sectors differ from each other in degree of simplicity, in the number of equations, and in the ratio between statistical and accounting equations. Some of the sub-models, like the welfare one, are internally simple and straightforward. Others, for example the manufacturing and employment sub-model, are quite involved to the extent that they are made of two sub-systems, one embedded in the other. Still others, like population and migrations, are computationally very complex.

An examination of some of the seven sectors into which the regional economy has been disaggregated, and of their economic underpinnings, is

Table 2. Synthesis of variables and equations.

Legend:

- O — Target variables
- S — Structural equations
- B — Balance equations
- D — Definitional equations

Column groups:

- Endogenous variables intermediate and target (columns 1–54)
- Instrument variables (columns 1–8)
- Data variables — Unlagged (columns 1–29), Lagged (columns 30–36)
- Lagged endogenous variables (columns 1–6)

Row groups (left margin categories and equation labels):

Iron and steel	D1, S1, S2, S3
Manufacturing and employment	S4, S5, S6, S7, D2, S8, S9, S10, B1
Output and investments	S11, D3, D4, S12, S13, D5, S14, S15, S16, S17, S18, S19
Households	D6, D7, D8, S20, D9, B2, S21, S22, S23, D10, S24, S25, B3, S26, S27, S28, B4
Governments and trade deficit	(continued B3, S26, S27, S28, B4)
Population and migration	D11, D12, D13, S29, D14, B5, D15
Welfare	S30, S31, D16, D17, D18

(The body of the table is a large sparse incidence matrix mapping the above equations against endogenous, instrument, data, and lagged endogenous variable columns. Individual cell entries include variable symbols such as K_{IS}, X_{IS}, Q_{IS}, e_{IS}, E_1, E_4, E_5, I_m, K_m, e_m, X_m, E_3, E, X_{CS}, X_G, GRP, I_{CS}, I_H, I, W, F_e, F_m, F_s, ip, SIP, MPA, Y_p, tr, T, Y_{DP}, Y_E, C_1, C_4, C_5, S, T_c, T_{IN}, GS_c, e_L, e_A, m, BRW, $\bar N$, L, D^L, M, $\bar M$, P, q_E, q_V, q_H, Y_A, and corresponding data/instrument/lagged variables.)

extremely fruitful in revealing their internal structure and the problems which regional models are facing. It also brings into sharper focus the analytical properties of the Model.

The *Iron and Steel Industry* sub-model is comprised of three equations (S.1), (S.2), and (S.3), and one identity (D.1). Several features of this sub-model reflect problems typically encountered in regional analysis.

The production function is extremely simple and describes value–added as a function of capital invested only. This is due to the fact that the extent of employment in the iron and steel plant at Sydney is largely the outcome of political considerations and of government policy and does not necessarily follow fluctuations in output. Several variants of production equation (S.1) were tested but no significant relationship over time between output and employment was found to exist.

The sub-model concentrates on the supply side without trying to establish separately the sector's supply and demand schedules and the resulting balance. This follows from the fact that Nova Scotia production forms only a small part of total Canadian output and does not influence appreciably price formation at the National level, which is clearly outside of the system.

On the other hand, only a relatively small proportion of the total output of the Sydney plant is consumed within the province. A corollary of this approach is that exports are treated as a function of output only; Table 3 illustrates the resulting system.

Table 3.

Equation number	Endogenous variables		Predetermined variables	
(D.1)	K_{IS}		$K_{IS(t-1)}, I_{IS}$	Capital formation
(S.1)	K_{IS}	X_{IS}		Production
(S.2)		X_{IS} Q_{IS}		Output
(S.3)		Q_{IS} e_{IS}		Exports

The causal chain of this sub-model, in its final version, is illustrated in Figure 1.

Actually a demand equation of the following form was also tried:

$$Q^D_{IS(t)} = 13 \cdot 316 \; + \; 1 \cdot 1886 \, GNP_{(t)}; \qquad R^2 = 0 \cdot 7507$$
$$(2 \cdot 4471) \quad (6 \cdot 336) \qquad\qquad d \; = 1 \cdot 8026$$

$$Q^D_{IS(t)} = Q^S_{IS(t)} \, .$$

The system including these two equations would, however, be clearly overdetermined, as is illustrated in Table 4.

The sub-model would comprise, in this alternative version, five endogenous variables and six equations. The reason why the more conventional approach fails in this case is that, in contrast to National models,
it is impossible to treat prices as endogenous variables.

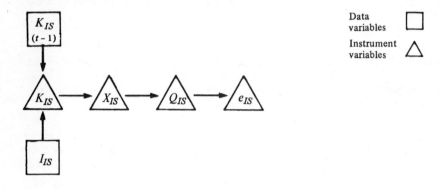

Figure 1.

Table 4.

Equation number	Endogenous variables		Predetermined variables	
(D.1)	K_{IS}		$K_{IS(t-1)}, I_{IS}$	Capital formation
(S.1)	K_{IS} X_{IS}			Production
(S.2)	X_{IS} Q^S_{IS}			Output
		Q^D_{IS}	GNP	Demand
(S.3)		Q^D_{IS} e_{IS}		Exports
		Q^S_{IS} Q^D_{IS}		Balance

The *Manufacturing and Employment* sub-model is comprised of seven
equations and two identities (D.2), (B.1). It deals with two closely related
problems: total employment in the regional economy, and developments
in the manufacturing sector (excluding primary iron and steel production).

Of the six basic components of employment in the regional economy,
two, namely employment in mining (mainly coal mining) and in the
primary iron and steel industry, are largely determined by political and
not by economic considerations. Consequently, their determination
lies outside of the system and they have been treated throughout as data
variables.

Employment in agriculture, forestry and fisheries; commercial services; and in government, including military personnel, depends to a certain extent at least, upon developments in the Nova Scotia economy and has been dealt with in Equations (S.4), (S.5), and (S.6). Yet these sectors have been treated in the model in a partial way only. Their full development was beyond the scope of the present study.

Employment in agriculture, forestry, and fishing has been explained as a function of commercial farming. In view of the heterogenous nature of this sector the explanatory and predictive power of the relation is open to doubt.

Employment in commercial services has been explained as a function of the degree of urbanization. This seems plausible because urban populations usually require a higher degree and greater concentration of commercial services than dispersed rural ones.

Employment in governments has been explained as a function of military expenditures. Military employment is, of course, the most flexible component of total employment in this sector and hence it proved to be statistically the most significant one. The equation contains also time as a shift parameter. The coefficient associated with time has a negative sign but is not very large.

With respect to manufacturing, the general paucity and low quality of data precluded the successful estimation of a production function of a conventional type. Equations (S.9) and (S.10) explain value added as a function of capital and of average size of plant.

The determination of capital invested in manufacturing hinged upon a successful estimation of an investment function. Investment in manufacturing has been explained in Equation (S.7) as a function of government investments in elements of infra-structure such as power plants, transportation facilities, and industrial estates, and of an accessibility index defined with the help of principal components. This last variable refers to changes in accessibility to centres of manufacturing activity in Canada (of importance to producers of intermediate goods), to accessibility to population centres (represented by aggregate personal income), and to the tonnage handled in Halifax harbour. Both explanatory variables were taken with a four-year lag, the length of which appears reasonable in view of the nature of the phenomenon involving location decisions by entrepreneurs. This is undoubtedly an interesting relationship but, unfortunately, owing to the short time series available, the number of degrees of freedom left is too small to feel quite comfortable about the explanatory or predictive power of this equation.

Finally, exports of manufactured products have been explained, in Equation (S.8), in terms of demand in the rest of the country, measured by GRP, and of the competitive ability of the Nova Scotia manufacturing production, represented by the difference in price levels for manufactured products in Canada and Nova Scotia. This relationship is statistically significant. Attempts to determine this relationship from the supply side did not yield satisfactory results, mainly it appears because of the relatively short time series on which the equation was estimated.

The causal chain of this sub-model is illustrated in Figure 2.

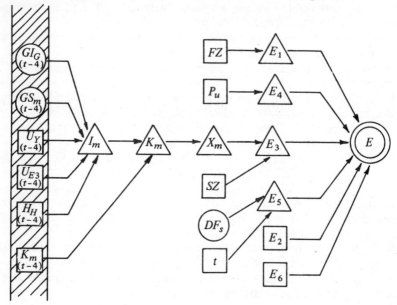

Figure 2. Manufacturing and employment.

(The system covering both the supply and the demand side and balanced at the level of exports is interdependent. It includes the following relationships:

$$e_{m(t)} = \underset{(2\cdot9136)}{26\cdot185} + \underset{(3\cdot1268)}{1\cdot2436 GNP_{(t)}} + \underset{(2\cdot3635)}{6\cdot6720(\bar{p}_m^C - \bar{p}_m^{NS})};$$

$$\begin{aligned} R^2 &= 0\cdot3932 \qquad\text{(S.8)}\\ d &= 1\cdot9141 \end{aligned}$$

$$X_m = \underset{}{-232\cdot805} + \underset{(2\cdot4572)}{5\cdot6234 E_{3(t)}} + \underset{(10\cdot0724)}{0\cdot4338 K_{m(t)}}; \qquad R^2 = 0\cdot9456$$

$$E_3 = \underset{(2\cdot5331)}{0\cdot0783 X_m} - \underset{(-2\cdot5018)}{0\cdot0384 K_m} + \underset{(19\cdot7267)}{0\cdot4441 SZ}; \qquad \begin{aligned} R^2 &= 0\cdot3745\\ d &= 1\cdot9939 \end{aligned}$$

$$X_{m(t)} = \underset{(126\cdot4873)}{0\cdot4126 Q_{m(t)}}; \qquad \begin{aligned} R^2 &= 0\cdot9729\\ d &= 1\cdot4042 \end{aligned}$$

$$e_{m(t)} = \underset{(20\cdot1460)}{0\cdot1319 Q_{m(t)}}; \qquad \begin{aligned} R^2 &= 0\cdot2604\\ d &= 0\cdot8015 \end{aligned}$$

Notice that there are here five equations and five endogenous variables. However, it is impossible to obtain a triangular matrix of endogenous variables. Hence, ordinary least squares is not applicable.)

The *Output and Investments* sub-model comprises three Equations (S.11), (S.12) (S.13), and three identities (D.4), (D.3), (D.5).

The first identity (D.4) defines *GRP* as the sum of value added in the six sectors with which the model is dealing. Value added in agriculture, forestry and fisheries, and in mining are treated throughout the model as data variables. Because of the complex nature of these primary sectors, no attempt has been made in the model to develop a comprehensive predictive system of their behaviour.

Value added in commercial services is explained as a function of employment in this sector, while value added in government is defined as the product of employment in the government sector explained in the sub-model dealing with manufacturing and employment and of average wages of government employees in Nova Scotia.

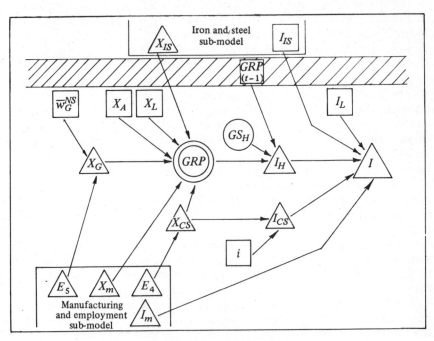

Figure 3. Output and investments.

Total investments in Nova Scotia are composed of investments in mining; in iron and steel; in manufacturing; in commercial services, and in housing. Investments in mining and in the iron and steel industries are treated as data variables because they are determined largely by political and not economic considerations, and thus fall outside the system. Investments in manufacturing have already been explained in the sub-model dealing with manufacturing and employment.

The remaining two components, namely investments in commercial services and in housing, are dealt with in Equations (S.12) and (S.13).

An interesting feature of the latter equation is the heavy dependence of investments in housing upon government investments and upon subsidies to housing construction.

The sub-model introduces six new endogenous variables, which did not appear previously, and six equations. The need to avoid simultaneous estimation methods resulted in some of the equations being somewhat oversimplified.

The causal chain in this sub-system, as illustrated in Figure 3, clearly shows the links with the iron and steel, and manufacturing and employment sub-models discussed above.

The *Households* sub-model is comprised of ten equations (S.14) to (S.23), and six identities, (D.6) to (D.10) and (B.2), and consists really of three parts. The first part, comprising a definition of total personal income, explains the components of income as a function of other variables. The second part defines direct personal taxes as a function of other variables and derives total disposable personal income as the difference between total personal income and total personal direct taxes. The third part starts with an identity between total personal disposable income and total personal expenditures and explains, by means of structural equations, various components of personal consumption in terms of exogenous variables. Out of this part, personal savings are derived as a difference between total personal expenditures and consumption in (D.10).

Total wage income is explained as a function of the level of operation of the local economy and of the price level. This appears reasonable because the price level is obviously an element in the establishment of the wage rate.

Net income of farm operators replaces a fully developed agricultural sector. This sector is, in fact, quite involved but is reduced in the Model to three equations which explain (a) net income of farm operators, (b) employment in agriculture, and (c) agricultural exports.

The net income of farm operators is explained in terms of the amount of cultivated land and of the number of commercial farms. In view of the fact that in Nova Scotia subsistence farming is extensive, this last variable was expected to affect the operation of the sector.

Interest, dividends, and rental income of persons is explained as a function of the existing number of relatively new housing units. Again this appears intuitively reasonable because in Nova Scotia rental income dominates other components of this variable almost to the point of exclusion. In order to arrive at net wage income accruing to households, employers' and employees' social insurance and government pension plans contributions have to be deducted. That their level is a function of total wages is shown in Equation (S.19).

In order to arrive at personal disposable income it is necessary to consider direct personal taxes. Their main component is personal income taxes. Other personal direct taxes, like succession duties, are less important and are treated as a data variable.

The equation explaining total personal income taxes is treated as a behavioural and not a technical relationship. The tax rates have been derived as a ratio of Canadian personal direct taxes to personal income and treated as a separate variable. In this equation tax rate and total personal income are the two explanatory variables.

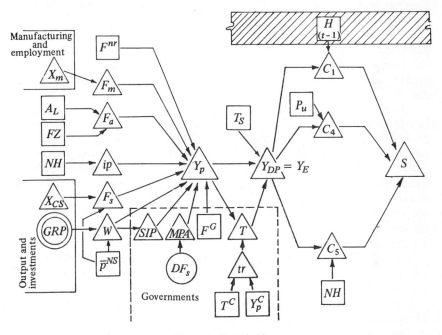

Figure 4. Households.

Turning next to the expenditures side, the three main components of household consumption are considered, namely consumption of goods, consumption of services, and rents and interest payments. The explanation of all three is straightforward.

Consumption of goods is explained as a function of total personal disposable income and of the number of households. There is surprisingly little multicollinearity between the two independent variables appearing in this equation.

Consumption of services has been derived as a function of total personal income and of the degree of urbanization of Nova Scotia. This seems quite reasonable because urban households usually spend a higher proportion of their income on services.

Finally, rents and interest payments by households have been related to personal disposable income and to the number of relatively new housing units.

The causal chain of this sub-model is illustrated in Figure 4. Despite the large number of variables involved, this chain shows a single uninterrupted flow.

The *Governments and Trade Deficit* sub-model is comprised of five equations (S.24) to (S.28) and two identities (B.3) and (B.4), and consists of two inter-connected parts, the first dealing with total government receipts and expenditures, and the second defining the external balance of the region with the rest of the world on transactions pertaining to income and product, embedded in an overall balance of the regional economy. The connecting link between the two parts of the model lies in that a large share of the substantial foreign trade deficit is covered by local expenditure of, and unilateral transfers from, the federal government.

An examination of the first part of the sub-model covering identity (B.3) and Equations (S.24) and (S.25) reveals that the overall government deficit (GD) is treated in the model as an instrument variable, whereas current government spending (GS_c) is introduced as endogenous to the system and defined as an intermediate variable. The two are clearly interdependent but it appears that in Nova Scotia the important components of current government expenditures cannot be changed at will by the federal or provincial governments. At the present stage of work on the model no real attempt has been made to explain statistically the behaviour of this variable.

Turning now to the structural equations, corporate profit taxes are explained by reference to the level of operation of the regional economy as represented by gross regional product.

Indirect taxes are satisfactorily explained as a function of total personal expenditures. This is what one would expect in view of the fact that sales taxes are the most important component of total indirect taxes. This relationship is statistically highly significant.

The causal chain in this part of the sub-model is shown in Figure 5.

In the case of the foreign trade of the region let us first examine the various components of total exports. Exports of services, (e_s), do not behave consistently and are treated as an exogenous variable. The necessity of remaining within the constraints of a diagonally recursive system requires that these variables be introduced before concluding the discussion of the regional economy with an overall balance (B.4).

Exports of mining products (e_L) consist mainly of coal and are the only endogenous variable left of the mining sub-model, which at an earlier stage comprised four equations. Investments in mining, employment, and value added, are treated in the final version as exogenous variables to be determined outside of the model.

The export equation is of the demand type, relating exports, (e_L) to *GNP*. Statistically it may be considered satisfactory, yet not too much faith can be placed in it in view of the fact that it has been derived on the basis of a small sample. Violent shifts might be expected in this sector of the Nova Scotia economy, which is both contracting and changing in character.

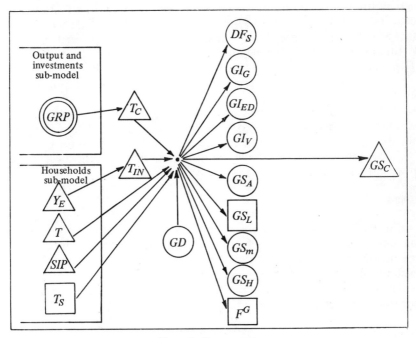

Figure 5. Governments.

The operation of coal mining, while now by far the most significant component of the mining sector in Nova Scotia, is only partly based on considerations of profitability. By and large, mining in Nova Scotia is a declining industry and the outputs and employment therein are governed by governmental subsidies rather than by the more familiar economic laws, which can be incorporated into the traditional production functions. Yet attempts to explore the impact of governmental regulations in the mining sector proved futile. As a result, time series on employment and value of output are not significantly correlated. Similarly, changes in capital invested in this sector stand in no relation to output, because the sector has been notoriously underinvested for a very long period of time.

Exports of agricultural products (e_A) have been explained as a function of the number of fishing boats and of the sum of government subsidies to, and investment in, agriculture, cumulated over a period of four years. This equation is statistically satisfactory but it is based on a small sample. More fundamental doubts as to its validity are raised by the fact that this sector covers several very heterogenous activities, namely subsistence agriculture, commercial farming, fishing, and forestry. Are we then to believe that the number of fishing boats is the main variable affecting its exports? The second variable refers to government subsidies to, and investments in, agriculture but these do not have as their main objective the fostering of exports. Besides, they were cumulated over a period of four years, a fact which reduced dangerously the number of degrees of freedom[7].

Imports have been explained quite satisfactorily in Equation (S.28). Their level was found to be a function of four types of demand:

1. consumption of final goods by private households represented by Y_E;

2. consumption of intermediate products by regional industries, itself a function of the level of operation of the main sectors of the provincial economy, namely mining, iron and steel, and other manufacturing;

3. consumption of investment goods fluctuating with the level of investments (I); and

4. requirements of the military establishment, represented by an index based on military pay and allowances in Nova Scotia (DF_s).

The *Population and Migrations* sub-model consists of one equation and six identities. At variance with the other sub-models, however, most of the relationships are expressed in compact matrix notation and hence each of them represents really a system of equations.

The following definitional equations represent a succinct statement of the sub-model, which is a closed system by itself:

$$\hat{N}_{(t)} = \tilde{\lambda} \hat{P}_{(t-1)}.$$

Population existing in the previous period is aged by the application of the survivorship matrix to yield population which would be obtained by natural increase. The survivorship matrix ($\tilde{\lambda}$) is a square matrix of order equal to the number of age-sex cohorts. The non-zero elements are on the sub-sub diagonal and in the first, second, and last two rows. The elements on the sub-sub diagonal and in the last two rows refer to probabilities of survival of an individual picked at random from the ith age-sex group to survive another year. The entries in the first two rows

---

[7] Ideally this sector should be split up into three or four separate ones. In each, the main factors affecting supply and demand should be introduced explicitly. The existing data basis would allow one to engage in a more detailed research, but, it was felt that this represents a major study all by itself outside the scope of the model here described. As it is, the sector is represented by three equations only.

Besides exports, employment has been explained in the sub-model dealing with manufacturing and employment (S.4) and income of farm operators has been dealt with among the relationships governing the components of personal income and consumption (S.15).

represent age specific fertility rates in the ith child-bearing age group.

$$L_{(t)} = \overline{R}\hat{N}_{(t)}.$$

Labour force at time t is the product of a row vector whose elements are the potential labour force participation rates in each age-sex cohort, and a column vector whose elements represent the size of each age-sex cohort obtained by natural increase.

The elements of $\overline{R}$ are typical labour force participation rates of each age-sex cohort. Average Canadian rather than Nova Scotia labour force participation rates were used because, in a declining region, labour force participation rates typically tend to be low. This is due at least partly to social customs prevailing in the more traditional rural parts of the province where women, as a rule, tend to stay at home. More importantly, however, in areas with high unemployment people do not register with labour exchanges and hence are not counted as members of the labour force. This lack of interest in registration is a direct outcome of the low probability of obtaining a job through the labour exchange.

$$D_{(t)}^{L} = E_{(t)} - (1-h)L_{(t)}.$$

Unsatisfied demand for labour (or labour surplus) equals the difference between total employment and potential labour force, taking into consideration the structural unemployment rate (h). By definition, employment is here taken to be equal to the total demand for labour.

$$M_{(t)} = -3 \cdot 007 + 0 \cdot 3718 D_{(t-1)}^{L}; \qquad R^2 = 0 \cdot 3687$$
$$(2 \cdot 5349)$$

Migrations are a function of unsatisfied demand for labour or of labour surplus (unemployment) in the previous period.

From a theoretical point of view, in addition to employment opportunities, relative wage levels or the relative level of earnings in the region should be a significant variable. Both propositions were explored as a ratio of average wages in Nova Scotia to average wages in Central Canada; as a difference between these two wage levels, and as differences between disposable incomes per capita but without yielding any statistically significant results.

$$\hat{M}_{(t)} = \hat{\pi}M_{(t)}.$$

The column vector of migrations, whose elements are the number of migrants in each age-sex cohort, is the product of a column vector, whose elements are typical relative shares of each age-sex cohort in migrating populations, and of a scalar representing the total balance of migrations at time t.

$$\hat{P}_{(t)} = \hat{N}_{(t)} + \hat{M}_{(t-1)}.$$

Population of each age-sex cohort equals the sum of population resulting

from natural increase in each age-sex cohort and the net balance of migrations (in each cohort) in the previous period.

$$P_{(t)} = \overline{\delta} \dot{P}_{(t)} \, .$$

Population at time t is the product of a unit row vector (whose elements
are all unity) and of a column vector whose elements are the population
in each age-sex cohort.

The whole sub-model is illustrated in Figure 6, and notice that there
are two loops involving migrations.

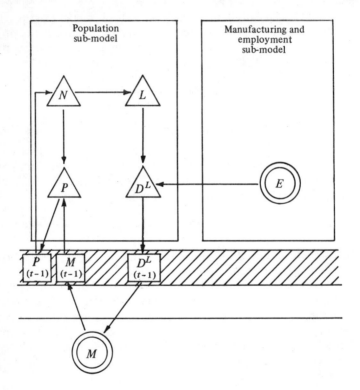

Figure 6. Population and migrations.

The major input into the model is total employment which is derived
from the manufacturing and employment sub-model. The two major
outputs of the model are migrations and the total population. Migrations
is one of the target variables because the desire to regulate migrations or
rather check out-migrations is a major policy objective of the provincial
government. This is understandable because of its welfare significance and
of the hardships involved in out-migrations of unskilled labour. Equally

important are the detrimental effects of out-migration upon the composition of the remaining population and labour force owing to the highly selective course which this process takes. During the period covered by the data, especially during the last few years, migrations have been growing steadily in line with the growing discrepancy between the potentially available labour force and actual demand for labour.

The *Welfare* sub-model consists of two equations (S.30), (S.31) and three identities (D.16) to (D.18).

The structure of this sub-model is extremely simple. Two of the indices, namely the index of educational standards and the index of health standards, are described simply as a functon of direct government investments in these two sectors. This over-simplifies the complex problem, but owing to the paucity of data it was impossible to probe deeper into the underlying phenomena.

The other index which has immediate welfare significance, namely the index of housing standards, is simply defined as a ratio of relatively new housing to total population.

All three indices are, admittedly, rather poorly defined and are determined by the model in a way hardly justifying their use for forecasting purposes. Yet per capita disposable income is, by itself, an insufficient indicator of the province's progress and hence an inadequate target variable. In fact, living standards are increasingly measured not only by the size of the per capita disposable income but also by the volume of intangible goods supplied to the inhabitants. Hence, this sub-model represents an admittedly crude attempt at measuring some of these values.

Quality of data and estimating procedures

One of the more important aspects of constructing a model is the confrontation of the various hypotheses embodied in it with actual data. In a very real sense a model, no matter how careful the construction of the various structural relationships, nor how elaborate and sophisticated the estimating techniques, cannot be better than the data basis upon which it is built.

Considerable difficulties exist in this respect at the regional level not encountered or no longer existing with national models. Many types of data, particularly those relating to interregional flows, are not collected at the sub-national level. In some cases the conceptual basis for many flows is lacking or controversial.

Furthermore, not only are published data for the Canadian Provinces far less abundant but they do not go back beyond 1951–1952, and many series end in 1963. With very few exceptions the Dominion Bureau of Statistics has so far released only preliminary data for later years.

Another source of considerable difficulties is the use of non-disclosure rules. For obvious reasons, these operate in a much more stringent manner in a small region than in the nation.

In view of the general paucity of and lack of reliability in data collected at the regional level, regional social accounts assume great importance. The discipline imposed by the double-entry system of social accounting goes a long way towards removing some of the inherent weaknesses of regional data, whilst helping in other places to fill in some remaining gaps.

Unfortunately, regional income and product accounts would have to be constructed according to a format designed to meet regional needs, and more particularly the needs of an econometric model.

There is another aspect of the data problem which may be worth mentioning here. Regional economic studies and regional models are concerned almost exclusively with long-run growth and consequently with breaks and shifts in regional structure. These structural breaks can hardly be derived and estimated on the basis of a study of past developments in the region considered. There is, for example, no way in which the future impact of a new industry can be estimated from the study of past developments in a region from which this particular industry was absent. Hence, interregional data or, generally speaking, cross-sectional data assume great importance. Such data are ordinarily not available. They could be derived only from a fairly uniform system of regional social accounting operating throughout the nation.

The above view stands in marked contrast to practices followed in the construction of national econometric models, where time series data are considered to be more relevant for analytical and forecasting purposes. However, national models dealing with business cycles are often based on quaterly or monthly data and consequently on fairly long series. Yearly time series data are often claimed to have a smaller variance than crosssection data, but this advantage is ordinarily more than compensated by the larger sample size of the latter.

Finally, at the regional level one is very often concerned with stock rather than with flow phenomena. Hence, wealth accounting and the quantitative evaluation of both tangible and intangible regional resources would be of fundamental importance for the construction of meaningful regional growth models. Again, such data do not exist, while the whole problem of wealth accounting, even at the national level, is still beset with many conceptual difficulties.

The lack of cross-section data and the shortness of time series available necessitates the use of simple estimating techniques and of simple equation forms. In the majority of cases the time series used in the present analysis were limited to fifteen years.

The data basis upon which the model described here has been estimated can be divided into several major categories:
1. data taken directly from published sources,
2. data derived indirectly by means of relatively simple techniques,
3. indices constructed by means of several techniques, and
4. data obtained from field surveys.

Data taken directly from published sources, supplemented by data derived by interpolation in order to maintain temporal consistency, represent approximately forty per cent of all data used. The major part of these data have been obtained from several Dominion Bureau of Statistics publications, such as *National Accounts, Income and Expenditure, Private and Public Investments in Canada, Vital Statistics*, and *Statistics on Employment and Unemployment*.

The second category, namely data derived indirectly, covers variables estimated as a ratio to a national total. In some cases fixed ratios were used while in others the ratio was extrapolated. In still other cases proxy allocators were used.

Data covering survival rates, fertility rates, age and sex structure of local and migrating populations derived from a study of vital statistics, and population studies also fall into this category. Data on foreign trade were obtained with the help of the technique based upon the modified location quotients approach (Czamanski, 1968).

The third category is comprised of indices which were computed from original data by using the technique of principal components. This category includes such variables as index of health standards (q_v) and index of regional attractiveness (Z_1). Other techniques applied in order to derive indices were accessibility studies, closely related to gravity and potential models.

The fourth and last category, namely data especially collected by means of field surveys, covers very few items. It is essentially limited to data pertaining to various components of government expenditures and investments in the province.

The multiple regression program used yielded the usual statistics of which the following were employed: (a) R^2, or, the coefficient of multiple determination; (b) t, or, Student's t. The t values are given in parentheses under each regression coefficient; (c) d, or, Durbin–Watson statistic.

In most cases where bias introduced by auto-correlation of residuals has been detected, it could be removed by the use of the auto-regressive model developed by Cochrane–Orcutt (Christ, 1966). The values of ρ, the coefficient of serial correlation of residuals, are given in all those cases in which the Cochrane–Orcutt model has been used.

Conclusions

Some interesting although still tentative conclusions can be derived from simulation experiments carried out on the above model. Their purpose is to test the model, its stability, and forecasting ability, rather than an analysis of the regional economy. Yet, interpretation of some of the results obtained underscores certain general features of regional econometric models.

Three types of simulation tests were performed on the model of Nova Scotia:
1. sensitivity analysis,
2. yearly solutions, and
3. forecasts.
The sensitivity analysis performed consisted of repeatedly solving the model for 1961, in each run increasing one of the exogenous variables by one hundred per cent. After each run the effects on all endogenous variables were noted and analyzed. In order to evaluate the voluminous results of these tests, they were grouped according to certain key problems.

The first important problem to be explored has been the relationship between the target and instrument variables. They are grouped in Table 5 which includes some other closely related variables.

An examination of Table 5 leads to some interesting conclusions. The target variables are scarcely affected by the main instrument variables representing various types of government spending. Of the eight instrument variables, only defence spending seems to affect significantly several of the target variables.

This negative and rather surprising result may be due to defects of the model. Yet another explanation offers itself: the values of the instrument variables during the period under study may have been insignificantly small. This would mean that the tools currently at the disposal of the Government of Nova Scotia are altogether insufficient for influencing the target variables and bringing about a major change.

Target variables, especially GRP and the related variables defining per capita disposable income, generally and in agriculture, and total employment are significantly affected by a number of other variables of which the degree of urbanization (P_u) is by far the most important.

The performance of the latter variable revealed by the tests points to an interesting and quite unexpected feature of the model. A 100 per cent change in the degree of urbanization influences almost every aspect of the regional economy. Besides the more obvious, although surprisingly strong, changes generated in the level of commercial services, investments in housing and general investments, such diverse elements as consumption level both of goods and services, imports, balance of payments with the rest of the world, savings, various tax revenues, current government spending, and the wage bill are affected. This otherwise plausible result is the more surprising because the model was not designed to test the effects of economies of urbanization.

A second group of variables, whose effects upon the economy are revealed by the sensitivity tests, are those connected with agriculture. This group is comprised of variables defining the number of commercial farms as a proportion of all farms, and changes in the amount of cultivated land. As might be expected, the variables relating directly to agriculture,

Table 5. Sensitivity Tests: Targets and Instruments.
Percentage changes in selected endogenous variables per 100% change in exogenous variables.

Instruments / Variables tested	Targets								Intermediate														
	GRP	$\bar{y}_{DP}$	$\bar{y}_A$	E	M	q_E	q_v	q_H	X_{CS}	L_{CS}	F_s	W	E_1	F_a	I_H	I	i_p	S	GS_c	T_c	T	T_{IN}	m
DF_s	21.9	13.3	10.5	16.9	20.2						16.6				56.0	18.8		69.3	-7.7	11.4	15.3	16.0	2.0
GS_H															55.8	18.8			-7.8				
GI_G																			-11.1				
GI_{ED}						10.3													-4.0				
GI_v							10.8												-0.5				
GS_A																			-0.4				
GS_m																			-1.0				
GD																			100.6				
Data																							
X_A	6.2	2.8	3.0									4.7			15.8	5.3		14.7	3.5	3.2	3.2	3.4	2.3
A_L		2.3	39.9															12.0	2.2		2.7	2.8	1.4
FZ		1.5	26.4	11.7										164.1				7.9	1.5		1.8	1.8	0.9
F^G		14.8	7.3										92.0	108.3				76.7	-35.7		17.0	17.7	8.9
F^{nr}		2.4	4.4															12.2	2.3		2.7	2.8	1.4
X_L	4.9	2.2	2.4									3.7			12.4	4.2		11.5	2.8	2.5	2.6	2.7	4.4
P_u		166.4	84.1	72.0	77.2				416.8	239.2	181.5	113.5			425.2	250.0		219.6	101.6	86.6	96.7	100.8	77.3
$\bar{w}^{NS}$		18.5	8.4	9.0								14.1			47.3	15.9		43.4	10.5	9.6	9.6	10.0	6.7
$\bar{p}^{NS}$		38.1	35.4								54.2	55.6						197.4	42.6		43.8	45.6	22.8
NH		15.8						100.8									184.4	-66.5	15.1		18.2	18.9	9.5

such as employment in agriculture, net income of unincorporated farm enterprises, and per capita disposable income of agricultural population, are those most strongly affected.

An interesting role is played by the variable describing the price level in Nova Scotia. This variable affects such diverse components of the regional economy as per capita disposable income in money terms, total wage bill, income of unincorporated enterprises, consumption, savings, tax revenues, and current government spending.

Interesting, though expected, results are produced by new housing construction upon housing standards and rental income of persons (an important component of i_p). Less obvious, though reasonable, results are revealed by a drop in savings and increases in indirect taxes, current government expenditures, and several other variables.

The second problem examined has been the degree of interaction between the national and regional economy as revealed by the model. This interaction is illustrated in Table 6, which more specifically explores the effects upon Nova Scotia of the five variables pertaining to the national economy. Their influence is, on the whole, almost negligible. GNP or Gross National Product for example affects only exports of mining and manufacturing products and the balance of the regional economy with the rest of the world.

Table 6. Sensitivity Tests: External Forces
Percentage changes in selected endogenous variables per 100% change in exogenous variables pertaining to Canadian economy.

External forces	Affected variables									Variables affected to a limited extent
	e_L	e_m	m	BRW	I_{CS}	I	$\bar{y}_{DP}$	T	tr	
GNP	23·6	87·4		−51·4						
i			2·0	−22·0	42·6	19·0				
$\bar{p}_m$		150·1		−75·0						
Y_p^c			0·9	8·4			1·5	33·0	−50·0	$C_1, C_4, C_5, T_{IN}, GS_c, S$
T^c			−1·8	−16·8			−3·0	66·0	100·0	$C_1, C_4, C_5, T_{IN}, GS_c, S$

It is difficult to establish without further analysis, whether this result is due primarily to the construction of the model and to the insufficient weight given to the export sector or simply reflects the fact that a relatively unproductive regional economy, depending upon government spending and unilateral transfers, does not respond strongly to changes in the national economy. Partial evidence from correlation analysis seems to validate the second argument.

On the whole, sensitivity tests reveal that the regional economy is sensitive to quite a number of variables, despite the fact that the model is relatively open with many exogenous variables. This characteristic would ordinarily dampen sensitivity. Similarly, the recursiveness of the system and the almost complete lack of lagged relationships should produce a similar outcome limiting the effects of changes in many exogenous variables beyond the equations in which they are directly involved.

The second test consisted in finding yearly solutions from the 1954 base for all years between 1954 and 1961. The solutions have been found over the estimation period and compared with actual values from the data listing. For each run the actual values of all exogenous variables and of lagged endogenous variables are used. The results show clearly that the vast majority of endogenous variables are estimated with an error below 10 per cent and most of them with an error less than 5 per cent. Occasionally, however, one or two variables show very large deviations from actual values.

The third text explores the forecast values of endogenous variables. Forecasts differ from the yearly solutions in that beyond the first year, the input values of lagged endogenous variables are generated by the model itself. This test, therefore, is a projection of the model from 1954 to 1961 using only the series for the exogenous variables. The time path of the key variables has been compared to that of actual values. This test gives some idea of the validity of results generated by the model for forecasting and policy purposes. If the series of endogenous variables generated by the model diverge from their actual values, or if errors tend to cumulate, the validity of the forecast will decrease with time. The forecast might also give an idea of admissible forecasting horizons, i.e. of the time period during which the actual and forecasted values of endogenous variables do not diverge significantly.

The tests carried out, on the whole, show satisfactory results. Again wide deviation from actual values are relatively rare. Yet, it should not be overlooked that both types of results have been obtained strictly within the sampling range. The results of both yearly solutions and forecasts have been plotted. The values for some of the more significant variables are shown in Figures 7 to 11.

What general conclusions can be drawn from the above? It appears that several premises upon which the model of Nova Scotia was based were right. The successful estimation of the model while working with insufficient data was largely due to its structural simplicity.

This single fact more than anything else forced the application of a recursive, relatively open, system with few lagged relationships. Under these circumstances ordinary least squares could be applied without introducing a bias.

The study also vindicates, at least partly, the view that market processes cannot be fully explored in regional models where price formation takes place outside of the system. To do otherwise leads to overdetermined sub-models.

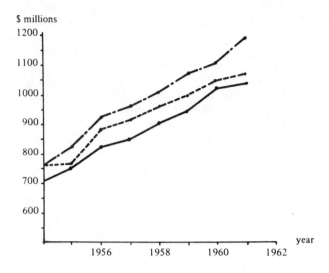

Figure 7. Gross regional product (*GRP*).

———— Actual
-▲----- Yearly solutions
—·— Forecast

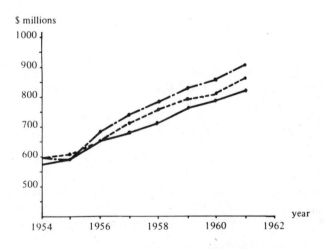

Figure 8. Total personal disposable income (Y_{DP}).

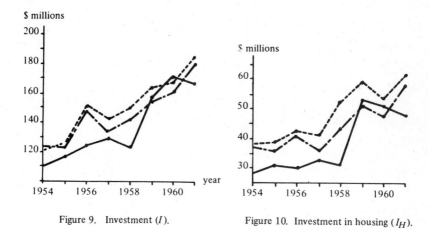

Figure 9.   Investment (I).   Figure 10.   Investment in housing (I_H).

—————— Actual
- - - - - - Yearly solutions
—— ·· —— Forecast

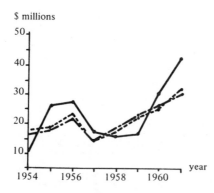

Figure 11.   Investment in manufacturing (I_m).

References

Christ, C.F., 1966, *Econometric Models and Methods* (John Wiley and Sons, New York).

Czamanski, S., 1964, "A Model of Urban Growth", *Papers of the Regional Science Association*, **13**, 177–200.

Czamanski, S., 1965a, "Industrial Location and Urban Growth", *The Town Planning Review*, **36**, 165–180.

Czamanski, S., 1965b, "A Method of Forecasting Metropolitan Growth by Means of Distributed Lags Analysis", *Journal of Regional Science*, **6**, 35–49.

Czamanski, S., 1968, *Regional Income and Product Accounts of Northeastern Nova Scotia*, Institute of Public Affairs, Dalhousie University, Halifax.

Fox, K.A., 1958, *Econometric Analysis for Public Policy* (Iowa State College, Ames, Iowa).

Goldberger, A.S., 1964, *Econometric Theory* (John Wiley and Sons, New York).

Isard, W., and Czamanski, S., 1965, "Techniques for Estimating Multiplier Effects of Major Government Programs", *Papers of the Peace Research Society (International)*, Vol.III.

Johnston, J., 1963, *Econometric Methods* (McGraw-Hill, New York).

Klein, L.R., 1953, *Textbook of Econometrics* (Row Peterson, Evanston, Illinois).

Malinvaud, E., 1966, *Statistical Methods of Econometrics* (Rand-McNally, Chicago).

Tintner, G., 1952, *Econometrics* (John Wiley and Sons, New York).

International and Interregional Economic Cooperation and Planning by Linked Computers

T.O.M.KRONSJÖ
University of Birmingham

General assumptions of the international-interregional economic plan

A general description may be briefly stated as follows for a group of cooperating national economies, regions, or units.

The variables of all cooperating economic units

The variable quantities and prices of *all* the cooperating national economies, regions, or units $k \in K$ may be denoted by the vector x. It will normally be required, in order to prevent activities from being run backwards, that

$$x \geqslant 0. \tag{1}$$

The preference function and constraints of the kth economic unit

The kth economic unit may be described by a preference function and a set of constraints.

The preference function may be assumed to be a function of all variables of all the cooperating economic units, that is

$$f_k(x) \tag{2}$$

This function may describe the preferences of the kth national government, regional authority, or economic unit.

The kth economy must fulfil certain political, economic and other constraints, which may be considered to depend upon all the variables of the cooperating economic units, or

$$g_{ki}(x) \leqslant 0 \qquad (i \in I_k) \tag{3}$$

where I_k denotes the set of indices of the constraints of the kth economy. These constraints are assumed to be of a rather general nature. They may describe fixed costs, increasing returns to scale, indivisibilities or the impossibility of compromise between some feasible solutions.

The common preference function

The cooperating economic units $k \in K$ may agree to formulate a common preference function and to optimize it subject to the set of constraints of Equation (3) above.

The common preference function may be established (*a*) by defining a function

$$\max f(x) \tag{4}$$

which in some way reflects the common preferences, or (*b*) by defining the common preference function in such a way that it only consists of raising the individual preference functions of *all* cooperating economic units from certain minimal levels and at certain relative rates of improvement.

A simple formulation could be: maximize a single variable x_0 expressing a basic index of improvement in the performance of all cooperating economic units at relative rates of increase a_k and above certain minimal levels b_k, that is

$$\max x_0 \tag{5}$$

subject to

$$b_k + a_k x_0 \leqslant f_k(x), \qquad (k \in K). \tag{6}$$

If the levels b_k can be chosen so that, at least, they represent the level of performance the economic units would attain in the absence of a common cooperation scheme, and if the coefficients a_k were strictly positive, then there would be an incentive for every one of the economic units to participate in the scheme. However, every one naturally would prefer, and bargain for, as large values as possible of b_k and a_k to be given to itself and as small values as possible to the others.

A straightforward generalization is to express the common preference function as some function of all the individual preference functions

$$\max f(x) = f[f_K(x)] \tag{7}$$

where $f_K(x)$ denotes the vector $f_k(x)$ obtained when k assumes all indices of the set K.

No matter which approach is used to formulate the common preference function it will inevitably have to be based upon politically decided coefficients and constants.

A summary of the problem of the cooperating economic units

The problem of the cooperating economies may be stated in the briefest possible way as the optimization of an objective function, say,

$$\min F(X) \tag{8}$$

subject to constraints concerning, possibly, the relationships of the individual preference functions; political, economic and other conditions of all cooperating economic units, and their relations with others. These constraints may be summarized by

$$G(X) \leqslant 0 \qquad (9)$$

and

$$X \geqslant 0. \qquad (10)$$

In the continuation, attention will be devoted to devising a convergent scheme to facilitate: (a) optimal decisions with respect to economies of scale and indivisibilities; (b) aggregation and disaggregation of the great number of economic balances and activities involved, and (c) parallel computations on a network of interconnected computers.

A MATHEMATICAL APPROXIMATION

The problem of international and interregional economic cooperation, which above was considered to be the problem

$$\underset{x}{\text{Min}} \{ F(X) \quad | $$

$$G(X) \leqslant 0$$

$$X \geqslant 0\}, \qquad (11)$$

will in the continuation be approximated by the problem

$$\underset{x}{\text{Min}} \{ f^0(x_0) \quad + \quad f(x) \quad | $$

$$g^0(x_0) \quad + \quad g(x) \leqslant 0$$

$$x_0 = 0, 1 \quad x \geqslant 0\} \qquad (12)$$

where x_0 is a vector of 'nothing' or 'all' activities
        x a vector of non-negative continuous activities
$f^0(x_0)$ a scalar function
$f(x)$ a *convex* scalar function
$g^0(x_0)$ a vector function
$g(x)$ a *convex* vector function.

The above formulation may seem odd, but it may indeed be expected that an economic system can be approximated to any practically required degree of accuracy by a mathematical programme of the form set out in Problem (12).

Suppose that the objective function $F(X)$ or a constraint function $G(X)$ could be represented by the function $H(X)$ indicated by the heavy line in Figure 1.

The function $H(X)$ could be approximated by a function $h(X)$ consisting of a line segment and a convex function segment, as shown in Figure 1. The approximation could be described by introducing 0–1 variables x_{01} and x_{02}, where $x_{01} = 1$ if the curve $H(X)$ is approximated by the first segment (the line) in Figure 1, otherwise $x_{01} = 0$; and $x_{02} = 1$ if the curve $H(X)$ is approximated by the second segment (the convex curve), otherwise $x_{02} = 0$. Thus, we may write:

$$x_{0i} = 0, 1 \qquad (i = 1, 2). \tag{13}$$

For any particular value of X only one of the curves is used to approximate the function $H(X)$, thus only one x_{0i} variable will be equal to unity and the remainder equal to zero. As each x_{0i} variable is either equal to zero or one, this last requirement can be expressed by the condition

$$\sum_i x_{0i} = 1. \tag{14}$$

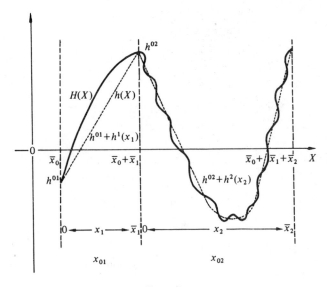

Figure 1.

In the ith segment the value of the variable X may be described by a new variable x_i. If a value of X is considered which belongs to the ith segment, then the value of the variable x_i should be within its lower and upper bound, that is:

$$0 \leqslant x_i \leqslant \bar{x}_i,$$

otherwise x_i should be equal to zero, which may be expressed as

$$0 \leqslant x_i \leqslant 0.$$

By using the corresponding x_{0i} variable this condition may be summarized as

$$0 \leqslant x_i \leqslant \bar{x}_i x_{0i}. \tag{15}$$

For $x_{0i} = 1$ this becomes $0 \leqslant x_i \leqslant \bar{x}_i . 1 = \bar{x}_i$, and for $x_{0i} = 0$ it becomes $0 \leqslant x_i \leqslant \bar{x}_i . 0 = 0$, where X is expressed as equal to the upper bounds of the x_j variables of the segments preceding the ith one plus the value of the variable x_i, i.e.

$$\sum_{j=1}^{i-1} \bar{x}_j + x_i.$$

However, as all the other variables x_j ($j \neq i$) will be equal to zero, X may be expressed as

$$\sum_{j=1}^{i-1} \bar{x}_j + \sum_i x_i.$$

Finally the x_{0i} variables may be used to select the correct sum $\bar{\bar{x}}_i = \sum_{j=1}^{i-1} \bar{x}_j$ by expressing

$$X = \sum_i \bar{\bar{x}}_i x_{0i} + \sum_i x_i. \tag{16}$$

The equation of the ith approximating segment may be expressed in terms of the functions

$$h^{0i} + h^i(x_i) \qquad \text{where } h^i(x_i = 0) = 0,$$

or since all variables $x_j = 0$ ($j \neq i$) as $h^{0i} + \sum_i h^i(x_i)$;

finally, the x_{0i} variables may be used to select the correct h^{0i} value and the approximating function be expressed by

$$h = \sum_i h^{0i} x_{0i} + \sum_i h^i(x_i), \tag{17}$$

where the functions $h^i(x_i)$ have been chosen to be linear or convex functions.

To continue with this example, it is evident that the minimization of a function $F(X)$, subject to constraints $G(X) \leq 0$, $X \geq 0$, may be approximated by the conditions expressed in Equations (13)-(17), to give the approximate problem:

$$\begin{aligned}
\operatorname*{Min}_{x_0, x} \{ &\sum_i f^{0i} x_{0i} + \sum_i f^i(x_i) && \text{cf. Equation (17)} \\
&\sum_i g^{0i} x_{0i} + \sum_i g^i(x_i) \leq 0 && \text{cf. Equation (17)} \\
&-\sum_i \bar{\bar{x}}_i x_{0i} - \sum_i x_i \leq 0 && \text{cf. Equation (16)} \\
&\sum_i x_{0i} - 1 \leq 0 && \text{cf. Equation (14), } \sum_i x_{0i} \leq 1 \\
&\sum_i - x_{0i} + 1 \leq 0 && \text{and } \sum_i x_{0i} \geq 1 \text{ is} \\
&&& \text{equivalent to } \sum_i x_{0i} = 1 \\
&- \bar{\bar{x}}_i x_{0i} + x_i \leq 0 \quad i \in I && \text{cf. Equation (15)} \\
&x_{0i} = 0,1 \quad x_i \geq 0 \quad i \in I \} && \text{cf. Equations (13) and (15)} \quad (18)
\end{aligned}$$

where, for simplicity, it has been assumed that the beginning and end points for the ith approximating segment are the same for all the functions being approximated.

The original problem, (11), has thus been approximated by a problem of the general structure of Problem (12). It may also be shown that this approximation method is equally applicable to problems of many variables.

STRUCTURE OF THE INTERNATIONAL COOPERATION PLAN

It is of great importance to devote increasing attention to the possibilities of applying mathematical methods to the problem of international and interregional cooperation and to joint economic planning based upon an efficient system of trade.

If several market or planned economies wished to cooperate in the economic field, they would be faced with the problem of deciding the optimal levels of the vectors of variables, namely

x_0 denoting 0-1 variables associated with the description of large investment projects, fixed costs, increasing returns to scale, etc.;

x_1 denoting the internal activities of the cooperating economies concerning production, consumption and investment started in one time period, continued and completed in some following periods;

x_2 denoting the export, import and stock activities in all time periods for commodities participating in international trade;

x_3 denoting the realization of social aims in the cooperating economies; the granting and obtaining of credits from other economies; the exchange of one type of currency holdings into another; the currency holding, and the trade in labour and transportation services in every one of the time periods of the plan.

In the development of such an international cooperation model, we should have to account for a large number of relations such as the objective function, the international balanced development constraints, the balance of payments constraints, the labour and transport balances, the commodity balances and marketing constraints, and the constraints concerning all internal activities. A brief indication of their nature may be useful.

The objective function

The cooperating economies may be interested in minimizing some social disutility function (or maximizing some social welfare function[1]). That is:

$$\underset{x_0, x_1, x_2, x_3}{\text{Min}} \quad f^0(x_0) + f^1(x_1) + f^2(x_2) + f^3(x_3) \tag{19}$$

[1] A non-optimizing equilibrium investigation of a related problem is presented by Mycielski (1967).

The international balanced development constraints

If some economies could cooperate, they would be likely to reach a better solution than that which they could achieve by each acting independently. The countries could conclude political agreements, concerning the sharing of the likely benefits from their economic cooperation, by the formulation of international balanced development constraints which ensure a mutually acceptable pace and structure of development in all of the cooperating countries. If such a decision is made, the internal balance of payment situation between the cooperating countries may be disregarded. The international cooperation scheme would ensure an optimal measure of development for all the cooperating countries as a whole, whilst the international balanced development constraints would ensure that this overall development is associated with a satisfactory measure of development within each cooperating state. The international balanced development constraints will, in a direct and rational manner, perform a function related to that which is usually performed indirectly by the internal balance of payments constraints of cooperating economies.

The external balance of payments constraints

A natural consequence of agreement on the international balanced development constraints would be for the cooperating economies to pool their external currency accounts. They would thus have a common external balance of payments in different currencies. However, in addition to the convertible currencies such as the U.S. Dollar and the Pound Sterling, there may be a large number of the currencies of under-developed countries which, although formally convertible, may not be in essence. This is due to such important factors as import and export regulations, which prevent exports to these countries unless they are matched by a corresponding amount of imports. In reality, therefore, such a currency is not convertible. For certain countries a large part of their trade, sometimes as much as 75-90%, is carried on in such inconvertible currencies. In this connection, constraints may be placed on the making of currency transfers, because requests to exchange fairly large surpluses in one 'convertible' currency into another may not be accepted. There may also be constraints on the availability of foreign credits.

The labour and transport constraints

As foreign trade activities usually involve the use of labour and transport services, the effect of foreign trade upon these balances has to be taken into account, and they must be considered differently from all other commodity balances.

The international balanced development, external balance of payments, labour, transport and some approximation constraints are expressed by the condition

$$g_1^0(x_0)+g_1^1(x_1)+g_1^2(x_2)+g_1^3(x_3) \leqslant 0. \tag{20}$$

The commodity balances

The commodity balances specify the various supplies and demands for a commodity, or group of commodities, in every one of the cooperating economies and include the external marketing constraints. If the model describes only one country trading with a number of other countries, then the external marketing constraints express that of a particular commodity in a particular country at a particular price; there is an upper bound upon the amount that may be sold or bought. If the model describes a group of cooperating countries, then the commodity balances state that for a particular commodity in a particular country at a particular price, there is an upper bound upon the sum total of quantities that may be sold or bought by all the cooperating economies together.

These commodity and other approximation constraints may be expressed by

$$g_2^0(x_0)+g_2^1(x_1)+g_2^2(x_2) \leqslant 0. \tag{21}$$

The constraints concerning only internal activities

These constraints are associated only with production, consumption and investment in the cooperating economies and not with international trade variables. The constraints may be due to the fact that no international trade takes place in certain commodities, or due to technological, capacity or other conditions concerning these internal economic activities.

The constraints concerning only internal activities and remaining approximation constraints are expressed by

$$g_3^0(x_0)+g_3^1(x_1) \leqslant 0. \tag{22}$$

Discrete variables

To permit the description of nonconvex functions it is required that

$$x_0 = 0 \text{ or } 1. \tag{23}$$

Non-negative variables

As usual, this requirement is included to prevent activities from being run backwards, thus:

$$x_1 \geqslant 0 \qquad x_2 \geqslant 0 \qquad x_3 \geqslant 0. \tag{24}$$

The optimal price, proportional and lump tax system

Assuming that it has been possible to reach an optimal solution to the problem expressed by Equations (19)–(24) with optimal dual variables,

u^1, u^2, and u^3, then these may be used to construct the price, proportional and lump tax (subsidy) system. This will make possible the same optimal solution by every economy acting according to its own preferences (except with respect to the 0-1 activities) under the corresponding financial budget constraint (Kronsjö, 1966).

DECOMPOSITION INTO A MASTER OF INDIVISIBLE ACTIVITIES AND A CONVEX SUBPROBLEM

The international, or interregional problem considered above may be stated in the form

$$\operatorname*{Min}_{x_0,\, x} \{ f^0(x_0) \quad + \quad f(x) \quad | \qquad \begin{array}{c} \text{Dual} \\ \text{variables} \end{array}$$

$$g^0(x_0) \quad + \quad g(x) \leqslant 0 \qquad\qquad u \qquad\qquad (25)$$

$$x_0 = 0, 1 \quad x \geqslant 0 \}$$

where

$$g^0(x_0) = \begin{bmatrix} g^0_1(x_0) \\ g^0_2(x_0) \\ g^0_3(x_0) \end{bmatrix} \qquad\qquad (26)$$

$$f(x) = [f^1(x_1) + f^2(x_2) + f^3(x_3)], \qquad (27)$$

$$g(x) = \begin{bmatrix} g^1_1(x_1) + g^2_1(x_2) + g^3_1(x_3) \\ g^1_2(x_1) + g^2_2(x_2) \\ g^1_3(x_1) \end{bmatrix} \qquad (28)$$

$$x = \begin{bmatrix} x_1 \\ x_2 \\ x_3 \end{bmatrix} \quad \text{and } u = [u_1, u_2, u_3] \qquad (29)$$

The assumption is made that for any possible x_0 solution, there will always exist a finite optimal and feasible solution to the remaining convex problem in the x variables. This assumption may be satisfied by the introduction of large positive upper bounds upon each variable or upon sums of variables; or by additional variables with large positive (penalty) terms in the objective function, each one of them with a negative coefficient in a different constraint, or one with a negative coefficient in each constraint.

Problem (25) may be solved by the author's method of decomposition in the dual direction (Kronsjö, 1967), which may be seen as a generalization of a decomposition method by Benders (1962).

This decomposition method is based upon a dialogue between one decision maker, the *discrete master* of indivisible (0-1) activities, e.g. large investment projects, occurrence of fixed production costs and increasing returns to scale activities, and another decision maker, the *convex subproblem* of continuous nonincreasing returns to scale activities.

The discrete master initiates the process by noting that the index r of the current iteration is zero, by recording that the cost of the hitherto cheapest solution is infinitely large, and by selecting an arbitrary solution x_0^r.

Next iteration.

The convex subproblem

The convex subproblem receives from the discrete master information about the net resource demands $g^0(x_0^r)$. It minimizes the cost $f(x)$ of satisfying these net demands of the discrete master by solving the problem

$$\underset{x}{\text{Min}} \{ \qquad f(x) \qquad | \qquad \begin{array}{c} \text{Dual} \\ \text{variables} \end{array}$$

$$g^0(x_0^r) + g(x) \leqslant 0 \qquad u \qquad\qquad (30)$$

$$x \geqslant 0 \}$$

and obtains the optimal solution $x = x^r, u = u_r$.

The convex subproblem quotes the discrete master its full minimal cost $f(x^r)$, in the form of the marginal cost prices u_r multiplied by the net demand proposal of the discrete master, and a (temporarily) fixed charge v_r amounting to the difference between the cost $f(x^r)$ and the revenue $u_r g^0(x^r)$ that may be obtained by charging the prices u_r per unit of the net demand proposal $g^0(x_0^r)$ of the discrete master, viz.:

$$v_r = f(x^r) - u_r g^0(x_0^r).$$

The discrete master

The discrete master calculates the total cost incurred, $f(x_0^r) + f(x^r)$. If this cost is less than that of the hitherto cheapest solution, then the discrete master records the total cost, the x_0^r solution, and requests the convex subproblem to record its x^r solution.

The discrete master increases the iteration index r by one unit and receives information concerning the charge v_r and the marginal cost price vector u_r. It decides upon the indivisible activities by evaluating their cost $f^0(x_0)$ and simultaneously underestimating the cost $f(x)$ of the corresponding optimal continuous activities. For every charge v_i and marginal cost price vector u_i that it has received, a corresponding cost estimate

$$v_i + u_i g^0(x_0) \qquad (i = 1, ..., r)$$

is formed, based upon the ith charge plus the product of the ith marginal cost prices of the resources and the net demand for these resources resulting from the discrete activity levels x_0. It is indicated elsewhere

(Kronsjö, 1967) that all of these estimates are either underestimates or correct estimates of the optimal value of the cost $f(x)$ corresponding to the net demands $g^0(x_0)$. The dual master therefore selects the largest underestimate as its best estimate. This it may obtain by minimizing a scalar variable y subject to the condition that it is larger than any one cost underestimate. The discrete master therefore solves the problem

$$\min_{x_0, y} \{ f^0(x_0) + y \qquad\qquad\qquad |$$
$$y \geqslant v_i + u_i g^0(x_0) \qquad (i = 1, ..., r) \qquad (31)$$
$$y \gtreqless 0 \qquad x_0 = 0, 1 \qquad\qquad \}$$

and finds, to the extended problem an optimal solution $y = y^r$, $x_0 = x_0^r$.

If the difference between the cost of the hitherto cheapest solution and the underestimate y^r is greater than ϵ, then another iteration performed, otherwise the previous best solution is accepted as an ϵ-optimal solution.

DECOMPOSITION OF THE CONVEX SUBPROBLEM INTO A PRIMAL MASTER OF FOREIGN CURRENCY, BALANCED DEVELOPMENT, LABOUR AND TRANSPORT, A DUAL MASTER OF NATIONAL PRODUCTION, CONSUMPTION AND INVESTMENT, AND A COMMON SUBPROBLEM OF INTERNATIONAL COMMODITY TRADE

So far nothing has been said about how the convex subproblem (30) could possibly be solved. It should be remembered that this problem is of the general structure

$$\min_{x_1, x_2, x_3} \{ f^{01}(x_1) + f^2(x_2) + f^3(x_3) \qquad | \qquad \text{Dual variables}$$
$$g_1^{01}(x_1) + g_1^2(x_2) + g_1^3(x_3) \leqslant 0 \qquad u^1$$
$$g_2^{01}(x_1) + g_2^2(x_2) \qquad\qquad \leqslant 0 \qquad u^2$$
$$g_3^{01}(x_1) \qquad\qquad\qquad \leqslant 0 \qquad u^3$$
$$x_1 \geqslant 0 \quad x_2 \geqslant 0 \quad x_3 \geqslant 0 \} \qquad (32)$$

where

$$f^{01}(x_1) \equiv f^0(x_0^r) + f^1(x_1)$$
$$g_i^{01}(x_1) \equiv g_i^0(x_0^r) + g_i^1(x_1) \qquad (i = 1, 2, 3)$$

The superscript 0 will be omitted in the continuation.

The problem (32) may in principle be solved by the author's method of decomposition in primal and dual directions to obtain a common subproblem (Kronsjö, 1968a, 1969).

This decomposition method is based upon communications exchanges among three decision makers, the *primal master* of foreign currency, balanced development, labour and transport; the *dual master* of national production, consumption and investments, and the *common subproblem* of international commodity trade.

The primal and dual masters initiate the iteration process by setting the iteration indices k and l equal to zero. The primal master selects a (temporarily) fixed charge $v_k^3 = \infty$ and marginal cost prices u_k^1 concerning foreign currency, internationally balanced development, transport and labour constraints (bearing in mind that the nonnegative prices u_k^1 must be such that all currency transfer, and other activities x_3 are associated with marginal losses); as well as a (temporarily) constant charge $w_k = -\infty$ for the joint use of international commodity and internal resources by the common subproblem and the dual master.

The dual master selects national production, consumption and investment activities x_1^l, which satisfy all internal constraints, and makes an underestimate $y^l = -\infty$ of the minimal cost $f^2(x_2) + f^3(x_3)$ of undertaking the corresponding international trade, currency exchange, and other activities x_2, x_3 of the cooperating economies; as well as to estimate the amount $v_l^1 = -\infty$ that it will have to pay the primal master for the social costs, foreign currency and other resource requirements arizing from its activities.

Next iteration.

The common subproblem

The common subproblem undertakes the international trade activities x_2 subject to given marginal cost prices for foreign currencies, etc., and given net demands for the internationally traded commodities.

The primal master charges the common subproblem for the costs $f^2(x_2)$, and for the use of the foreign currency and other resources $g_1^2(x_2)$ at prices u_k^1. The common subproblem therefore incurs the costs $f^2(x_2) + u_k^1 g_1^2(x_2)$ in undertaking the international trade activities x_2.

The dual master requires the common subproblem to satisfy its net demand $g_2^1(x_1^l)$ for internationally traded commodities, which result from its proposal to operate the national economies at the activity levels x_1^l.

The common subproblem minimizes the net cost of international trading, subject to meeting the net demand for internationally traded commodities, by solving

$$-df^0 = dh^0 = \operatorname*{Min}_{x_2} \{f^2(x_2) + u_k^1 g_1^2(x_2) \qquad \Big| \qquad \begin{matrix} \text{Dual} \\ \text{variables} \end{matrix}$$

$$g_2^1(x_1^l) + \quad g_2^2(x_2) \leqslant 0 \qquad\qquad u^2$$

$$x_2 \geqslant 0\} \qquad\qquad\qquad (33)$$

and obtaining the optimal primal solution $x_2 = x_2^l$ and optimal dual solution $x_2 = x_2^k, u_2 = u_k^2$.

If the dual master and the common subproblem find that together they achieve a profitable solution, i.e. their joint loss

$$v_l^1 - \mathrm{df}^0 + w^k < 0, \tag{34}$$

then they submit a joint proposal to the primal master indicating the cost $f^1(x_1^l) + f^2(x_2^l)$, together with the foreign currency and other resource demands $g_1^1(x_1^l) + g_1^2(x_2^l)$ that are associated with the proposed activities.

If the primal master and the common subproblem together find that, in meeting the demand proposal $g^1(x_1^l)$ of the dual master, their costs $f^2(x_2^k) + f^3(x_3^k)$ exceed the amount y^l which the dual master has declared itself willing to pay, that is

$$f^2(x_2^k) + f^3(x_3^k) - y^l > 0, \tag{35}$$

which condition, after suitable transformations[2] may be replaced by the condition used in (Kronsjo, 1968a, 1969)

$$\mathrm{dh}^0 + v_k^3 + u_k^1 g_1^1(x_1^l) - y^l > 0. \tag{36}$$

They then jointly inform the dual master of their costs in the form of marginal cost prices for foreign currency etc., u_k^1, and internationally traded commodities u_k^2 per unit of the demand proposal $g_1^1(x_1^l)$, $g_2^1(x_1^l)$ of the dual master, together with (temporarily) fixed charges v_k^3 and v_k^2 amounting to the difference between their cost and revenues, where

$$v_k^2 = f^2(x_2^k) + u_k^1 g_1^2(x_2^k) - u_k^2 g_2^1(x_1^l) = f^2(x_2^k) + u_k^1 g_1^2(x_2^k) + u_k^2 g_2^2(x_2^k) .$$

The primal and the dual master may *simultaneously* solve their respective problems.

The primal master

The primal master increases the iteration index l by one unit; it receives and remembers the net costs $f^1(x_1^i) + f^2(x_2^i)$ and the net foreign currency and other resource demands $g_1^1(x_1^i) + g_2^1(x_2^i)$ associated with the present and earlier plan proposals $[x_{12}^i \equiv (x_1^i, x_2^i)]$ of the dual master and the common subproblem. It minimizes an overestimate of the cost and resource requirements associated with a compromise plan $x_{12} = \sum_i x_{12}^i t_i$,

where the fractions t_i are nonnegative, $t_i \geqslant 0$, and their sum equal to

[2] The transformations involved are: i) statement of the relationship between the primal and dual of Equation (32) when $x_1 = x_1^l$; ii) use of the optimality of the x_3 and slack variables of Equation (37) and the x_2 and slack variables of Equation (33), from which follows that the corresponding $x_2^l, x_3^k, u_k^1, u_k^2$ solution satisfies the constraints of the previously stated dual problem and also that a number of terms in the objective function of the latter will be equal to zero owing to complementary slackness; iii) use of the definitions of dh^0 and v_k^3 given by Equation (33) and Equation (38).

unity, $\sum_i t_i = 1$, by solving

$$\underset{t, x_3}{\text{Min}} \{ \sum_i [f^1(x_1^i) + f^2(x_2^i)] t_i + f^3(x_3) \qquad | \qquad \text{Dual variables}$$

$$\sum_i [g_1^1(x_1^i) + g_1^2(x_2^i)] t_i + g_1^3(x_3) \leqslant 0 \qquad \mathbf{u}^1$$

$$\sum_i t_i \qquad = 1 \qquad w$$

$$(i = 1, ..., l) \quad t_i \geqslant 0 \quad x_3 \geqslant 0 \} \tag{37}$$

and obtains, the optimal solution

$$t = t^k, \quad x_3 = x_3^k, \quad \mathbf{u}^1 = \mathbf{u}_k^1, \quad w = w_k.$$

The primal master informs the dual master and the common subproblem of the marginal cost prices $\mathbf{u}_k^1$ of foreign currency and other resources, of a charge v_k^3 concerning its x_3 activities

$$v_k^3 = f^3(x_3^k) + \mathbf{u}_k^1 g_1^3(x_3^k) = f^3(x_3^k) - \mathbf{u}_k^1 \sum_i [g_1^1(x_1^i) + g_1^2(x_2^i)] t_i^k \tag{38}$$

and of a charge w_k for the use of international commodity and internal resources by the dual master and the common subproblem.

The dual master

The dual master increases the iteration index k by one unit; it receives and remembers the net charge v_k^3 concerning the foreign currency and other activities, the marginal cost price of foreign currencies etc., $\mathbf{u}_k^1$, from the primal master, and the net loss of international trade activities v_k^2, together with the marginal cost prices of internationally traded commodities $\mathbf{u}_k^2$ from the common subproblem.

The dual master decides upon the national production, consumption and investment activities x_1 by evaluating their cost $f^1(x_1)$ and simultaneously underestimating the cost $f^2(x_2) + f^3(x_3)$ of the corresponding optimal international trade and exchange operations x_2, x_3. For each loss and price information which it has received, it forms a corresponding cost estimate

$$v_i^2 + v_i^3 + \mathbf{u}_i^1 g_1^1(x_1) + \mathbf{u}_i^2 g_2^1(x_1) \qquad (i = 1, ..., k)$$

based on the ith charge upon exchange and international trading plus the marginal cost prices for resources multiplied by the net demand for these resources corresponding to the internal activity levels x_1. It is elsewhere indicated (Kronsjö, 1969) that all these estimates are either underestimates or correct estimates of the optimal value of the cost $f^2(x_2) + f^3(x_3)$ for the particular activity level x_1. Therefore, the dual master selects the largest underestimate as its best evaluation of the minimal cost of $f^2(x_2) + f^3(x_3)$ for the particular internal activity level x_1, which it is considering. It finds this largest estimate by minimizing a scalar variable y, subject to the condition that it is larger than or equal to each cost estimate. In selecting the particular x_1 values the dual master also takes account of the internal constraints concerning these activities. It therefore solves

$$\begin{array}{lll}
\underset{x_1, y}{\text{Min}}\, \{f^1(x_1)+y & | & \qquad\qquad\text{Dual} \\
 & & \qquad\quad\text{variables}
\end{array}$$

$$y \geqslant v_i^2 + v_i^3 + u_i^1 g_1^1(x_1) + u_i^2 g_2^1(x_1) \qquad (i = 1,...,k) \qquad\qquad s^i$$

$$g_3^1(x_1) \leqslant 0 \qquad\qquad\qquad u^3$$

$$y \gtrless 0 \qquad\qquad x_1 \geqslant 0 \qquad\qquad\quad \} \qquad (39)$$

with the optimal solution

$$x_1 = x_1^l, \quad y = y^l, \quad s = s_l \text{ and } u^3 = u_l^3.$$

If the difference between the overestimate and the underestimate of the optimal objective function value, provided by the primal and the dual master respectively, is greater than ϵ another iteration is undertaken, otherwise the process is concluded and a *feasible primal solution* is available by selecting

$$x_1 = x_1^k = \sum_i x_1^i t_i^k \qquad x_2 = x_2^k = \sum_i x_2^i t_i^k \qquad x_3 = x_3^k,$$

and a *feasible dual solution* by selecting the following conditions: if the dual constraints corresponding to x_2, x_3 define a convex solution set, which will be the case if the corresponding functions $f^2(x_2)$, $g_1^2(x_2)$, etc., are linear, then

$$u^1 = u_l^1 = \sum_i s_l^i u_i^1 \qquad u^2 = u_l^2 = \sum_i s_l^i u_i^2; \qquad u^3 = u_l^3;$$

otherwise $u^1 = u_l^3$ may be obtained as the dual solution of

$$\begin{array}{lll}
\underset{x_3}{\text{Min}}\, \{ & f^3(x_3) & | \qquad\qquad \text{Dual} \\
 & & \qquad\quad \text{variables}
\end{array}$$

$$g_1^1(x_1^k) + g_1^2(x_2^k) + g_1^3(x_3) \leqslant 0 \qquad\qquad u^1$$

$$x_3 \geqslant 0\} \qquad\qquad\qquad (40)$$

and $u^2 = u_l^2$ from

$$\begin{array}{lll}
\underset{x_2}{\text{Min}}\, \{f^2(x_2)+u_l^1 g_1^2(x_2) & | \qquad\qquad \text{Dual} \\
 & \qquad\quad \text{variables}
\end{array}$$

$$g_2^1(x_1^k) + \quad g_2^2(x_2) \leqslant 0 \qquad\qquad u^2$$

$$x_2 \geqslant 0\} \qquad\qquad\qquad (41)$$

and finally, $u^3 = u_l^3$ by solving

$$\begin{array}{lll}
\underset{x_1}{\text{Min}}\, \{f^1(x_1)+u_l^1 g_1^1(x_1)+u_i^2 g_2^1(x_1) & | \qquad\qquad \text{Dual} \\
 & \qquad\quad \text{variables}
\end{array}$$

$$g_3^1(x_1) \leqslant 0 \qquad\qquad\qquad u^3$$

$$x_1 \geqslant 0\} \qquad\qquad\qquad (42)$$

DECOMPOSITION OF THE DUAL MASTER INTO A COMMON MASTER OF NATIONAL DEMAND PROPOSALS, EVALUATED ACCORDING TO DIFFERENT PRICE QUOTATIONS AND PRIMAL SUBPROBLEMS OF NATIONAL PRODUCTION, CONSUMPTION AND INVESTMENT

So far no concern has been given to the fact that the dual master is supposed to be solving an extremely large problem embracing all the internal economic activities x_1, all the generated constraints of cost underestimates, and the internal constraints $g_3^1(x_1) \leqslant 0$ of all the cooperating economies.

The internal production, investment and consumption activities of the kth cooperating economy ($k = 1, ..., r$) may be denoted by the sub-vectors

$$x_{1k} \qquad (k = 1, ..., r).$$

The corresponding internal economic constraints of the kth cooperating economy may similarly be denoted by the vector functions

$$g_{3k}^1(x_1) \leqslant 0 \qquad (k = 1, ..., r).$$

From a computational point of view it is preferable, but by no means necessary, to assume that the internal production, consumption and investment activities of one national economy have no direct effects, or at least no effects which are dependent upon the activity levels of some other economy, upon the cost function and constraints of another economy. The functions $f^1(x_1)$ and $g^1(x_1)$ of the production, consumption and investment activities x_1 of the cooperating economies may then be formulated as

$$\sum_k f^{1k}(x_{1k})$$

$$\sum_k g_1^{1k}(x_{1k})$$

$$\sum_k g_2^{1k}(x_{1k})$$

$$g_{3k}^{1k}(x_{1k}) \qquad (k = 1, ..., r). \qquad (43)$$

The solution of the dual master (39) by use of the decomposition method of Dantzig (1963) for a convex programme, and decomposing it into a master problem and r subproblems, is immediately evident.

The resulting master problem will be a master both in the primal and the dual directions, and may therefore be named the *common master* of national demand proposals evaluated according to different price quotations. The corresponding subproblems could be called the *primal subproblems* of national production, consumption and investment.

The common master may initiate the iteration process by setting the iteration index h equal to zero, and deciding upon some arbitrary prices u_h^1, u_h^2, and (temporarily) fixed charges w_h^k for the use of the national resources.

Next iteration.

The kth national subproblem ($k = 1, ..., r$)

This subproblem receives from the common master the marginal cost price information about foreign currencies etc., u_h^1, imported or exported commodities u_h^2, and a charge w_h^k. The national subproblem evaluates the cost

$$f^{1k}(x_{1k}) + u_h^1 g_1^{1k}(x_{1k}) + u_h^2 g_2^{1k}(x_{1k}) + w_h^k$$

associated with the national production, consumption and investment activities x_{1k}.

To determine the minimal loss it solves the problem

$$z_k = \underset{x_{1k}}{\text{Min}} \{ f^{1k}(x_{1k}) + u_h^1 g_1^{1k}(x_{1k}) + u_h^2 g_2^{1k}(x_{1k}) + w_h^k \mid$$

Dual variables

$$g_{3k}^{1k}(x_{1k}) \leq 0 \qquad u^{3k}$$

$$x_{1k} \geq 0 \} \qquad\qquad (44)$$

If the minimal loss is negative, i.e. if it achieves a net profit, then it submits to the common master the corresponding proposal concerning net cost and net demand for foreign currency, etc. and internationally traded commodities.

The common master

The common master receives and remembers the costs $f^{1k}(x_{1k}^j)$, the net foreign currency and other resource demands $g_1^{1k}(x_{1k}^j)$, and the net demand of internationally traded commodities $g_2^{1k}(x_{1k}^j)$ associated with the present and earlier plan proposals x_{1k}^j of all the national subproblems. It minimizes an overestimate y_0 of the cost and resource requirements associated with a compromise plan $x_{1k} = \sum_j x_{1k}^j t_j^k$, where the fractions t_j^k are non-negative, $t_j^k \geq 0$, and their sum adds up to unity, $\sum_j t_j^k = 1$. Before doing this it calculates a current underestimate $\underline{z_0}$ of the optimal objective function z_0 of the common master, where

$$\underline{z_0} = z_0 + \sum_k z_k. \qquad\qquad (45)$$

It then minimizes the overestimate z_0 of the cost associated with a compromise plan by solving the problem

$$z_0 = \underset{t_j^k, y}{\text{Min}} \{ \sum_k \sum_j f^{1k}(x_{1k}^j) t_j^k + y \qquad\qquad \mid$$

Dual variables

$$y \geq v_i^1 + v_i^2 + \sum_k \sum_j [u_i^1 g_1^{1k}(x_{1k}^j) + u_i^2 g_2^{1k}(x_{1k})] t_j^k \qquad s^i$$

$$(i = 1, ..., K)$$

$$\sum_j t_j^k = 1 \qquad w^k$$

$$(k = 1, ..., r)$$

$$y \geq 0 \qquad\qquad\qquad\qquad\qquad t_j^k \geq 0 \} \qquad (46)$$

[3] K is identical with the iteration index k of the preceeding section.

and increasing the iteration index h by one unit.

If the difference between the current value of $z_0 = \bar{z}_0$ and the underestimate $\underline{z}_0$ is greater than ϵ, then it informs the national subproblems of new charges w_h^k and prices

$$\mathbf{u}_h^1 = \sum_i s_h^i \mathbf{u}_i^1, \qquad \mathbf{u}_h^2 = \sum_i s_h^i \mathbf{u}_i^2,$$

whereafter another iteration is undertaken. Otherwise, it forms an ϵ optimal solution to the original dual master problem, viz.:

$$\mathbf{x}_{1k}^l = \sum_j \mathbf{x}_{1k}^j t_j^{kh} \qquad (k = 1, ..., r)$$

with corresponding values for y and z_0, and informs the primal master and the common subproblem of the corresponding costs $f^1(\mathbf{x}_1^l)$ and net demands $g_1^1(\mathbf{x}_1^l), g_2^1(\mathbf{x}_1^l)$.

THE STRUCTURE OF THE INTERNATIONAL TRADE SUBPROBLEM

Block diagonal structure implying independent part problems

Of importance for the efficient solution of the international trade subproblem is that all variables concerned with trade and stocks in any one commodity have no constraints in common with the variables concerned with trade and stocks in any other commodity, as the levels of interconnecting activities are temporarily kept constant.

The subproblem is separable, and its optimal solution may be obtained by finding the optimal solution to as many independent problems as there are commodities. Each of the independent problems concerns the trade in a particular commodity and has, therefore, as many variables as there are trade and stock activities in that commodity over all time periods, plus as many constraints as there are cooperating and other economies with which the commodity is traded at different price levels in all of the time periods. These independent problems are thus of manageable size, the more so as they have a computationally favourable structure.

The structure of the international trade problem and the dynamic transportation problem

A careful study of the independent problems reveals that they may be dealt with as dynamic transportation problems, for the solution of which some special algorithm may be employed.

If the out- and in-going stocks have been grouped and dealt with as internal activities, or if the international cooperation plan only embraces one time period, then the independent part problems will contain no stock variables and may be dealt with as transportation problems.

The problem of trading in one commodity between the cooperating economies (internal markets) and other economies (external markets) may be understood as follows. The surplus of one cooperating economy, say market 1, may be used either to cover deficits in some other cooperating economies (say k to m, which have been assumed to have deficits), or it may be exported to some other economies, or simply, it may remain in the cooperating economy as unused surplus. Similarly, the potential export of some other economy may be used either to cover a deficit of a cooperating economy, or to be imported by some other economy, or simply remain unexported. The same applies to the deficits. A cooperating economy with a deficit, say the market k, may cover this deficit by buying from some of the cooperating economies with surpluses, or by importing from some of the other economies, or simply retain an unsatisfied deficit. Similarly, the import demand of some other economy may either be utilized by selling the surplus of some cooperating economy, or by export from some other economy, or simply not be satisfied at all.

To assure the existence of finite primal and dual solutions, it was assumed in a previous section that upper bounds were introduced upon the variables to prevent infinite solutions. This is in addition to artificial supply variables associated with large positive coefficients in the objective function to ensure that they would be used only when necessary to achieve a feasible solution.

Research has been undertaken by Liggins (1967) on the formulation of a computational algorithm for the optimal solution of the above subproblem of international trade and a report is at present in the final stages of preparation.

UNDELAYED IMPLEMENTATION BY INTERACTION BETWEEN A FORMAL EQUATION AND A PRACTICAL PLANNING ELEMENT

The formulation of the complete model as a large equation system with real numerical coefficients, to be solved by the interaction of one or more computers, may at present require too many changes in actual planning practice and put too many requirements upon the creation of an efficient data processing system, thereby preventing its immediate implementation.

Immediate application of these concepts may be achieved, however, by allowing practical economic planning organizations, using traditional methods essentially, to solve the large subproblem of internal constraints and by calculating macro-vectors of net requirements and availabilities of various commodities in various countries for communication to the large master of international constraints.

Only the solution of the master of international constraints would be obtained by solving a large system of equations by one or several intercommunicating computers. The result of the improved solution of the master of international constraints would be a new set of prices of currencies, balanced development, labour, transport, commodities and marketing constraints. This may again be communicated to some or all of the practical planning organizations, who may be asked to propose new net requirement and availability vectors for the internal activities of the cooperating economics. A further improved solution would then be attempted, and so on, until the cost and time spent in obtaining improved solutions from the practical planners is not compensated by the expected improvement of the overall solution. The slowness and costliness of the present planning mechanism may, perhaps, warrant this already after a few practical solutions. The most favourable solution for the overall problem will then provide (*a*) balanced and achievable international trade and internal activities; (*b*) targets for balance of payments, balanced development, employment, transport, net deliveries to and from foreign trade and other sectors; and lastly, (*c*) a set of realistic prices based upon the substitution possibilities offered by international cooperation.

References

Benders, J.F., 1962, *Numerische Mathematik*, **4**, 238-252.
Dantzig, G.B., 1963, *Linear Programming and Extensions* (Princeton University Press, Princeton).
Kronsjö, T.O.M., 1966, *Centralization and Decentralization of Decision Making, the Formulation of a Linear Economic Plan for Implementation by an Optimal Combination of Command and Financial Stimulus.* University of Birmingham, Centre for Russian and East European Studies, Discussion Papers, Series RC/A, No.8, and *Economics of Planning,* **7**, 30-38.
Kronsjö, T.O.M., 1967, *Centralization and Decentralization of Decision Making, Decomposition of an Economic System consisting of a Convex and Non-Convex Section.* University of Birmingham, Centre for Russian and East European Studies, Discussion Papers, Series RC/A, No.9.
Kronsjö, T.O.M., 1968a, *Centralization and Decentralization of Decision Making, Decomposition of a Non-Linear Convex Separable Economic System in Primal and Dual Directions.* University of Birmingham, Centre for Russian and East European Studies, Discussion Papers, Series RC/A, No.16.
Kronsjö, T.O.M., 1968b, *The Primal and Dual Programming Formulation of a Non-Linear Convex Economic System.* University of Birmingham, Centre for Russian and East European Studies, Discussion Papers, Series RC/A, (forthcoming).
Kronsjö, T.O.M., 1969, Optimal Co-ordination of a Large Convex Economic System (Decomposition of a Nonlinear Convex Separable Economic System in Primal and Dual Directions to Obtain a Common Subproblem), *Jahrbücher für Nationalökonomie und Statistik,* (forthcoming).
Liggins, D., 1967, *A Computational Procedure for the Solution of a Sub-Problem of International Trade.* M.Soc.Sc. dissertation, University of Birmingham (unpublished).
Mycielski, J., 1967, *Papers of the Regional Science Association*, **18**, 111-125.

Two-stage Planning in the Irish Context

M.ROSS
The Economic and Social Research Institute, Dublin

In his survey of regional economics some years ago Meyer (1963) saw as a major current task the synthesis of two basic approaches to regional analysis. The first he characterised by its search for the reasons underlying changes in structure and conduct by, for example, hypothesis testing and the analysis of trends. At the other extreme he put the programming approach. For Meyer this was more oriented towards quantification, forecasting, and the development of a logically rigorous framework for analysis. These are not rigorous distinctions but arise mainly out of the circumstances and philosophy of the individual economist. The advocates of the hypothesis approach are often concerned to make a series of short-term piecemeal adjustments over time in existing institutions; the programmers are frequently faced with the task of compiling comprehensive development plans of considerable magnitude.

The programming approach is capable of handling greater degrees of complexity and produces consistent results from the assumptions made. However, the enormous data requirements of such a model lead to inevitable, and often excessive, simplifications. Thus the underlying assumptions may not reflect reality accurately enough, either because the postulation of economic rationality is too crudely made, or structural relationships are not properly specified, or simply as a consequence of excessive aggregation. The hypothesis approach, whether based on regression analysis or general familiarity with the field, can afford better insights into change but may run into difficulties when the *ceteris paribus* assumptions cannot be validly made, when resources become restricted [1] or when the field of study becomes too complex.

A rather analogous comment was made by two Swedish agricultural economists but with one difference (Folkesson and Renborg, 1967). They introduced a new dimension into the discussion by tending to associate the programming approach with central planning while suggesting that the analysis of trend etc., was more a feature of studies by local development agencies. Insofar as local experts are likely to be in closer touch with the realities underlying change and the central planners more

---

[1] An Institute, which summarised all the local plans made in Sweden in the decade after World War II, found that for them to be feasible they would require a tenfold rise in the Swedish population over a very short period (Folkesson and Renborg, 1967).

familiar with overall resource availabilities, the problem becomes one of evolving a procedure whereby each can contribute his expertise in the interest of better decision-making for the economy as a whole.

Many interesting and promising suggestions have been advanced as possible routes towards such a synthesis. This paper proposes yet another. It is not proposed at this stage to review the alternative proposals, though they are highly relevant in the current context. Such discussion will be deferred until later in the paper. The suggestion being advanced here builds on the existing pattern of Irish planning and in particular, the use of the planning by stages method and the work of the county development teams.

Planning by stages is the natural discovery of planning pragmatists. It was given academic respectability by Tinbergen and Bos (1962), who preferred this method of successive approximations to the more ambitious method of establishing one very complicated model for the simultaneous solution of all problems. Its mixture of mathematical programming and judgement is in itself a synthesis of the two approaches we discussed earlier.

The Irish team, that formulated Ireland's first and second programmes for economic expansion, were guided in their choice of methodology by practical considerations rather than by overt reference to Tinbergen's work. The general procedures used were presented to the Irish Statistical and Social Inquiry Society in two successive papers in early 1964 (Geary, 1964; Ryan, 1964). In the second of these the Economic Advisor to the Irish Government, Ryan, showed how, at the first stage, target levels were set for the more important strategic variables such as the growth rate, the balance of payments position, etc. Feasible levels for each variable were first selected by judgement and then made consistent with one another by means of a macro-economic study which used an iterative process.

At the second stage, production targets were set for a number of sectors over a fairly long period. The checks for internal consistency at this stage were more elaborate and based on an input–output decision model developed by Geary. It is of the essence of planning by stages that the result of any stage should be used to suggest revisions to the previous stage and this flexibility is a crucial part of the entire exercise.

At the third stage, the programme specifies the targets for a greater number of sectors and in greater detail. For example, in the second programme a growth rate of 4% was one of the variables determined initially. This was then refined to a growth of 2.5% for agriculture compared to one of 7% for manufacturing industry.

At the third stage the detailed targets for individual agricultural industries were drawn up as set out in Table 1. The achievement of these goals would ensure that the desired growth rate was obtained and, since they are based on estimates of the quantities marketable at home and abroad, they would also be consistent with the balance of payments variables. If in the elaboration of these detailed goals a different weighting of products was deemed preferable, or if market forecasts changed, this would be reflected back on the previous stages and either the necesary revisions undertaken or measures introduced to counteract the disturbance.

Table 1. Agricultural output in 1960 and targets for 1970.

Commodity	Unit	Quantity (thousands)		Value £ Million (Constant 1960 Prices)	
		1960	1970	1960	1970
Horse	No.	17	16	3·5	3·5
Cattle	,,	1046	1500	55·0	80·0
Milk	'000 gal.	480	760	42·0	64·9
Sheep	No.	1582	2500	9·5	15·0
Wool	lb.	17818	27000	3·5	5·3
Pigs	No.	1407	2000	20·8	30·0
Poultry				4·1	5·0
Eggs	120	6980	8460	9·9	12·0
Wheat	Tons	430	300	11·1	7·9
Oats	,,	64	50	1·4	1·0
Barley	,,	266	500	5·8	12·4
Sugar Beet	,,	935	1200	6·0	7·7
Potatoes	,,	563	600	6·1	6·5
Fruit, Vegetables and other Crops		(value only)		6·8	10·5
Gross Value				185·5	261·7
Gross Value Adjusted*				193·1	270·2
Current Operation Expenses				57·4	90·0
Gross Product plus Subsidy under Land Acts				136·4	180·9

* Adjusted for value of turf and changes in livestock numbers.
Source: Republic of Ireland (1964).

The fourth stage of the programme involves filling out the plan with individual projects and the devising of schemes to guide the various industries towards the levels of output etc., reckoned to be desirable. In this connection the Irish Government decided to establish county teams to supplement other initiatives undertaken. These teams were confined to the public officials but had as their aim to harness local initiative for the purposes of local development (Harmon, 1963).

Already from such reports as have come in the difficulties of local planning have become apparent. Each county team has been planning in complete isolation and ignores the external economies and diseconomies of its activities. It is obvious, that if all the suggestions put forward by these teams were to be acted on, the investment capital required for western development would be greater than that available. In these circumstances some system of priorities must be established. It is hoped to show how such a priority system could be worked out by the mutual co-operation of the local planning groups and the Department of Finance, or central planning authority.

The basic technique employed is that of decomposition, which was developed by Dantzig (1963) as an extension of linear programming. It is based on a generalised interpretation of the dual prices in linear programming. These dual prices have often been referred to in the literature as 'accounting prices' (see Qayum, 1960) and as such have been advocated as a means of determining investment priorities. More specifically they have two uses:

1. They replace market prices for the factors of production when used to evaluate public sector investment.

2. They enable the Government to evolve a system of taxes and subsidies on the use of these factors in the private sector. The purpose of these calculations is to encourage private entrepreneurs also to base their calculations on these prices and so ensure correspondence between the interests of individuals and of society as a whole.

The dual prices used for this purpose are those associated with the optimal solution of a linear programme. However, the dual prices associated with sub-optimal solutions have an important role, in that they indicate which processes could be profitably included in the basic solution and the opportunity costs of including other processes which are not optimal. Following the practice of Baumol and Fabian (1964), let us call these dual prices 'provisional dual prices'. Using these provisional dual prices we can now develop a coordinating mechanism, which will prevent local decisions from working at cross-purposes by ensuring that external economies and diseconomies are fully considered. At the same time, this mechanism arranges for the localised decisions to work towards an optimum consistent with national objectives and the resources available nationally for new investment. In this paper the coordinating role is regarded as being logically the responsibility of the central planning authority i.e. the Department of Finance in Ireland.

To illustrate the procedure let us construct the simplest possible linear programming model of two regions, A and B. In each there are two alternative processes. Let x_1 and x_2 represent the amounts, as yet undetermined, of the goods produced by the two processes in region A, and y_1 and y_2 the corresponding unknown output levels in B. Each unit of output produces a specific amount of revenue of some sort e.g., p_1, p_2, q_1, q_2, respectively. There are two fixed resources in each region to produce these goods and these are available in the following amounts: v_1, v_2 for the two resources in region A, w_1, w_2 for those in region B. Initially we will assume these fixed resources can only be used in their own region. In addition, there is an amount, F, of a common resource available. This is also required by the four processes and is freely transferable between the regions without cost.

The object is to maximize revenue, R, i.e.

$$\text{Maximize } R = p_1x_1+p_2x_2+q_1y_1+q_2y_2.$$

This is restricted by the restrictions imposed by resource availabilities. These restrictions give the following inequalities:

$$
\begin{aligned}
a_{11}x_1+a_{12}x_2 &\leqslant v_1 \\
a_{21}x_1+a_{22}x_2 &\leqslant v_2 \\
b_{11}y_1+b_{12}y_2 &\leqslant w_1 \\
b_{21}y_1+b_{22}y_2 &\leqslant w_2 \\
g_1x_1+ g_2x_2+ h_1y_1+ h_2y_2 &\leqslant F
\end{aligned}
$$

where a_{ij} and b_{ij} are the quantities of the ith fixed resource required by the jth process in region A and B respectively, and g_j, h_j are the requirements of the common resource i, for $j = 1$ or 2.

When this system is put into the dual form it becomes

$$\text{Minimize } S = r_1v_1+r_2v_2+s_1w_1+s_2w_2+uF,$$

where r_1, r_2 and s_1, s_2 are the required unit values of the fixed resources, v_1, v_2, w_1, w_2 respectively and u is the required unit value of the common resource F. These are subject to the conditions:

$$
\begin{aligned}
a_{11}r_1+a_{21}r_2 &+ g_1u \geqslant p_1 \\
a_{12}r_1+a_{22}r_2 &+ g_2u \geqslant p_2 \\
b_{11}s_1+b_{21}s_2+h_1u &\geqslant q_1 \\
b_{12}s_1+b_{22}s_2+h_2u &\geqslant q_2
\end{aligned}
$$

It is well known that the maximum value of R will be found equal to the minimum value of S, the optimal solution of their respective programmes. From the presentation above it is clear that the dual gives us individual regional values for the fixed regional resources, so that what may be the same resource physically may have different marginal values depending on its location. On the other hand, there is only one value for the common resource.

One way of obtaining these accounting prices would be to develop a large scale linear programming study on the lines of the simple model used in the illustration, but at a much higher level of sophistication. This proposal can be rejected for many reasons. It would be difficult to construct and would possess all the defects of mathematical programming mentioned earlier. It would defeat the whole spirit of planning in stages, and, most important of all, it is unnecessary. The alternative is to give greater scope to the local planning authority and to concentrate on establishing the accounting prices of the common resources alone. Decomposition enables this to be done.

The method works on the basis that the model used in the illustration above can be decomposed into blocks. This is clear from the method of presentation above. Region A has its own activities and its own resource restrictions; so does region B. Thus each region could plan in isolation, if it knew the costs (accounting prices) of the common resources.   The centre, on the other hand, could determine the accounting prices of the common resources if it knew how much each region needed and the revenue expected to derive from its use.   The problem of the centre is to try and arrive at a weighted average of the plans submitted by each individual region, which will maximise national income within the limits imposed by the levels of common resource available.   As a by-product of this exercise it obtains the dual, or accounting, price for each common resource and an indication of the value of the weighted plan for each region.

To help visualize the procedure let us continue with the basic model presented earlier.   If the requirements of the common resource are left aside, region A has a simple problem:

$$\text{Maximize } R_a = p_1 x_1 + p_2 x_2$$

subject to the limitations

$$a_{11} x_1 + a_{12} x_2 \leqslant v_1,$$

$$a_{21} x_1 + a_{22} x_2 \leqslant v_2.$$

Let the values of x_1 and x_2 in the solution be x_1^1 and x_2^1.   Therefore $R_a^1 = p_1 x_1^1 + p_2 x_2^1$.   The requirements of the common resource are $g_1 x_1^1 + g_2 x_2^1$; let us call this total G_a^1.   (In all cases the superscripts indicate that these are the results of the first plan.)   The central coordinator receives from region A two items of information i.e. R_a^1 and G_a^1.   As will be shown later, the exchange between the region and the centre will give rise to revisions of the region's plan and with it the value of R_a and G_a. Let R_a^i and G_a^i be the information transmitted by region A after the ith calculation or the ith plan.   Similarly region B would transmit two items of information:

$$R_b^i = q_1 y_1^i + q_2 y_2^i \quad \text{(revenue)},$$

$$H_b^i = h_1 y_1^i + h_2 y_2^i \quad \text{(common resource)}.$$

In all, four items of information would be transmitted after every fresh plan has been calculated.   It is noteworthy that this information tells the centre nothing about how the regions arrived at these figures.   In fact, the centre can be completely ignorant of production processes, resource bottlenecks, psychological difficulties in increasing production, and so on in the individual regions.

Now the problem facing the centre is to obtain a weighted average of the plans of an individual region, so that total national revenue is maximised within the limits of the resources available.   If m_i and n_i are respectively the fractions of the ith plan from regions A and B, the objective of the centre is as follows:

$$\text{Maximise } R = R_a^1 m_1 + R_a^2 m_2 + \dots + R_a^i m_1 + R_b^1 n_1 + R_b^2 n_2 + \dots + R_b^i n_i$$

subject to the restrictions

$$m_1+m_2+...+m_i = 1,$$

$$n_1+ n_2+...+ n_i = 1,$$

and

$$G_a^1 m_1 + G_a^2 m_2 + ... + G_a^i m_i + H_b^1 n_1 + H_b^2 n_2 + ... + H_b^i n_i \leqslant F,$$

i.e. the total amounts of the common resource required by the weighted average of all regions' plans does not exceed the supply available. When this is solved, a dual price is obtained for a common resource as well as one for the weighted average of each region.

The centre now tells the regions that they have to reckon with a charge on their use of the common resource (or, perhaps, a subsidy). Call this f. Given this information, region A realises that the revenue it can expect from a unit of the first process, is not in fact p_1. It uses g_1 units of the common resource at a cost of $g_1 f$. The revenue it should reckon with is, therefore, $p_1 - g_1 f$. Similar calculations are made for other processes. Region A now has a new objective:

$$\text{Maximise } R_a = (p_1 - g_1 f)x_1 + (p_2 - g_2 f)x_2$$

and this will probably result in a new set of proposals i.e. a new value for x_1 and x_2. It should be noted, however, that the R_a value submitted to the centre is always based on the actual p_i values, not the modified $(p_i - g_i f)$ values.

Another important feature of the central programme is that it provides a criterion for deciding when the optimum is reached. This is the dual price of the weighted average plan of a region. The value of a new proposal from the region can be compared with it and if it is an improvement, a new weighted average may be calculated. When no region can propose any improvement the national optimum is reached. The result will be the same as that obtainable by the centre solving the entire programme for the two regions without consulting them (i.e. by developing a large scale national model).

Before discussing the merits and demerits of this system, a report will be given of some experiments with it in the Irish context. These were undertaken to demonstrate that it would provide a way of coordinating the work of the county teams and the architects of the national programmes for economic expansion. The work was theoretical and did not involve any actual cooperation either from the local bodies or the centre.

The target outputs for agriculture, which were developed in stage three of the plan, were taken to be the national objectives of the central planner (see Table 1). The local bodies were assumed to be mainly concerned with improving farmers' income and not unduly worried about the consequences of their proposals. Thus if milk were the most profitable enterprise at existing prices, they must of necessity ignore the fact that

increased production of milk would lead to an external diseconomy—
either a fall in the price of milk or an increase in the price support costs
to the Exchequer.

A national goal is analogous to a national resource. It can be thought
of as a negative resource. For a common resource the problem is to keep
the sum of regional demands down to the national level of supply. For
a goal it is a question of ensuring that at least the target level is reached.
When excessive demands are made on a resource a penalty is put on its
use (e.g. a rate of interest for capital). For a deficit in a goal a subsidy
may be added to the price. Thus the same principles can be applied in
each case, with the difference that the signs may have to be interpreted
differently.

The county teams were not contacted to put forward proposals, since
they were not set up to cover all regions but merely the eleven less-
developed counties[2]. Instead, farming type, structure, soils, terrain, and
other characteristics were employed to construct seven regions covering
the entire country. The pretence was made that these regions were the
responsibility of seven regional councils.

The first task of these teams would be an inventory of resources. This
was simulated by the author, who prepared for each such details as soil
classes, current and investment capital, available labour, etc. The second
task would be to define possible enterprises for the individual regions.
This was also simulated using all the records of the 1964 Irish National
Farm Management Survey. The return from these activities was expressed
in terms of Gross Margins. Given this data, it would be a simple matter
to develop a separate linear programme for each region. The objective
would be to maximise family farm income, i.e. the sum of Gross Margins
less the overhead costs of the farms.

Thus, the exercise consisted of developing six linear programmes (one
region was excluded, in that it involved mainly non-commercial agriculture
practised on small and fragmented holdings with extremely impoverished
soil resources). These programmes were designed as a crude simulation of
local planning practices. The results from each plan would be "submitted"
to the central coordinator and here again, the author posed as the centre
and calculated the dual prices for the common goals. It was hoped that
the insights gained from this use of the model could then be extended to
a procedure for the county teams, if they became established for the
country generally or if special resources, or targets, were proposed for the
area covered by the existing teams. These procedures would be valid for
other industries besides agriculture.

Table 2 presents the results of the six linear programmes, i.e. the first
set of proposals for the centre. Some goals (sheep and pigs) are vastly
over-supplied, others not at all (cattle and barley). Although the basic

---

[2] These teams, of course, had as their objective to expand not merely agricultural but other
industries and services as well.

model used in this pilot study was rather crude, it shows the potential dangers from local planning divorced from national objectives. If sheep made the best use of resources, advisory effort would be focused on increasing the national flock, even though cattle were the mainstay of exports and could be disposed of without costly export subsidies. Clearly there was a need to correct the relative prices, in order to arrive at a more satisfactory development in accordance with export possibilities, and general national goals.

Table 2. The first proposal submitted by each region to the central coordinator. The proposals were designed to achieve maximum regional income while contributing to the achievement of the national goals for 1970.

Activity or Enterprise	National Goals to be achieved by 1970 (excluding region 1)		Vector of proposals submitted by region:					
			2	3	4	5	6	7
	Quantity	Unit of Measure						
Milk	670	million gal.	0	152	56	0	0	0
Cattle	1350	thousand head	0	0	0	0	0	0
Sheep	2·16	million head	2·65	2·81	2·15	4·72	8·62	4·99
Fat Pigs	1·90	" "	0	0	0	4·13	6·33	5·85
Wheat	5·84	" cwt.	0	0	0	1·79	0	0
Barley	11·70	" "	-0·9	0	0	0	0	0
Calves*	0	thousand head	0	-362	-103	0	0	0
Bonhams*	0	million head	+16·59	0	0	+2·30	-6·33	-2·93
Expected family farm income from the proposals: £ millions			52·5	24·4	11·1	41·4	48·9	50·6

*Calves and bonhams (piglets) are not national goals but intermediate products necessary for the achievement of these goals and which enter inter-regional trade.

The central planning authority was assumed to have received the information set out in Table 2. From it a central programme was constructed, which aimed at maximizing the expected family farm income, subject to 14 restrictions. Of these, 8 were lower bounds to ensure the achievement of the 8 common goals (including 2 for the intermediate products). In addition there were 6 upper bounds to ensure that the weighted average of the proposals, accepted from any one of the 6 regions, did not exceed unity. This latter possibility did not occur in the first central programme, since each region submitted only one plan.

In the solution of the first central programme the proposals from regions 3, 4, 5, and 7 were accepted completely, that from region 6 was only accepted to the extent of 82.5%, while the proposal from region 2 was rejected. This latter proposal had required barley which was not available from any other region. If the proposal had been accepted, a target for barley would have been further from achievement than if it was rejected.

More important, however, were the dual prices associated with the
goals. Since pigs, sheep, and calves were over-produced, they had dual
prices of zero. On the other hand, the deficit goals, milk, cattle, and
cereals, were associated with large positive values. This would induce the
central planner to increase their relative attractiveness to farmers, either
by a subsidy, or by excluding them from a price reduction or levy imposed on other products. Whatever approach was used the message
relayed to the local planners would be that, for the present, the central
authority would welcome proposals which put less emphasis on sheep and
pigs. In the simulated study this took the form of a subsidy on the
under-produced products.

After five iterations between the local groups and the centre all the
goals had been achieved. At this stage the proposed changes in product
prices were much finer than was the case earlier, when some goals were
still unachieved. At this point, family farm income for the 6 regions was
£147 million or 5½ per cent short of what was found to be the optimum
by a direct solution for all regions using a large linear programme. This
has important implications for a methodology which proceeds by successive approximation.

Table 3. Regional proposals accepted in the fifth programme of the central planning authority.

Region	Proposal Number	Weighting %	Value* £'000	Regional* Total Value £'000
2	3	81·7	7252	
,,	4	18·3	12075	19327
3	1	95· 2	23199	
,,	4	4·8	839	24039
4	2	100·0	7648	7648
5	2	13·7	428	
,,	4	62·3	17525	
,,	5	24·0	6427	23524
6	5	100·0	42171	42171
7	1	11·2	5682	
,,	2	62·0	11318	
,,	4	26·8	13295	30295

Total Value £147004252
Excess Milk 39919100 gallons.
Excess Sheep 8979614 head.

  * These figures were not given in the solution but were easily calculated
from the matrix.

This, then, is how the procedure works. It is not proposed to examine
it in greater detail. Table 3 gives the twelve proposals used to arrive at
the weighted regional plans. It also shows that milk and sheep were over-
produced. Table 4 indicates the background to the proposals accepted
for region 5 and gives their content. This was a region which submitted

a fresh proposal each time, or five in all, and so contrasts with region 4 which only changed its proposals once. It will be noted that the weighted proposal for region 5 in Table 4 included each enterprise, though the optimal established by a direct solution was more specialised, i.e. 123 million gallons of milk, 617 thousand head of cattle, 5.8 million cwt. of wheat, 3.4 million cwt. of barley, −412 thousand calves (i.e. to be imported from elsewhere).

Table 4. The five proposals from region 5 and the composite proposal emerging from the fifth central programme

Enterprise	Unit	Proposal Number					
		1	2	3	4	5	weighted proposal
Milk	million gallons	0	0	280	0	162	39
Cattle	thousand head	0	0	0	785	0	489
Sheep	million ,,	4·7	0	0	0	3·4	0·8
Fat pigs	,, ,,	4·1	0	0	1·6	0	1·0
Wheat	,, cwt.	1·8	12·7	0	6·6	0	2·1
Barley	,, ,,	0	0	0	0	9·7	2·3
Calves	thousand head	0	0	466	−785	270	−484
Bonhams	,, ,,	2.3	0	0	4·4	0	2·7
Expected family farm income (net of subsidies)	million £	41·4	−3·1	14·5	28·1	26·8	23·5
Weighting in Table 3	per cent.	0	13·7	0	62·3	24·0	100·0

It might be objected that the process of entering new proposals and obtaining new solutions is a cumbersome one. However, where the revised simplex method is used, any new proposal can be evaluated by a single pivotal step of the programme (see Baumol and Fabian, 1964). Furthermore, any proposal which is rejected by the central programme can be eliminated, as it will not be acceptable at a later stage. These considerations can result in a very considerable saving in computational time.

It may also be felt that there is excessive communication between the local teams and the centre. However, the practical administrator will quickly find various heuristic methods to reduce the number of information flows. The first and obvious way is to get the local teams to submit a number of alternative proposals at the initial stages. These could be based on different assumptions about relative price trends, or the availability of Government financing. In practice, it was found that, even where very sub-optimal proposals were put forward, the decomposition technique uses its weighting procedure to combine them with others nearer the optimum in such a way, as to reduce very considerably the amount of time required to arrive at a satisfactory system of dual prices (see Table 4).

Another possible anxiety is whether the method can cater for special regional policies of the central Government. This was investigated by Johansen (1965), who relaxed some of the assumptions of the basic model. His six modifications were respectively:

1. Some fixed resources can be transferred to another region, but at a cost.

2. Specified levels of demand arise in each region and there is a possibility of inter-regional trade in products.

3. Policy-makers are anxious to subsidize production in a particular region.

4. Minimum production is required in a particular region.

5. A minimum value of production is required in a region.

6. Certain minimum use must be made of a resource in a region, e.g. labour.

He found, that in these cases, the dual price of both the regional resources and the common resource or goal might be considerably modified but in no case did the method of arriving at the dual prices need to be changed.

It is not only at the centre that the technique can accommodate considerable modification of the basic model. The same is true of the local planning agencies. In the Irish study, the objective was to demonstrate that the results obtained by decomposition and using linear programming are the same as those which would be obtained by the solution of a large multi-regional matrix. There is no reason why this procedure should always be followed. There is more to the technique than merely an alternative method of solving large linear programmes. Baumol and Fabian (1964) argued that the regional plans could be based on a non-linear programme without requiring an adaptation of the procedure. The central coordinator is indifferent as to how the information supplied by the regions is obtained. While such a modification would not pose any mathematical difficulties to him, it would enhance the realities embodied in the proposals and the criticism of the linearity assumption would be avoided to some extent. This would also be true, if it was considered advisable to use separable objective functions or integer programming in the regions.

However, the possibilities might be developed still further. There is no reason why any form of mathematical programming needs to be used to develop regional proposals. The task of the local development groups is to make a detailed and thorough investigation of their own individual regions. In so doing, there are no limitations on the method they will use or the degree of disaggregation they will employ. Thus they can benefit from the expert knowledge of local conditions and trends provided by economists, sociologists, physical scientists, etc., when establishing the probable pattern of production in given circumstances. Such a study could include adjustment costs, resistance to innovation, and the like. It could be based on one representative firm or a hundred, on average resource endowments, or on a detailed inventory of a multiplicity of soil types, land–labour relations, yield responses, and so on. In short, it can have all the advantages of expert local opinion in the study of a manageable local problem. Whatever its basis the central coordinator will merely wish to get a summary of what is planned in terms of the national goals or resources and some indicator of the cost or the profit or whatever happens to be the objective. In this way a synthesis can be achieved between the 'hypothesis' and 'programming' approaches. In particular, it seems likely to overcome the difficulty outlined by Folkesson and Renborg at the outset of this paper, when they contrasted the realistic local plans based on expert knowledge of the region and its internal trends with the highly aggregated and over-simplified national model. In this synthesis the national coordinator considers the interactions of local investments with activities in other regions—a feature which was lacking in the local studies. At the same time, by being based on these local plans, the decomposition device maintains a close touch with reality which was lacking from the national model.

If this step was taken to provide for those aspects of economic rationality which are "too complex to be readily incorporated in presently operational programming models" (Meyer, 1963, p.36), there still remains the question of determining when an optimum has been reached. Research is needed to discover if the dual prices can provide such a criterion. If not, this might be arrived at either when the difference between two successive central programmes is sufficiently small or, better still, if the modified prices transmitted to the regions lead to no fresh proposals. In the former case the solution would tie in very neatly with the flexibility implied in the philosophy of successive approximations.

Another query posed was whether the objective function of the centre and the local groups must necessarily be the same. What would happen if the central coordinator was more consumer-oriented and wished to minimise costs, while the local development group was producer-oriented and anxious to secure maximum income for producers within its region? In a study of Norwegian agriculture Langvatn (1964) showed that this was in fact the case. He used a linear programming model to allocate Norway's food production to those areas where it could be produced at a minimum cost to the nation. In interpreting the results he found it extremely difficult to reconcile the interests of farmers and those of the economy generally. The same problem was investigated by two Hungarian planners, Kornai and Liptak (1965). They developed a game theoretical model, which they claimed was superior to decomposition though it would appear to have many similarities. The players, on the one hand, are the centre and on the other hand, the team of sectors. The Hungarian National Planning Bureau works out general targets for the sectors. These process the targets and suggest modifications. This stage is called 'counter planning'. The National Planning Bureau then revises the targets and so on. The strategies of the centre are the feasible accounting price systems in the duals of the sector problems. The pay-off function is the sum of the dual sector objective functions. This method has not as yet been applied in the Irish context but it would appear to be a very useful development in the whole field of decentralised planning.

Another planning situation which is worthy of research is where the centre, instead of merely coordinating inter-regional activities within an industry, such as agriculture, coordinates several industries simultaneously. In this case the subsidies and levies will be calculated, not merely on the proposals of the agricultural regions, but on those of other sectors as well. The basis for the proposals could be whatever was deemed suitable by the sectoral planning groups.

This approach by decomposition and successive approximations has certain attractions compared to simple mathematical programming. One of these arises from the way in which the method makes the planner aware of sub-optimal solutions and their cost. In general in a large linear programme all that will be presented is the optimum solution. The policy-maker might have preferred to accept some deviation from the optimum and select a sub-optimum solution. This could arise if the latter is closer to his social aims, for example in the regional distribution of income. It might require less adjustment cost, being a less extreme departure from the current pattern. It might be based on a regime of subsidies which would be more politically acceptable, or less expensive to the Exchequer, and it might present a more balanced agriculture within each region.

A concrete example of how this can happen was reported by Blyth and Crothall (1965). In their linear programming study of investment in New Zealand, the programme selected one manufacturing industry. Sensitivity analysis indicated that nine other industries could have been included in the solution with a reduction of less than one per cent in gross national consumption—the maximand in this case. There are many reasons why this latter solution would be deemed more acceptable.

To overcome this tendency in linear programming to yield solutions characterised by specialisation and concentration, various devices can be employed such as dummy constraints, or at a more sophisticated level, stochastic programming and risk studies[3]. Alternatively, sensitivity analysis and parametric programming may be used. However, all these devices are difficult to use in practice. It is here that the decomposition technique comes into its own. Any proposal submitted by a region can be specified in extreme detail in the regional office. This detail will not

---

[3] A method which shows a great deal of promise is recursive programming (see Day, 1963) which starts out from the existing pattern of production and studies the time path of change initiated by innovation, technology, structural changes, and market developments. Such an approach could be integrated into the method studied here.

be forwarded to the coordinator—only those aspects required for the central programme. This proposal will be evaluated and the result may be that it would be combined with another. Because of the underlying detail of each proposal the composite proposal itself would be exceedingly detailed. An insight into how this is so can be gained by considering the composite proposal for region 5 discussed above. It included all possible activities in the region at some positive level while the optimum contained fewer. If the basis for these proposals had been better (e.g. based on local expert opinion) then the detail would have been further enhanced.

A great attraction of the method is the wide powers of discrimination and discretion afforded to the local planners, in arriving at their objectives. If there is any purpose in having local development groups at all, it is because they are regarded as having insights into local affairs, which are not readily available to the central planner. Granted this premise, decomposition provides a convenient method of coordinating local investigations and arriving at a means of ranking the regional investment priorities.

In this paper, the emphasis has been more on a possible system for arriving at this flexibility rather than the statement of actual achievements. Some simple models have been worked out, to show that theoretically at least, the approach does seem to have considerable potential.

References

Baumol, W.J., and Fabian, T., 1964, "Decomposition Pricing for Decentralization and External Economies", *Management Science*, 2, 1.

Blyth, C.A., and Crothall, G.A., 1965, "A Pilot Programming Model of New Zealand Economic Development", *Econometrica*, 33, No.2.

Dantzig, G.B., and Wolfe, P., 1965, *The Decomposition of Mathematical Programming Problems* (The Rand Corporation, Santa Monica).

Dantzig, G.B., 1963, *Linear Programming and Extensions* (Princeton University Press, Princeton).

Day, R.H., 1963, *Recursive Programming and Production Response* (North Holland Press, Amsterdam).

Erza, E., 1967, "Regional Development Policies in the United Kingdom", *OECD Observer* (OECD, Paris).

Folkesson, L., and Renborg, U., 1967, "Optimum Inter-Regional Allocation of Agricultural Production and Resources in Sweden", *The Use of Operational Research in the Public Domain*, Symposium organised by the Economic Research Institute, Dublin, and OECD, 1965, DAS/CSI/66.369 mimeo OECD Paris.

Geary, R.C., 1964, "Towards an Input/Output Decision Model for Ireland", *Journal of Statistical and Social Inquiry Society of Ireland*, 21.

Harmon, J.F., 1963, "County Development Teams", *Administration*, 2 (Institute of Public Administration of Ireland).

Johansen, L., 1965, "Regiønalokonomiske Problemer Belyst ved Lineaer Programmeringsteori" ("Regional Economic Problems Illustrated by L.P.Theory"), *Sosialøkonomen*, 19, special number for Dr.R.Frisch's 70th Birthday.

Kornai, J., and Liptak, Th., 1965, "Two Level Planning", *Econometrica*, **33**.

Kresge, D., 1965, "A Simulation Model for Development Planning", *Harvard Transport and Development Seminar, Discussion Paper No.32* (Cambridge, Mass.).

Langvatn, H., 1964, *Produksjonstilpasning i Norsk Jordbruk Gjennom Naeringsokonomisk, Regional, Individuell Planlegging* (Allocation of Production in Norwegian Agriculture through Industry, Regional, and Individual Planning), Report No.32, Norwegian Institute of Agricultural Economics, Oslo, Norway.

Meyer, J., 1963, "Regional Economics: A Survey", *American Economic Review*, **53**.

Orcutt, G., Greenberger, M., Korbel, J., and Rivlin, A., 1960, *Microanalysis of Socioeconomic Systems: A Simulation Study* (Harper and Row, New York).

Qayum, A., 1960, *Theory and Policy of Accounting Prices* (North Holland Press, Amsterdam).

Republic of Ireland, 1963, *Second Programme for Economic Expansion*, Pr.7239 (Stationery Office, Dublin).

Republic of Ireland, 1964, *Agriculture in the Second Programme for Economic Expansion*, Pr.7697 (Stationery Office, Dublin).

Roberts, P.O., 1966, *Transport Planning: Models for Developing Countries*, Ph.D. Thesis (Northwestern University, Evanston, Illinois).

Ross, M., 1967, *Regional Allocation in Irish Agriculture: An Application of Operations Research*, Ph.D. Thesis, National University of Ireland, Dublin.

Ryan, W.J.L., 1964, "The Methodology of the Second Programme for Economic Expansion", *Journal of Statistical and Social Inquiry Society of Ireland*, **12**.

Schaller, W.N., 1966, *The FPED National Model: Background and Progress*, USDA, Production Adjustment Branch, Washington.

Tinbergen, J., and Bos, H.C., 1962, *Mathematical Models of Economic Growth* (McGraw-Hill, New York).

Erratum

Page 48, Table 8.

Values in this Table were computed incorrectly. Corrected, it should read as follows:

Statistic	Value of Statistic		Standard Deviation		Standard Deviate	
	observed	expected under H_0	N	R	N	R
1. All links						
Moran, I	0·0446	−0·2333	0·2667	0·2660	1·0424	1·0449
Geary, c	1·0394	1·0	0·2437	0·2499	−0·1616	−0·1576
proposed, $r, \alpha = 1$	0·1414	−0·1111	0·2125	0·2116	1·1882	1·1933
proposed, $r, \alpha = 2$	0·2497	−0·1111	0·4123	0·4103	0·8751	0·8794
2. Bristol–other only						
Moran, I	−0·1219	−0·1000	0·1206	0·1246	−0·1819	−0·1760
Geary, c	1·1097	1·0	0·6030	0·6231	−0·1819	−0·1760
proposed, $r, \alpha = 1$	−0·3714	−0·1111	0·1757	0·1786	−1·4810	−1·4572
proposed, $r, \alpha = 2$	−0·5239	−0·1111	0·2380	0·2393	−1·7345	−1·7249
3. Non-Bristol links only						
Moran, I	0·1249	−0·1667	0·2789	0·2793	1·0455	1·0438
Geary, c	1·0145	1·0	0·2981	0·2968	−0·0486	−0·0488
proposed, $r, \alpha = 1$	0·2308	−0·125	0·2965	0·2969	1·2000	1·1985
proposed, $r, \alpha = 2$	0·1939	−0·125	0·4667	0·4673	0·6834	0·6825

N = Normality
R = Randomisation

6.3. J Ĥ

Erratum

Page 48, Table 8.

Values in this Table were computed incorrectly. Corrected it should read as follows:

Statistic	Value of Statistic (if normal is expected mean $\bar{x}$)	Standard Deviation		Standard Deviation	
		N	R	N	R
1. All data					
Mean $\bar{x}$	0.1406	0.2177	0.2087	1.1424	1.0469
Cv $s/\bar{x}$	1.0	0.2565	0.432	0.676	1.1376
proposed $\alpha z, \alpha = 1$	0.1411	0.1131	0.2135	-0.2146	1.261	1.1973
proposed $\beta, z_{\alpha} = \infty$	0.5897	1.111	0.8103	0.8103	0.8751	0.8774
2. Broad water only					
Mean $\bar{x}$	-0.2319	-0.1008	0.1706	0.7236	-0.1870	0.1760
Cv $s/\bar{x}$	1.1099	1.0	0.9510	0.6431	-0.1517	-0.1760
proposed $z, \alpha = \infty$	-0.0274	-0.1111	-0.1387	0.1786	-0.0478	-0.0476
proposed $\alpha = 2$		-0.0216	-0.1111	-0.0216	1.1745	1.1748
3. Narrow land line only					
Mean $\bar{x}$	0.1395	-0.1867	-0.2186	0.8197	1.0654	1.0826
Cv $s/\bar{x}$	1.0195	1.0	1.081	0.9463	0.0480	-0.0488
proposed $z, \alpha = 1$	0.2208	-0.1254	-0.2962	0.2963	1.3600	1.3955
proposed $\alpha = 2$	0.1954	-0.115	0.2682	0.2682	3.9634	0.9822

N = Normality
R = Randomisation

213